JUDGE NOT

A biographical account of true events.

Written by

PAT FLEWWELLING;

As lived and told by

JONATHON PARKER

To all who have been judged while their story remains untold, I pray that you come to experience the fullness of the inner peace and joy you surely deserve.

And to all those who have judged others without first hearing their story, I pray you will diligently yearn to seek that forgiveness, which in due time is bound by greater laws to find you, regardless.

And to my loving wife, who remains forever impartial and hopeful; if there are words to express how extraordinary and terrific you are, they elude me. And to her family for their enduring faith, I am so very honoured. And to our most wonderful children, and particularly our youngest daughter, for being my most precious inspirations, I am truly blessed.

Thank you all for being with me.
Jonathon Parker; 2012

"Do not judge, or you too will be judged. For in the same way you judge others, you will be judged, and with the measure you use, it will be measured to you. Why do you look at the speck of sawdust in your brother's eye and pay no attention to the plank in your own eye? How can you say to your brother, 'Let me take the speck out of your eye,' when all the time there is a plank in your own eye? You hypocrite, first take the plank out of your own eye, and then you will see clearly to remove the speck from your brother's eye." *Matthew 7:1-5*

Judge Not

CHAPTER ONE

Dresden, Ontario - 1974

Jonathon Parker's work boots clunked on the floorboards, and behind him, the screen door slammed shut with such force it bounced and banged again. It was a day of lasts: the last time he'd sleep in that room, the last time he'd eat at that breakfast table, the last time he'd let the porch door bang; so it was disappointing not to hear his mother shout at him one last time.

He wasn't sure where his mother had gone to. He squinted against the late spring sun, scanning the green hills that interlocked like fingers folded in prayer under a robin's egg blue sky. The air was freshly rain-washed and easy to breathe, but white haze in the west foretold of a hot day to come. *Great. And no air conditioning in the truck.*

He traced the contours of the farmland, the river flats in the distance, the tree-lined creek bank, the deer track and the fences between adjoining properties. He wished he hadn't packed his camera; he wanted to capture this moment and fix it in his memory. Then again, he was glad, too. A picture would only make him regret the situation even more.

This was all supposed to be his. This was supposed to be his inheritance.

Things change. He sighed and leaned against the porch railing. Change was one thing; but leaving everyone he knew and cared about behind, that was another thing.

The last he'd seen of his mother Norma, she'd been in the sewing room, crying. She'd been doing a lot of that. One minute, talking about what's for dinner, the next minute, crying. One minute talking about the last few things she wanted to buy from Stedman's before closing up the truck, the next, crying. One minute she'd be watching a shampoo commercial, the next…

1

And no air conditioning in the truck, he thought again.

But she was moving away from all her friends, too; so was his father Edward, and his grandfather, Jake. It wasn't easy for anyone.

A car door slammed. Men exchanged long-distance, meaningless greetings. Norma called for Jonathon, so he jogged down the steps of the back porch. He passed the place where he'd broken his leg after jumping out of his bedroom window on a dare. He passed the place where his best friend Rick had accidentally set fire to one of the awning struts – the result of a midnight, drunken barbeque bet. He came around the side of the house where the ground had been so well trampled by feet and machinery that no grass grew.

Edward had cut down the tractor tire from the elm.

Jonathon ground his fist across the empty feeling in the pit of his stomach. He was a grown man, practically; like hell he'd cry about something like a tire swing. *But why'd he have to take it down?*

Under the gap where kids had swung for generations, the soil had been hollowed out. Kids, cousins, sweethearts, drunken uncles – no one knew how many people had swung from that branch as the old tree grew. It had been there when the Parkers took possession of the land, already decades old. Only God knew how many thunderstorms and tornadoes it had outlasted; and God only knew what it would have to face, now that the farm was out of Parker hands for the first time in four generations. The growing town had burst its traditionally urban banks and was seeping out into the surrounding farms. And towns weren't known for growing *around* farmland.

A man shouted, "Jonathon! Let's go!" Edward's voice couldn't carry like it used to.

Jonathon was about to quit the side yard when an older voice grunted, "Hey." His grandfather was sitting on the front porch in his old Muskoka chair, a sweaty glass of water in his hand and a thousand yard stare in his eyes. Jonathon would have sworn his grandfather had been calling to Jonathon's parents, until the old man said, "Got a light, kid?"

Jonathon leaned against the porch, feeling his shirt pockets. "You won't tell?"

"Who'm I gonna tell, fer cripe's sake?" It was an old joke between them. He accepted the matches Jonathon pressed into the palm of his scarred, calloused hand.

Jonathon's grandfather was watching the world go by, though there was a parked U-Haul and a sleek Cadillac blocking the view. The Cadillac was black – a bad idea out here where only half the roads were paved – but it was a very nice car.

Jonathon's father was all smiles, but he was no match for the grinning realtor that shook his hand. The realtor looked like he needed a Colonel Sanders tie and a ten gallon hat; it would have suited his oil-baron grin. He told Edward a joke, and Edward laughed because he was supposed to. Mid-conversation, the realtor leaned against the Sold sign with a sense of pride and possession. Edward said something profound as he took out his keys. The realtor didn't reply; he only took the keys and quickly pocketed the whole ring.

Jonathon's grandfather Jake struck a match from his grandson's pack, and he applied it to the end of his hand-rolled cigarette. His puckered lips made dry smacking sounds as he brought the flame to life. Jake was staring at the sign under the realtor's elbow. He seemed to have the ability to simply shut off what he was feeling; Jonathon had always envied that. If his grandfather was starting to feel sad, he'd simply pinch off the emotion and chuck it away. *What's done is done,* he'd always say. *The world will go on tomorrow, with or without us.* At the very least, Jake never let anyone see him show emotion.

Nearby, Edward laughed and tried his hand at making a joke of his own; the realtor didn't mind so much, but he checked the time while he laughed.

Jonathon never had to explain things to his grandfather, nor vice versa. They didn't need so many words. They shared a common experience. Jonathon had known from infancy that, like Jake, he would get up every morning to do his chores on the farm, that he would go to school and get his degree in Agriculture, and that eventually he would take over the farm operations. That was the only future he had envisioned, and it was the one he had worked toward; but Jonathon was young – only eighteen – and very adaptable. But as for Jake, this was the only life he'd ever lived. Now, instead of retiring in the one home he'd known, Jake was compelled to uproot himself, follow his family westward into uncertainty, and leave Parker Farms behind.

"Jonathon!" Edward's shout faltered when he spotted the younger man so near at hand. "Jonathon, there you are. I said, let's go! Get in the truck."

Jonathon offered his grandfather a handshake. The old man grunted, "Get up here and say g'bye properly." Jonathon slipped between the rungs of the porch railing. By the time he was on his feet on the porch, so was Jake. They clapped arms around each other. There was nothing weak about the old stalwart. He was like the elm tree; the older he got, the more inflexible he became, but the stronger he was. And when he pounded somebody on the back, most times they'd walk away coughing and bruised.

Jake sighed. When he let go of his grandson, the old man's eyes were dry and far away. "I'll see you in a few months."

Jonathon nodded. In a couple of months, the rest of their family's holdings would be transferred over to the new owners, and his grandfather could join them in Regina and retire in the middle of nowhere.

Jonathon turned and didn't look back. He did glance sidelong at the blue '53 Ford truck, an old fixer-upper that was supposed to be his, come his twenty-first birthday. Jake had already sold the truck to somebody else, since Jonathon couldn't very well take it with him all the way from Dresden to Regina, not with a busted rear axle and a shot piston. It was someone else's project now.

For Jonathon, it was just one more thing to say goodbye to.

Jonathon eyed the realtor's Cadillac again, and he nodded to himself. *That* was a fine car. He wondered what it would be like to own and drive one of his own. He wondered what it would be like to have that kind of disposable cash, and to command that kind of respect. Farm boys didn't typically own Cadillacs.

And suddenly it occurred to Jonathon: he didn't have to be a farm boy. They'd sold the farm. They were moving into the city. This was a new start for the family; all bets were off. Anything was possible. Even a Cadillac of his own.

A new start. New friends – maybe even a new girlfriend – new everything. He didn't have to follow in his father's footsteps. Didn't have to follow in his grandfather's footsteps either. He breathed the fresh air. A new start. A world of possibilities. Limitless horizons.

Norma's eyes were swollen and red. She threw herself into her work, tossing her overnight bag into the front cabin of the U-Haul, tossing her purse into the foot well, and hauling up the cooler onto the middle seat. There'd be three of them sitting shoulder to shoulder and hip to hip: one driving, one against the passenger's window, one sitting in the middle with a picnic basket and overnight bag between his legs. *And no air conditioning.*

Edward Parker pushed back his John Deere ball cap so that it rested on the back of his balding head. Gravel crunched under his sneakers. "Ready to go?" he asked. He passed by his wife, cheerfully whistling and jangling the U-Haul keys in his hands.

Norma's eyes steamed up, her nose turned red, and she thrust her hand into her jeans pocket for a well-used handkerchief.

And no air-conditioning.

Jonathon opened the U-Haul door for his mother and let her in first. While she sniffed and scrambled up into the elevated seat, Jonathon turned – not to look at the porch, but to watch as the realtor picked his way across his mother's well-tended lawn to the front path, and toward the stairs that led up to his grandfather. Jonathon pulled shut the U-Haul door, wound down the window and hooked his elbow through the frame. Edward started the diesel engine, sighed pleasantly, and threw the transmission into drive. "Yes sir. Best decision we ever made." He kissed his wife on the cheek. "You won't regret it."

Norma opened her handkerchief and planted her face in it.

CHAPTER TWO

Regina, Saskatchewan. Spring, 1974

Norma had been struggling with the fluttering map, blocking Jonathon's view, when Edward pointed and shouted over the road noise, "Hey. You see what I see?"

Jonathon hoped it was something other than more prairie. He was getting tired of the hypnotic effects of the Saskatchewan highway.

When Jonathon had thought that the move west would mean limitless horizons, he hadn't meant it so literally. Saskatchewan was nothing but a thin, straight surface under a dizzyingly wide sky. Flat. Dry. Farmland. That was the sum total of Saskatchewan. He knew, because when he looked out the one window, the land was so flat to the north that he could see the Arctic circle; through the windshield, he swore he could see the Rockies; in the reflection of the side view mirror, he could see Manitoba behind them; he was positive that if he looked out through the driver's side window, he could see clear to the Gulf Coast of Mexico. Flat, dry farmland – good for Edward's arthritis, great for the sinuses, but it sure made a body feel small and low to the ground.

Norma folded the map widthwise. Jonathon could see the jagged, boxy outline of buildings in the distance. "What am I looking at?" Norma asked.

"The sign," Edward said. He was pointing over the steering wheel at something up ahead. "I think..." They came closer, and Jonathon began to make out the shape and colours of the sign down the road. "Ha! Yes." It was a plain sign with blue letters, and attached to its upper border, there was the cut-out of a man in a red uniform, holding a red pike with two pennants on it. "City of Regina," Edward announced. "Home of the Mounties. And now, home of the Parkers."

The man in uniform was a smiling example of the Royal Canadian Mounted Police, his free hand extended in welcome.

"Oh thank God," Norma groaned. She yawned. "There – there's the turnoff."

They followed the off ramp for Regina South. Within a few minutes, they were puttering down a quiet suburban street.

"I hope the water's turned on already," Norma said.

"Why?" Edward laughed and asked, "You need a shower?"

"I need the toilet!"

Edward smiled and nodded. Then he leaned forward over the steering wheel, squinting at the numbers on the ranch style homes. "Well, Pat should have already taken care of that."

"Who?" Norma asked.

"Pat Burton. The real estate agent."

"Oh, right. Sorry."

"He said he was going to make sure everything was in order before we got here. He knew we were arriving today."

"You sure?"

"Yep. I called him before we left Winnipeg."

"Good," Norma replied. She glanced at Jonathon, who was gazing out the truck windows at his new environment. Jonathon didn't care one way or the other about the place; he only wanted out of the truck to stretch his legs. Still, it was nice to have arrived after such a long, dull drive along the Trans-Canada Highway. And now that they had arrived, Life Part Two could get underway.

Edward's lips moved as he read the house numbers. "There...That's it."

There was a sold sign on the front lawn. Edward nodded, satisfied, and smiled briefly to himself. He pulled the rumbling diesel truck over to the curb, put it in park, idled the engine for a moment as if caught up in some strange nostalgia, and then he finally shut off the engine. Jonathon was the first one out, and he could barely move. He stretched his legs and his back, getting a face full of prairie sunshine. It was still early in the afternoon. They could get a lot of work done yet, before the sun went down.

He wondered if he should start looking for a job. But doing what? He didn't know where to begin. There were too many options.

By late afternoon, they'd unloaded better than half of the boxes from out of the truck. Edward went into town to visit Max, an old family friend. It was because of Max that Edward decided to move to Regina in the first place. Edward and his uncle had helped out on Max's farm back in the mid-Fifties, and now that Max was of retirement age, he'd asked Edward to come help look after the farm once again. Unfortunately, Max had taken suddenly ill, and Edward had been eager to visit him in hospital, now that they'd arrived. He left Norma and Jonathon with the rest of the disembarkation of all their worldly goods.

It was nearing dinnertime. Jonathon held up an apple corer and pointed at the cupboards nearest the sink. "Here?"

"No, um..." Norma pointed at the cupboard closest to the refrigerator. "Yeah, that one."

"Top shelf?"

"Middle. I can't reach the top shelf."

"Okay."

Jonathon slid the corer onto the shelf, and when he delved into the next box, he heard a noise from the front door. He turned, and there was a man standing in the hallway outside the kitchen door. Norma noted Jonathon's surprise, and she turned as well to see what the problem was.

The unexpected visitor was a tall, lanky man, maybe in his late twenties to early thirties, with short curly hair and mutton chops. He wore wide sunglasses, a green paisley shirt with wide lapels, brown pants, polished brown shoes and a chrome watch. He hooked his thumbs in his pants pockets, and said, "Good afternoon." Norma and Jonathon had both stopped their work to stare back at him. "How was your trip, Mrs. Parker?"

Norma frowned. "Fine, thank you." It sounded like a question.

The man smiled awkwardly, then strolled into the kitchen as if he owned the place. He looked over the rusty-orange paint on the walls with a cool, mildly disapproving look. "I guess I should welcome you to our fair city!" He glanced into one of the open boxes. He absently chucked his thumb over his shoulder. "Your door was open." He laughed to himself and picked a mug out of the box to inspect it. "I guess this place does give people a real sense of security, what with all the Mounties crawling around. You know about the training school in town?"

Norma cleared her throat impatiently and asked, "Can I help you, Mr...?"

He smiled, confused, then he nodded and set the mug down on the kitchen table. "Right. Sorry." He thrust out his hand to Norma first. "Burton," he said, shaking her hand. He offered it to Jonathon next. Jonathon extended his hand, and Burton reached out to claim it and pump it. "Pat Burton, Imperial Realty. I helped Ed purchase this property. Nice to meet you." When Jonathon released his hand, Burton smiled again and pointed at Jonathon. "And *you* must be..."

"Jonathon."

"Jonathon. Nice to meet you," he said again.

"Nice to meet you," Norma said. She picked up the box closest to Burton's elbow and moved it onto the kitchen counter. Jonathon rescued the mug before Burton could pick it up again. Neither Jonathon nor Norma spoke any further. They continued unloading the contents of the boxes.

Burton ran his tongue over his teeth. "Say, Jonathon. Can I call you Jonny?"

"No thanks."

"Jonathon, listen. I've got some great properties you and your Dad should look at. Great investment opportunity – perfect start-up jobs for a young man like yourself. After all," Burton added with a bit of chagrined pride, "gotta help you get started on the right foot, since you're new in town."

"I think we'll manage," Jonathon said. "Thanks." Jonathon cut through the packing tape of another box and set back to work.

Burton stood behind them, breathing audibly. Jonathon could hear the soles of his shoes creaking on the linoleum as he fidgeted. "Say, where is Ed anyway?"

"Visiting a friend in hospital," Norma answered.

Burton nodded enthusiastically. He was staring at the box of silverware. "Great...great..." He ran his fingers over his lips. "Listen, could you ask him to call me when he can? I have a hot investment property I think he should look at."

"I'll tell him," Norma said.

"Fantastic." Burton smiled broadly, bade them a good afternoon, waved at Jonathon and exited with long, confident strides. Norma watched him go, and they listened for the click of the front door.

Norma glanced at her son and murmured, "Can you believe that guy?" Jonathon grinned. "Like he owns the world and everything in it," Norma added. She put a pair of coffee mugs on the shelf and closed the cupboard door. "You'd better keep your hand on your wallet, the next time you see him."

Jonathon laughed. "Mom, come on. He doesn't exactly look like a pickpocket. A flake, maybe..."

"No," Norma said. "I know his type." She squinted at the kitchen door. "He doesn't have to pick your pocket to get your money away from you. Whatever he wants to take away from you, he'll *talk* away from you."

REGINA. SPRING, 1975

"Number two meal deal, hold the onions, extra pickles, side of fries, three cans of Coke," Jonathon said to the cook, who nodded and set to work. At the same time, Jonathon took what was on the short order counter and packed it in the paper bag. "And how are we doing on the family meal?"

Living the dream, Jonathon thought. He dragged his sleeve across his brow. *Limitless horizons*. Still, it was better than his first job with the Department of Agriculture. At least here, he didn't have to drive all over the prairies with his wheels turning and the scenery never, ever changing.

"Steve!" Jonathon called.

"It's coming!" was the reply.

Jonathon turned with the paper bag, folding over the top edge to make a kind of handle. "There you go," he said to the woman on the other side of the front counter. "Thanks. Enjoy your meal and please come again." She smiled back politely. To the man checking out the dessert display, he called, "Sir?" The man looked up. "Your meal should be ready in just a minute." The customer raised his hand in thanks and as a sign that he was content to wait.

Jonathon took a breath and returned to the cash. He lifted his eyes. She was stunning.

She was all class, willowy and fine, with waves of black, waist-length hair. She had enormous brown eyes, an inviting red mouth and just a hint of freckles across her cheeks. Over a lean body, she wore a light blue blouse, tight beige pants, and a spring jacket that matched her purse.

What is a woman like that doing in a place like this? he thought. The answer was obvious. She glanced at her watch and sighed. She was here for food, fast, and not for conversation.

Jonathon cleared his throat. "May I help you?"

"Your number four meal deal, and a coffee with two cream, please."

All class, all business. She was a nine at least – a ten if she smiled. She stared back at him, pursing her saucy lips. Her eyes were captivating, and a little angry.

"Uh..."

She softened her gaze a little, she averted her eyes, and colour bloomed on her cheeks.

"Sorry," Jonathon said. He swallowed. "Number four meal!" he called out.

"Right," shouted a voice behind him.

"Let me...just...get you that coffee," Jonathon said. He lurched for the pot and a takeout cup. Hot coffee sloshed over the back of his hand. The woman sighed and checked the time again. Jonathon filled the cup, added the cream and set it on the counter between them. She reached for it before he'd pulled his hand away.

Her fingers were cool, smooth and soft.

His ears burned. "One eighty-five, please," he said. He felt like he was being strangled from the inside out. His mouth had gone dry. He took the five dollar bill from her, made change and placed it securely and slowly in the palm of her narrow hand. "Enjoy your meal and please come again," he said. He sounded robotic, and it took an effort of willpower to bring his eyes up to hers. She wasn't looking at him. She was looking everywhere *but* at him.

"Sure," she said. "I can hardly wait."

"Order up!" someone shouted behind him.

She had picked the perfect pair of pants.

She had walked away, hand on one hip. Clothes weren't her only perfections. He'd never seen a figure like that outside of the movies or magazines. He couldn't believe his eyes – and when she moved –

A round, wrinkled face leaned into his line of view. The next person in line smiled sweetly, encouragingly, and hopefully.

"Jonathon – order up!"

"Excuse me," he said sheepishly to the next customer, and he dove for the outstanding family meal deal.

The black-haired young woman watched him, and she rolled her eyes.

Jonathon handed over the family meal deal and took the next order. Out of the corner of his eye, he watched her move, wondered what her name was, what she did, what she liked. She didn't seem like a steak and beer kind of woman. *White wine and seafood, maybe, like you could get at Stavros' Mediterranean. Candlelight and soft music...*

A tall, dark-haired business man entered the restaurant, wearing a suit and cowboy boots. He took off his hat and smoothed back perfect hair. A gold watch flashed under the lights. Bright, feminine eyes regarded him with cool interest, and when he smiled, so did the black-haired beauty.

Jonathon nodded to himself, and while he worked away with an edge to his voice and gestures, he thought, *Give it time.* He wasn't going to be working fast food forever. This was just a means to an end. *Give it time.*

REGINA. FALL, 1975

Jonathon checked his pockets again. His suit didn't quite fit anymore, but it was clean and it was the best he had.

He glanced at the sign over the door: Imperial Real Estate. He was in the right place. Still, looking up at the sun-reflecting windows of the financial district, he felt out of place. The streets were busy with businessmen, tourists and cars, everyone with some place to be, and everyone moving either too quickly or too slowly.

A family passed behind him; the youngest boy trotted a model Mountie on the air, and his mother tugged him along. The boy pointed the Mountie at Jonathon and shouted, "Pew-pew! You're under arrest!" Jonathon smiled at him, and the mother scolded her son for being so rude to a perfect stranger. "Mounties only capture criminals," she told him. "They *protect* honest people like that young man. They don't shoot first and arrest later." She mouthed an apology at Jonathon, but he grinned and raised his hand. The boy was only having fun.

Jonathon took a quick, deep breath and went in before he changed his mind.

A secretary at the front desk said goodbye into the telephone, adjusted her glasses and smiled at the young man who'd come in. "Can I help you?"

"I'm looking for Pat Burton."

She smiled more broadly. "You have an appointment?"

"Uh…no."

"All right, let me see if he's available." She picked up the phone again, and this time, she hovered her finger over a button for a pre-programmed extension. "Your name?" she asked him.

"Jonathon Parker."

When there was an answer on the other end of the line, the secretary relayed all the information.

It was a modest but neatly decorated office, with poster boards displaying photographs, prices and features of properties recently sold and those still up for sale. There were a few listings in Jonathon's neighbourhood, which gave him an idea of the value of his new family home. There were a few different areas of the city that were shockingly affordable, and his optimism was rekindled.

"Mr. Parkins?"

"Parker."

"Sorry. You can go right in. He's a friend of your father?" She looked him up and down. She seemed mildly satisfied by his looks. "Just down this way. First door on the left."

Jonathon followed the directions and found the door opening as he arrived. Today, Burton was wearing a tasteful brown suit with a sharp tie, and no glasses. When he put out his hand, he didn't seem as aggressive about it. "Jonathon, great to see you. Come in!" He extended his arm toward the window at the rear of his office, and Jonathon entered. "How's Ed? Is he all right?"

"He's fine."

"I haven't heard from him in a while," he smiled, but he seemed genuinely concerned. "And his friend? Who was it now...Max?"

"Yeah." Jonathon would have smiled too, impressed at Burton's faculty for remembering names, but the news was grim. "He's not doing too well."

"I'm sorry to hear that."

To prevent the inevitable uncomfortable silence, Jonathon said, "Dad's looking after Max's farm while he recuperates."

"Ah." Burton took out a pack of cigarettes. "That explains why he's been so busy." He offered the cigarettes first to Jonathon, but Jonathon declined, so Burton lit one for himself. "And how have you been holding up lately?"

"I'm all right."

As his secretary had done, Burton looked over the quality and cut of Jonathon's suit. "You look like a young man on a mission." He exhaled and tapped his cigarette into the ash tray. "You're in the market for something."

Jonathon smirked. "I just got my real estate license."

Burton grinned. It was a warm and sincere expression. "Really!" Then the smile sharpened. "And now what do you plan to do with it?"

"Well..." Jonathon had rehearsed on the way over, but now he felt like he was missing his cues, and so he spoke off the cuff. "I'm looking for a good starter property."

"To live in? Or to fix up and put back on the market?" Burton's eyes narrowed.

"To flip," Jonathon answered with a nod.

Burton pursed his lips. "How good are you at manual labour?"

"I used to help out on the farm with all the repairs."

Burton asked a few more specifics – what his price range was, what neighbourhood he'd been eyeing, how good he was at plumbing, at electrical work, the like – as he led Jonathon out of the sunny corner office. They were still speaking in three word questions and one word answers when Burton stopped them in front of one of the displays. A moment of silence, and then Burton picked one of the pictures off the board. It was a bungalow on the edge of town.

"Got just the place, I think." Burton handed him the picture. "Have you uh…"

"I've saved up enough for a down payment," Jonathon replied.

Burton measured the honesty and moxie in Jonathon's eyes. "Okay. You have time right now to check it out?"

"I've got the whole day."

"Great." Burton fished the car keys out of his pants pocket, checked for his wallet, then grinned and led the way to the reserved parking spot out front. Burton drove a Mercedes.

"Nice car," Jonathon remarked.

"Still less than ten thousand on it." Burton opened the passenger's door for him. "You in the market for a car, too?"

"…Maybe…"

Burton looked him over again, the way a man might judge a crackling, steaming steak on his plate. "Good. I know a guy."

A couple of weeks later, Jonathon was up in the master bedroom, running the paint roller down the southern wall. Behind him, John Denver's *Calypso* was playing on the a.m. station – the third time so far that day. But it was catchy, and it seemed to fit the mood of the day. It made his work go quickly. He caught himself humming along as he worked.

The window to his left was naked and open, and through it, he caught sight of a car slowing down out front. Burton's Mercedes parked beside the curb. Burton himself was quick to open the rear door for a young woman. A man stepped out of the front passenger's side and waited for the woman to join him. *Young married couple,* Jonathon thought. No sign of kids yet, but they were smiling at each other like it was Christmas morning, and like Burton was Santa Claus. Jonathon finished the section of wall while Burton walked the couple through the front hall. Jonathon brushed his hands on his painter's coveralls, and he strolled out of the bedroom to meet the prospective buyers.

"And all new hardwood flooring in the hall here. We tore out all the old cupboards and replaced them. The bathroom's been overhauled, too. Ah – and here's the man himself. Jonathon Parker, this is Mr. and Mrs. Albert Grant."

Jonathon shook their hands. "I'm just finishing the paint work upstairs today. Other than that, the place will be ready for move-in by the end of the week." He introduced them to the specific improvements in the kitchen. "I tried to give it a country feel." The husband and wife were both nodding and asking questions. The missus opened the cupboards top and bottom, and she measured the depth of each with her forearm. The husband pulled open the refrigerator, and while he bent to peer at the interior space, Burton gave Jonathon a knowing smile and a thumb's-up.

The sale was practically in the bag. He felt good about this couple. They seemed to fit the place.

Then it occurred to him: he and Burton were going to sell the house, and there was a good chance that Jonathon was going to turn a sizable profit doing what he liked to do. He could take that money and reinvest it…buy another place, fix it up…invest that…*This might just work*, he thought. *Hell, this is easy!* He allowed himself the freest, biggest smile he'd smiled in years. *This could work!*

The husband stood up suddenly, and Jonathon assumed a studied poker face, as did Burton. "Is the basement finished?"

"With a wet bar," Jonathon answered.

The young husband stood very tall and very straight. "Can I see it?"

"Right this way," Burton said. He invited them into the hallway, and as the husband asked more intrigued questions, Burton winked at Jonathon.

CHAPTER THREE

REGINA. FALL 1975

Jonathon pushed his fist through the sleeve of his jacket and grabbed his cup of coffee in the same motion. He drained as much as he could before setting it on the kitchen counter and putting on the other sleeve.

"Jonathon?" Norma joined him at the sink, looking tired. Her eyes were rimmed with red.

"Sorry Mom, I've gotta fly." He kissed her on the cheek.

"Off to another property, so soon?" She toyed with the collar of his chequered shirt.

"Selling like hot cakes," he said. He smiled apologetically and finished his coffee. "Can't believe we're onto our third sale already."

"Jonathon," she said. Something in her tone made him stop in his tracks and turn. "It's Max."

Jonathon's shoulders dropped. "What about him?" She hardly needed to respond aloud. The answer was clear in her eyes.

"He passed away last night." She held Jonathon's hand. "Your father wants you to go with us to the funeral."

Jonathon frowned. He'd been on a roll, and he wanted to wrap up this sale before the end of the month. "Mom, I hardly knew the guy."

"I know."

"And I'm really busy on this new house."

"I know that, Jonathon. But you never spend any time with your Dad anymore, and he really wants you to be there." She squeezed his hand. "Jonathon, there's more to life than work. Don't let life pass you by. If you keep working at this pace, you're going to miss something important, and you're going to regret it."

Jonathon frowned.

"Please."

"When is it?"

"Thursday afternoon, around 1:00."

Jonathon sighed. "I'll come home in time for lunch, get cleaned up, and we can go right after that. Okay?"

She smiled wearily and nodded. He smiled for her, kissed her briefly on the cheek, and scurried out of the kitchen with a quick goodbye.

There weren't many at the funeral. The preacher kept forgetting Max's name, and every time he referred to his notes, Max's wife sobbed and wiped her eyes. Jonathon's eyes were watering too, but that was because of the wind and the cold. A fine dusting of snow fell from the sky to cover the open grave and the coffin suspended above it. Winter was on its way, and Jonathon was not especially looking forward to it. He'd been on a roll. He couldn't wait for spring. Winter was a drag. Everything was dead and buried. But spring! Spring was life, busy-ness, prosperity, second chances, fresh starts…

Jonathon had looked up at a sudden rush of activity. Edward had quit his wife's side, because Max's widow had faltered under the weight of her grief; but beyond Edward, Jonathon caught sight of a figure walking away – a tall, lean figure with waist-length black wavy hair. Norma patted her son on the arm and went to help Edward with the grieving widow. That left Jonathon without much to do but watch and wander. His parents weren't in a hurry to leave, so Jonathon trailed after the young woman who was walking away.

It *was* her.

He caught up quickly enough. "Hello."

The young woman startled and turned. Conflicting reactions made her eyebrows dance. "Hi." She turned to him fully, scrutinizing his face. "You knew my uncle?"

"Max? Yeah. Sort of. When my Dad was a teenager, he and my uncle worked on Max's farm for the summer. They've kept in touch ever since."

She almost smiled. "Well…thank you for coming to pay your respects. I'm sure my aunt appreciates you coming today." Jonathon shrugged and tried to think of something smart to say. She looked

20

tired, confused and impatient. "I'm sorry, do I know you from some-where?"

Jonathon reached into his inside coat pocket and pulled out a busi-ness card, which read "Jonathon Parker, Imperial Realty." He gave it to her, and smiled warmly.

The last time she'd seen him, he'd been wearing the goofy uniform of the fast food place, not the finely tailored suit and the overcoat he wore now. Norma had said that the suit aged him five years – in a good way. He didn't look nineteen. He looked like a lawyer. The raven-haired woman regarded him again, this time with a thoughtful smile.

"Rita," she said, putting out her delicate hand. They shook on it. "Rita Osterman. You sure we've never met somewhere before?"

"Are you in the real estate business?"

"No. The hospitality industry."

"You mean hotels?"

She smiled widely. She really was a ten when she smiled. She blushed and averted her eyes. "I'm working my way up the manage-ment ladder."

Jonathon nodded and crossed his arms. "I'm thinking of buying a hotel, myself."

Rita laughed skeptically. "Really?"

"Yeah!"

She crossed her arms, too, and she flipped her hair over her shoul-der. "Which one?"

"A place out of town. Way out of town. About six hours north of here."

She nodded. "Sounds like a…a good investment."

"Yeah," Jonathon sighed. "Yeah, it will be."

Incredible eyes, he thought.

She cleared her throat and fished for her keys.

"It'll uh…" He cleared his throat. "I'm probably going to need someone to run the place…" He scratched the back of his head, think-ing, *Now there's a pick-up line for you…* "Someone with experience and uh…"

"Ambition?"

"Yeah."

She smiled. "Listen, Jonathon…" She pointed feebly at the car behind her. "I'm sorry, I've…"

"Yeah! Yeah, I've gotta get going too."

"Work," she said.

"Same."

"Well…" She smiled again, bobbing her head and shoulders uncomfortably. "I guess I'll be seeing you around."

"Yeah," he said. He rushed to hold open the door for her, and she slipped onto the driver's seat with grace and determination. She reached for the door handle. "Listen. Rita." He cleared his throat. "Do you, uh…Would you like to go out for dinner some time?"

She froze, hand on the door handle. Then, a slow, knowing smile played out across her lips from the left corner to the right. "Dinner."

"Sure. Why not?"

The smile was saucy, now. "Will it be a number four meal deal?"

He flinched. "Oh God, no." *So she does remember me after all.* Then he thought, *I must have made quite the impression!*

She laughed and said, "I'm in the phonebook."

"Tomorrow?"

"Later this week," she said.

Boyfriend, he thought suddenly. *I should have asked…*

"I have a management meeting tomorrow night."

He beamed. "Later this week, then!"

She grinned back at him. "Bye now. Jonathon." She closed the door and started the engine.

"Rita," he said to himself. He crouched a little so he could smile at her through the driver's side window and wave. She waved with her fingers, and pulled away from the parking spot. "Rita."

Graveyard or no, he couldn't hide the smile. He'd be smiling all day. Tomorrow, he'd be a nervous wreck. Until then…

He cleared his throat, smoothed down his smile behind his hand, and trudged toward his parents, the very model of sobriety.

Jonathon measured his steps as he approached Burton's desk. Burton sat with his hands folded behind his head and his knees wide apart. "And?" Jonathon asked.

Burton's smile was somewhere between a grin and a leer.

"...*And*...?" Jonathon drew out.

"Full list price."

Jonathon clenched his fist in triumph. "That's the best news I've had all month. And the way this month has been going, that's really saying something." Burton lowered his arms and sat forward to start drafting the cheque. "Really? Full list price?"

"We've got the magic, partner."

Jonathon dumped the air from his lungs and sat in the chair on the opposite side of the desk. "What about the hotel deal? Any news?"

"What's the rush?" Burton asked as he scribbled his signature on the bottom the cheque. "Hot date or something?" When Jonathon didn't immediately respond, Burton looked up. "You dog," he laughed. "You do, don't you?"

Jonathon answered with a blush and a smile.

"When do I get to meet her? Is she hot?"

"Hot doesn't cover it. She's a *knock-out*," Jonathon answered. "As for meeting her..." He laughed drily and said, "Let's see how this date goes, first."

Burton handed him the cheque. Jonathon hummed as if satisfied by an excellent meal laid out before him. "That oughta help impress her, huh?" Burton asked.

Jonathon nodded. "No drive-thru for us tonight."

"Bank that cheque first. Put it someplace safe." He sat back again with his fingers interlaced behind his head. "Take it from me, Jonny. Hot broads are all alike."

Jonathon scoffed. "No, not her. You don't know her."

"Do you?"

Jonathon sighed. "Don't be so quick to judge." Burton shrugged. "The hotel," Jonathon said again. "Do we have it, or do we start something else?"

"No flies on you, huh?" Burton lit a new cigarette. "Relax. They're calling this weekend. Come back on Monday, I'll have news for you. So get out of here. Go get a haircut or something, you hippy."

Jonathon laughed and rose. "Thanks for this."

"Just keep working your magic, Jonny," Burton said. "That'll be thanks enough for me. And kiss her once for me. You going to meet up with her this evening?"

"Yeah. But I have a stop to make first."

Once Jonathon had signed the last page, the dealer wrote up the receipt and temporary registration.

"Don't lose this," the dealer said. "In a couple of weeks, you'll get your formal registration from the government in the mail. So hang onto this. Without it, it's illegal to drive."

"Great," Jonathon said, accepting the receipt and temporary registration form. They both stood up, and the dealer handed over the keys.

"Congratulations."

Jonathon beamed and shook the dealer's hand. "It's a very nice car."

"I know," the dealer said, extending his hand toward the parking lot, and to the brand new Cadillac awaiting its young driver. "And don't forget: you need anything, any kind of maintenance or repairs, you come back and see us, all right?"

"It's a deal."

Candlelight glimmered off the rim of Rita's glass, making her eyes twinkle. She caught him staring, and she smiled. It seemed almost surreal: everything was going perfectly, all day long. And it could only go up from here. Even if it didn't, he'd always have this one perfect night.

"Better than coffee?" he asked, pointing at the champagne flute in her hand.

"*Anything* is better than your coffee." Adopting an expression of profound surprise, she added, "I can't imagine why you quit."

"Hey, it wasn't all that bad."

"Really."

"Sure. It had its perks."

"What," she asked, "unlimited fries?"

He shrugged. "Responsibility, a steady pay, overtime..."

He felt the edge of her shoe against his shin.

"Upward mobility?" she asked, lifting an eyebrow. She hid her smile behind her champagne flute, and her foot went up his pant leg.

He cleared his throat and laughed self-consciously. "Only once that I can recall."

Her smile widened, and suddenly she loosed a free laugh that rang across the softly lit restaurant.

"Honestly," he said, "you were the only good thing to come out of that place."

She leaned toward him, her elbows on the table cloth. He could see down the front of her dress. "I can think of one other good thing that came out of that place."

He slid his hand across the table. She folded her fingers around his.

A two man band in the opposite corner of the restaurant began playing a soft tune. Jonathon couldn't quite place it, but he knew if he listened long enough, the words would come to him.

"Do you dance?" Rita asked.

Jonathon glanced at her. She smiled understandingly, though with a twinge of disappointment. "Sure I do. With both left feet." She snickered. "Want me to prove it?" Without waiting for her answer, he took her by the hand and led her toward the dance floor.

They danced until Jonathon lost track of the time. He ran his hand up her back, and she gazed into his eyes, as if asking a question. He kissed her gently on the lips. She smiled and pressed her cheek against his chest as they danced slowly, more or less in time with the music. She looked up again, and this time, she kissed him back.

They sat in the Cadillac, watching the full moon as it hung suspended over a clear, star-filled night. It was crisp outside, but Jonathon kept the engine running to keep the car warm. Anne Murray was on the radio singing *Cotton Jenny*.

He found her gloved hand and squeezed it.

"I had a great time tonight," she said. She was still buzzed from the champagne. Her cheeks were rosy. "Thank you."

He kissed her on the lips. She wanted more. He slipped his fingers through her hair. She looped her arm around his neck and slid her hips closer to his. She made a small, animal noise in her throat.

He had no idea when the song ended, but when they came up for air, the radio announcer was telling the time. It was already late, but they were both wide awake.

She smiled at him, gazing, teasing him through long eyelashes, and she bit her bottom lip. She tossed her hair over her shoulders. She was waiting for him to make the next move.

"You live alone?" he asked.

"I have a roommate," she answered.

Damn it.

"But she's gone for the weekend."

He put his hand on her knee. "You must be freezing." He brushed his hand along her thigh. She caught his hand and held it there.

"We probably shouldn't..."

He touched her face, slipping a lock of hair behind her ear.

"Call me old-fashioned," she explained.

He gently pulled her closer and kissed her again, tenderly. He turned off the car engine. "Shall I get the door for you, Miss Old-Fashioned?"

"Such a gentleman!"

She waited in the front passenger's seat while he stepped out and opened the door for her. He even held his hand out, to help her from the seat.

"You know," she said, "we old-fashioned girls have a thing for true gentlemen." He offered his elbow, and she hooked her arm through his. "I'm sorry I had to cut our evening short." Her heels echoed on the flagstones leading up to the apartment building doors.

"You have to work in the morning?"

"I'm up for a promotion soon," she said, "at the hotel. And when the boss needs you to report for duty..." They stood on the front steps, loosely embracing each other. "I really did have a great time tonight."

"Can I see you again?"

"Wrong question," she said, touching his lips with her gloved fingertips. They smelled of her perfume. "The real question is...*when* will you see me again?"

"And the answer is...As soon as possible. How's tomorrow night?"

She opened her mouth to answer. Then her face relaxed, and she said, "That's the correct response! You win the big prize."

"I hope it's a pony."

She laughed. "Really? Really, that's what you want?"

"No, not really." He hugged her closer. "I want a hotel. And someone to manage it for me. And a couple million bucks. That's not too much to ask, is it?"

She squeezed him around the middle with her arms. She was the perfect height. She could rest her head on his shoulder. When the wind blew, her hair brushed his face.

"No, not too much at all," she answered. "I think it's just right."

REGINA. SPRING, 1976

They walked out of the church into the smell of lilacs and fresh cut grass. It had rained earlier that morning, but now, the sun was bright and warm. A million beads of water dappled flowers, leaves and new spider webs, each aglow with the sunlight; people wearing their Sunday best seemed all the brighter and more colourful outside. Church bells rang overhead.

A cheer went up as the wedded couple emerged from the shadows of the church's front doors. Burton roared with glee and threw handfuls of rice at Jonathon and Rita. His secretary tossed rice onto the steps before them. Jonathon's parents stood at the bottom of the steps; Norma was crying, and Edward was smiling. Jonathon's grandfather

Jake winked and nodded with stoic approval, as if to say that Jonathon had done a good job.

Jonathon smiled at his prized catch. *How did a country boy land something this beautiful? What the hell does she see in me?*

Rita giggled and adjusted her veil. The large diamond in her ring sparkled in the sun. Someone had tied old soup cans and used boots to the rear bumper of Jonathon's Cadillac, and a sign said "Just Married!" The roof, trunk and hood were festooned with gaudy bows.

"Do you want to make a run for it?" Jonathon asked out of the side of his mouth.

"And go back to your place before the reception?" Rita whispered back.

Jonathon smiled eagerly at her.

They kissed, to the enormous delight of the rowdy crowd on the church lawn. Cameras clicked on all sides.

"On the count of three?" Jonathon asked her. She nodded and grinned. "Three!" With Rita squealing at his side, running under a torrent of rice, they ran down the church steps toward the car. Burton ran with them so he could open the door and help Rita with her dress while Jonathon fired up the engine. Once she was in, Burton slammed the door and waved them off. Burton stood in the road, his hand lifted, until Jonathon navigated a corner and disappeared out of sight.

They were thirty-five minutes late for the reception, and a little out of breath. Her hair wasn't as camera-perfect as it had been a couple of hours ago. Neither was his. Both were a little flushed. They couldn't stop smiling.

Jonathon lifted her off her feet, screaming and squirming. He rushed her past the Imperial Realty "For Sale" sign – now marked "Sold!" – and up the porch steps. Jonathon carried her across the threshold, and he'd barely closed the door before she clawed at his shirt buttons. They got as far as the living room before his feet tangled and he fell on the couch. She pounced on him, sitting on his thighs and tugging at the button of his jeans. He pulled her close and kissed her urgently until he could hardly breathe.

He came home from work, reeking of sweat and coated in drywall. "Rita?" It was dusk already. "Rita? Honey, are you home?"

There was a note on the kitchen counter. "Working late. Dinner in the fridge. XOXO."

He set the note down and smiled. He'd clean up before he ate. He was tired of the gritty feeling between his teeth and up his nose.

He'd been rinsing out his hair when he felt the temperature in the bathroom change. The shower curtains moved behind him.

Hands slid up his back to his shoulders, and two hot lips pressed against his spine. Her hands roved around to his chest, massaging, lathering him up. He turned and leaned her against the shower wall, kissing her hungrily as the water tumbled against them.

The sun had barely cleared the horizon. Her fingers swirled through his chest hair. She kissed his chest. He kissed the top of her head. As good as it was, all he really wanted was another half hour of sleep.

She stretched her arm across his chest. "I always like it best first thing in the morning," she purred. She reached down and aroused him. "Don't you?"

He smiled and said, "Mm-hmm..." He wasn't getting much sleep these days, but when he slept, he slept like the dead.

CHAPTER FOUR

He hated the drive. He'd always hated the drive. Regina wasn't so bad, but once they were out in the countryside, they had to change drivers frequently. Even with his foot to the floor, Jonathon couldn't make the prairies move. The wheels kept turning, sometimes potholes jostled the chassis, but the countryside never changed. He had one particular red barn in the corner of his eye for twenty minutes; he kept driving and driving and driving, and the barn was still there, like a bug on his driver's side window. The road eventually veered east around a patch of scraggly trees. Beyond it, there was a new barn to ride along with him. They were stuck on an asphalt treadmill.

Sometime after noon, Jonathon traded places with Burton. Rita sat in the front seat beside Burton, while Jonathon stretched out his legs in the backseat and rested his head against the passenger's side window. They'd lost radio reception some time ago, so the only thing to keep them entertained was the road noise. Rita had been reading a book for a while, but it was too dull to keep her attention. She struck up a conversation with Burton, talking about real estate, cars, music and film. Jonathon tried to follow the conversation, but, after so many hard-working days and so many acrobatic nights, he couldn't keep his eyes open for long. He caught a glimpse of Burton glancing in the rear view mirror, and as sleep crept over him, he could have sworn he saw Burton running his tongue over his teeth and wagging his eyebrows at Rita. In his dreams, he heard Rita cackling, humming, murmuring...

He snorted awake some time later. Rita had turned in her seat and taken a snapshot of him with her little Kodak. "Gotcha!" she laughed. She gestured with her fingers, indicating that he had to wipe his mouth. He blushed when he realized he'd been drooling in his sleep.

"What time is it?" Jonathon asked. The road wasn't well paved here. He heard gravel rumbling under the tires, and he worried about the paint job.

"Good timing," Burton said. "We're about five minutes away from Buffalo Narrows."

"Which puts us smack dab in the middle of nowhere," Rita sighed. "Who would put a hotel way out here?"

They passed through an intersection that could be laughably called 'Town'. There was a liquor store, a post office, the local RCMP office, a general store, a roadside diner, a Hudson's Bay store, and a bait and tackle shop. After that, there was a gas station, a couple of broken down houses, another garage, and a hunting supplies store. There was a string of houses set far back from the road, most of them looking ragged and unkempt. Every lawn looked like an extension of the local automobile junk yard. Burton eased the car onto a wide driveway and parked before the long patio.

The sign at the front of the parking lot said "Buffalo Narrows Hotel." Over the office door, another sign said "Vacancy". Beaten trucks of every shape and colour filled the southern end of the lot; Jonathon's Cadillac was the only car among them.

"You're sure this is the place?" Rita asked.

Burton pointed at the sign over the office door.

Rita wasn't convinced. "This isn't a hotel, it's a *motel*. And a cheap one at that!"

There were five or six men standing on the patio, some Native, some White, each of them wearing work boots, lumberjack coats and ratty hair. Rita lingered in the car, until Jonathon opened the door for her and tugged her out. Catcalls greeted her. Between all the men on the patio, there may have been one complete set of teeth. Every one of them had a bottle of beer in their hands. One of them was missing an eye.

"Ever feel like you've just stepped into a bad movie?" Rita asked.

Burton glanced at her curiously.

"Like...*Deliverance*, for example?" Rita said under her breath. Even bracketed by Burton and Jonathon, Rita looked concerned for her safety. Jonathon leaned close and hummed the first bars of *Dueling Banjos*.

"It isn't much to look at," Burton said, casting a wary eye over the two-storey, wide-hipped eye-sore. Its only striking feature was the slight but disturbing twist in the roof. There was an office at one end and a saloon-like bar at the other end, with a string of disreputable rooms between them, and all of it was painted a dull sand colour. "But you can't beat the price," Burton added with renewed optimism.

A man poked his head out from the office door. With a smile, he stepped outside and locked the office door behind him. He was a well-dressed grizzly bear of a man, easily six foot four or five, and for a man as heavy as he was, he was quick on his feet. He had an impressive, and seemingly unconscious, impact on the men outside the bar. They moved out of his way and quieted down. "Hello!" he called out. He smiled against the sun and strode across the parking lot with sure steps.

"Besides," Burton added, pointing roughly in the direction of the loiterers on the patio, "with the new uranium mine opened up, there's bound to be a bus-load of bored men with lots of money and nothing to do but entertain themselves."

"Uranium mine?" Rita asked.

"What, you thought they'd come out here for the tourist value?" Burton asked. "They make good money, and they have nothing better to spend it on but booze and..." He pointed at a female figure in a window. "And stuff."

"Hi there," said the stranger from the office. He looked like he didn't know whose hand to shake first. "You're the folks up from Regina?"

"That's us," Burton said. "Pat Burton, Imperial Realty."

"Bob Myers," was the reply. "Global Realty." He made his acquaintance with Rita and Jonathon next. "You're the couple that are thinking of buying the place?"

Rita was disinterested. Her nose wrinkled as if someone had passed gas.

"We're thinking of it," Jonathon answered.

"Would you like to take a look around?" Myers asked. He smiled and extended his hand toward the rowdier end of the hotel. "Starting with the bar?"

Dubiously, almost apologetically, Jonathon said, "The place looks like it could use a few renovations."

Myers winced and said, "A little elbow grease couldn't hurt, no."

"What's the annual sales revenue?"

Myers scratched his beard. "Close to a million, maybe?"

Rita's eyes flashed open. She exchanged glances with Jonathon. "How much?"

"At least, on the books, that's the gross we're pulling in," Myers said.

Rita quickly asked, "What's that net?"

"A couple hundred grand," Myers answered.

Her enthusiasm wavered. "A couple hundred thousand dollars."

"Yeah, maybe more," Myers answered. "The real volume should easily be that, but the current books are a disaster. Cash sales at the back door, if you get my meaning." His smile was tense. "The liquor store in town has rotten hours of operation, and the previous management wasn't so good at keeping things above board."

Rita glanced at Jonathon. "We could afford a few repairs," she commented.

"The asking price is low," Myers said, "but the problem is getting the financing. Low sales on the books...being this far north...It makes for a tough decision, for most buyers."

"We've got it covered," Burton replied smoothly.

"We have some investment properties we're about to sell off back home," Jonathon said.

"Wait." Rita hissed as if she'd been scalded. "We're not putting up the house for *that*, are we?" She was pointing at the bar and its patrons.

"Trust me," Jonathon whispered.

Rita was pale. "Jonathon."

Jonathon turned to Myers and said, "Why don't you show us around?"

"Great idea," Myers said. "Follow me!"

Rita had nothing but choice words for her husband, and it was all Jonathon could do to keep her from running back to the car and driving back to Regina without him. Myers looked uncomfortable, but Burton laughed, clapped him on the shoulder and said, "Newlyweds. Know what I mean?" Burton snorted and shook his head, then found his own way into the dark and dusty bar.

Willie Nelson was playing on the juke box. Two men were quarrelling over the next song. One wanted to listen to Johnny Cash; the other wanted to listen to nothing but more of Willie Nelson. Laughing Natives drank at the bar, while a few of the morose Whites sat at any one of the many tables, playing card games and bragging about sexual exploits they probably never had. It was a huge, open room, crowded with mismatched chairs and wooden pillars that supported a sagging, stained ceiling, and all of it was a dingy shade of burgundy and brown.

Pool tables, Jonathon thought. *That's what this place needs. Pool tables and pinball machines.*

Myers led them to a corner booth near a pair of dewy windows. When the waitress came over, he ordered drinks for everyone. He then pulled out a folded contract. "It's a great buy if you can spend the time managing and repairing it yourself. But the key is starting a real set of books, and keeping an eye on the employees."

"Why?" Rita asked.

"There's been some employee theft," Myers said. "Cash sales at the back door, remember?"

"That's why so much of the profit has been off the books," Jonathon said.

"You got it," Myers replied. "And that's what's killing the current owners. They're dying from a thousand cuts. This place...it needs a personal touch."

Jonathon looked at his wife, who already had management experience, and who took no guff from anybody. She startled. "Wait – you mean we'd have to *live* here?"

"Only until we find someone we can trust to run the place," Jonathon said. "Or until we sell it."

"Oh God," Rita groaned. "Are you kidding me?"

Myers jumped in, laying his hand on the table in front of her. "Rita, this could be your once in a lifetime opportunity here. With the right skills and a little bit of luck, you could make more here in one year than most people make in *ten*."

She bit her tongue.

Burton shrugged and said, "And I'd be happy to look after your house and other properties back in Regina."

"Thanks," Jonathon said. "I'd appreciate that."

Rita rolled her eyes and got up from the table. Jonathon followed her. "Excuse me," she said, once she was at the bar. The waitress turned. "Where's the washroom?"

"Around that corner, toward the back." the waitress said. "You'll need the key."

"Thanks."

"Rita," Jonathon said.

"Jonathon, I've got a good job back home, I'm up for a promotion..."

"Honey, you've been telling me you're up for a promotion for almost a year now."

She raised her hand as if to slap him. Instead, she pursed her lips and folded her fingers into a fist. "If we stay here," she said under her breath, "you've guaranteed that I'll *never* get promoted." The waitress held out the key for her. "And if we stay here..." she said, dangling the key in front of him. "What about our home, Jonathon? It has a toilet. A clean toilet – and I don't have to share it with *anybody* else except you."

He wrapped her in a hug. "Honey, we're not going to live in the *bar*." She was rigid against him. "It won't be forever."

She didn't answer.

"Honey, this is my dream! You remember? A hotel, someone to manage it, and a couple million dollars?"

"A couple million," she muttered against his chest. "We'd have to stay here way too long to make that much."

"And how many years would we have to spend at home to make that kind of money?"

After a moment, she released the tension from her shoulders. He gave her a squeeze and kissed her on the head.

"You'd better be right about this," she grouched. She broke the embrace and went off in search of the washroom. "Because if you're not..." she warned from across the bar floor.

A pack of hungry men watched her as she wagged her finger at Jonathon, and for want of stronger words, she turned and walked along the hallway, following the sign for the washrooms. At a hot glance from Jonathon, the patrons all found something new and interesting to drink at the bottom of their bottles.

CHAPTER FIVE

BUFFALO NARROWS. FALL, 1976.

By the glow of the brake lights, Jonathon helped close up the back of the beaten pick-up truck, and he dusted himself off. "I could use an extra pair of hands around the hotel," he commented as one of the two men peeled off bills from a roll. The man with the money snorted, and the other one laughed and climbed into the driver's side of the truck. "Nothing much – just some odd jobs here and there. We could call it barter," Jonathon said, jerking his chin at the cases of beer in the back of the truck. He took the money just the same, knowing that the best answer he could accept was a friendly laugh and a shake of the head. Jonathon pocketed the cash without counting it, and he waited until the truck pulled away before crossing his arms against the night's chill and heading inside.

It's my hotel, it's my booze, and I can do as I please, he thought, feeling the neat packet of dollar bills in his pocket. The problem wasn't whether or not he was selling beer by the back door. They'd kept track of the inventory and the revenue, and making sure that the two balanced at the end of the night; he was still doing so. Really, what was the difference if he sold liquor by the glass or by the gallon, so long as he kept it on the books?

The problem was, once he left, what would his customers do to the new management, if they stopped selling things so cheaply?

In the office, Rita was giggling and batting her eyelashes. Jonathon could see her through the window. Two stumbling drunks were at the front desk laying down cash for a room where they could sleep off the booze. One of the miners leaned hard against the counter. He was slowly spinning an extra twenty dollar bill. Rita smiled sweetly and said, "Upstairs and to the right."

"I dunno," said the man with the twenty dollar bill. He sucked his teeth and said, "Frank and I are both pretty drunk. We might get lost along the way."

Jonathon lingered by the office door. Despite the window in the door, no one saw him standing there. He could hear them as clearly as if the door was open.

"Maybe you oughta play the nice hostess," said the man with the money. "Show us our rooms in person?"

The other one stood at the far end of the counter, blocking Rita's path of escape. He had one hand against the wall and one against the counter. His top two shirt buttons were undone, and he was hairy. "And you should make sure we're all tucked in, so we don't fall out of bed."

Rita crossed her arms on the counter and leaned. She was wearing a low-cut blouse and a black bra. She toyed with the twenty. "You know..." She tossed her hair over her shoulder. "For twenty, I could show you where your rooms are. Anything more than that..." She shook her head thoughtfully.

Jonathon opened the door with a bang. "Hey Rita, I just came in to..."

Rita stood up, suddenly straight. She was pale.

"Oh – excuse me," Jonathon said, never taking his eyes off his wife. "I didn't realize we had paying guests." Rita's colour returned with a vengeance. She couldn't make eye contact with him. "Same rooms as before, hey boys?" he asked.

Both men coughed into their fists and muttered something about "upstairs" and "to the right." They didn't seem to need any further assistance finding their way.

Jonathon joined his wife behind the counter. He checked the roster. Two more guests, and they'd have to hang up the "No Vacancy" sign. He rubbed her shoulders. "How are you holding out?"

Rita smiled and turned between his hands.

"You're bored, aren't you?" he asked, running his hands up and down her arms.

"The money keeps me entertained," she answered. "But what I wouldn't do to have a night out with the *girls* for a change."

"Well, why don't you ask Peggy from the bar if she wants to do something some night? It'd do you both a world of good."

"And go where?"

She had a point. Buffalo Narrows Hotel was the place where everyone went for entertainment. What were they going to do, hide out behind the bar and paint each other's toenails?

"Civilization, Jonathon. Do you remember it?"

"We haven't been here *that* long," he said, kissing her on the nose.

"Feels like forever already. It's getting so I can't even stand the smell of the place anymore. One more drunk asking me to tuck him in, and I'll scream. I don't know how you can stand it."

Jonathon kissed her again. "For me it's easy. No one ever asks me to tuck them in." She laughed drily. "Not much longer now, okay? All the work's been done on the east end of the hotel, the bar's completely refurbished, and we can't work on the roof until spring…"

"And what about the guy in the States? Are you any closer to selling the place?"

"That's what I came to tell you. We've worked out a deal with the American."

Her eyes widened and sparkled.

"He's sending his management team in soon, and if the sales stay up at this rate, he'll buy us out in no time."

"You mean…we can go home?"

"Sooner than you think."

"Jonathon, that's *great* news! Is it a good deal?"

"It's a *very* good deal."

"Everything you ever hoped and dreamed of?"

"It's close enough."

She embraced him and sighed against his chest, genuinely relieved.

"Listen honey…" Jonathon could hear the guests walking along the upstairs hallway. "I think you should go on ahead. Take the car. I'll stay until the Americans get here and get settled into the routine."

"You're sending me home?" she asked.

"I'll be home a few days after you leave."

She gazed into his face. "You don't want me hanging around anymore?"

"I want you to go home and check on the house and everything. Go for a night on the town with the girls. I know you miss your girl-friends."

And he knew she wasn't happy there. He knew she'd been finding ways of keeping herself entertained while her husband was busy else-where. She was the most beautiful thing on two legs for two hundred miles in all directions, and she liked the attention.

"I'd love to go home," she confessed. She pressed her ear to his chest and caressed his back. "But what about *us*? I'll miss you."

"It'll be hell for me too, knowing you're at home alone and I'm not there with you."

"So I guess that means we'd better say goodbye properly," she purred.

He kissed her deeply, searchingly. *You're mine*, he thought at her. *You're my wife*. With his kiss, he imprinted upon her lips a memory of himself, of his devotion, of their vows.

Rita reached behind her and turned the sign from "Office Open" to "Office Closed."

Jonathon disembarked from the Cessna with a vague sense of urgency. He'd been away a full week longer than he'd hoped. He needed to see Rita. They'd been apart three weeks. Three long, difficult, tense weeks. She'd sounded distant on the phone.

Jonathon claimed his baggage and headed for the terminal doors. Burton was standing beside the door, smirking. His sunglasses reflected the setting sun behind Jonathon. There was something bitter about Burton's smile, as if his teeth had contracted dry rot. Once Jonathon was close enough, Burton took one of the suitcases from him and led the way across the small airport.

"Where's Rita?" Jonathon asked.

"Huh?"

"Rita. My wife. I thought she was going to pick me up."

"Oh. Had to take care of some business. How'd everything go with the sale? You got the bank transfer all right?"

"Pat," Jonathon said. "What business?"

"How the hell should I know? She's your wife. She said she'd meet you at home later tonight."

"What, is she working again?"

"Huh? Yeah, maybe, I guess so. I don't know. She mentioned something about talking to an old boss about a job."

On the phone, Rita had bitterly complained about having no job to come home to. She'd officially quit her old job in order to be with Jonathon in Buffalo Narrows, and since no one knew when she would come back, they had backfilled her position.

"Did she find a new job?"

"Maybe that was the business she had to take care of."

Jonathon shrugged. "I hope so. She gets bored easily."

"Yep," Burton said.

Jonathon squinted at him, but between the sunglasses and the guarded expression behind them, Jonathon didn't know what to make of Burton's prompt response.

"The deal," Burton asked. "How'd it go?"

"Almost too good to be true," Jonathon said.

"So it was worth the effort."

Jonathon wasn't so sure. He wouldn't be, not until he got home. Not until he talked to Rita.

Jonathon parked in front of the house and left his suitcases in the car. He opened the door quietly.

"Rita?" He closed the door behind him. "Honey, you home?" He stuck his head in the living room. The TV was on, but no one was watching it. Rita had spent some time redecorating the place, as she'd said on the phone. He liked it. Everything seemed to go together. But something felt off, too.

There were no pictures on the walls anymore. No pictures of their time dating, no wedding portraits, no photos of their honeymoon. Their home had become a showcase of good taste, but it was as anonymous as a page out of an Eaton's catalogue.

"Rita?" he called.

"I'll be out in just a sec!" She was in the bathroom. She closed the door.

Something smelled funny in the kitchen. She'd left a window open a crack, which was strange for so late in the fall, but the smell lingered. He closed the window to pinch off the bitterly cold breeze. He poured himself a glass of water from the tap.

There was a letter on the counter. He flattened it. It was some kind of medical document dated for earlier that same day.

The toilet flushed. Jonathon finished his glass of water and turned to rinse out the glass when he spotted cigarette ashes in the drain.

"Jonathon," Rita breathed. She was barefoot and wore tight jeans, and above the waist, she wore only her bra. "God am I glad to see you." Her eyes were misty, and she ran at him kiss-first, wrapping her arms and legs around him, forcing him against the kitchen counter. She stole the breath from his mouth.

"Rita," Jonathon started.

"No," she whispered. She kissed his lips. "No, just say hello."

"Hi," he said impatiently.

"Not that way." She silenced him with a plunging, desperate kiss. "Please."

It had been a very long three weeks. Whatever it was, it could wait until morning. He carried her as far as the refrigerator before he lost his balance the first time. *Three weeks*, he thought. He kissed her behind the ear, and she dragged her nails across his back.

He roused sometime in the night. Rita was climbing back into bed beside him. He touched her shoulder. She rolled onto her side, facing away from him.

Jonathon flung back the covers and got out of bed. Something wasn't right. He went into the kitchen for another glass of water. The medical document was gone. It wasn't in the trash – in fact, the trash was empty, with no new bag in the bin. The cigarette ashes had been washed away. The kitchen smelled of Lysol, masking any trace of the cigarette smell.

He drank, he went to the washroom and he went back to bed, but he lay on his back, arms crossed, and he stared at the ceiling. *No pictures on any of the walls.* He rolled over and felt around the top of his night table. A picture frame was missing there, too. He opened the drawer, and there he felt the familiar metal edges of a 5"x7" frame. He lay on his back until dawn, putting the pieces together.

When Rita woke again, she rolled over and touched his chest. He plucked her hand off his body. Her fingers were clammy. He got out of bed and began to dress for work. She sighed a hissing sigh. While he dressed, she rose and raked a brush through her hair.

In my house! In my own bed? He wrestled his tie into a half-Windsor. "Who was it?"

She paused, the brush halfway down her long black hair.

"Your friend who was over," he said. "The one who smokes."

She pulled the brush through the tangles as if pulling out her hair. She was thinking. "Carla. She came over and we watched some TV."

"Yesterday afternoon?"

She narrowed her eyes.

"I don't care," he added with a laugh. "I'm just curious, that's all." He cinched his belt. "What was on TV?"

"I don't know. We got talking about her husband. They've been having some problems lately, and she needed someone to talk to."

"Pat told me you had some business. I figure whatever was on TV must have been damned interesting, if you couldn't spare a few minutes to pick your own husband up from the airport."

She shrugged. "I know Pat wanted to talk to you as soon as possible about the hotel deal. I knew I'd have all night with you. It made sense at the time."

He combed his hair. "Cigarette ashes in the sink," he said. "And if I remember the smell correctly, it's the same brand Pat smokes."

She slapped her brush on the dresser. "A lot of people smoke the same brand. That's how brands stay in business."

"It's just an observation," he said. His voice was flat.

"It's an accusation," she said, "and I don't appreciate it."

"What would I be accusing you of?" Jonathon asked. "Tucking someone in?"

She shot to her feet, fists clenched at her sides. "You bastard."

Jonathon gritted his teeth.

"Come out and say it," she said. "Say it."

"Who was it?" he asked.

Her eyes reddened and watered. She looked at him as if he was a maggoty side of beef. "Well, it wasn't *his* fault," she said.

Jonathon took his wallet, his keys and his suit jacket and he slammed the bedroom door behind him. Rita screamed, "Jonathon!" He marched down the hall and slid his feet into his shoes. She came out of the bedroom with her dressing gown flapping behind her. "Jonathon, come back here. Listen to me!" He threw on his suit jacket. "Jonathon, please." He carried his winter coat outside, and he slammed the front door between them. He had his key in the Cadillac when she flung open the front door and screamed his name again. "You walk away from me, Jonathon, and you'll regret. I swear to God, you'll regret it."

He got into the car and started the engine.

- § -

Burton's secretary looked up, aghast at the crack and bang of the front door. She stood up, exclaiming, "Jonathon! You're back!"

He ignored her.

Burton was joking with a pair of prospective buyers. They turned and looked like they were about to invite him in on the good humour. One by one, the smiles faded.

"Pat," Jonathon said. His voice was low and quiet. "Can I talk to you for a second? Alone?"

Burton grinned. "Can't you see? I'm in the middle of some important business here. You know. Grown-up stuff."

Jonathon's cheeks burned. "Now."

"Jonny," Burton laughed.

"*Now.*"

"Listen, Pat," said one of the two men as they rose. "I could sure use a coffee. You want anything?"

46

"Yeah, sure," Burton said. He was smiling, but the corners of his mouth trembled with the effort of keeping the rictus in place. "I could use something to drink."

The two businessmen left, and one of them softly closed Burton's office door.

Burton interlaced his fingers behind his head and smiled.

In three strides, Jonathon covered the distance between them. He leaned across Burton's desk and wrapped his fists in the front of Burton's shirt. Burton laughed and said, "What's the matter, partner? Have a rough night?"

"You had no *right!*" He bunched up Burton's collar and pulled Burton's face closer to his own. "You were my *friend.*"

Burton's grin faltered. He was sweating. "What the hell was I supposed to do? She was on me like *lice!*" He grabbed Jonathon's wrist and pried at Jonathon's fingers. "We were drunk and she was bawling her eyes out. One thing led to another." His voice was rising, and his face was turning a shade of purplish-red. "Damn it, I'm sorry!"

Jonathon released him with a shove.

"She's bad news, Jonny. I told you that. I warned you. Broads like her, they're all alike. If she likes you, she'll bleed you dry with a smile. If she hates you, she'll bleed you dry by stabbing you in the back, and you won't even see it coming." Burton scoffed. "That's the problem with you. You're naïve. You look at people and you only see the good in them. You're just a kid, Jonny, and you don't know *shit* about the real world. You can't read people." He leered. "You're a sucker and you're a patsy. And one of these days, somebody's gonna take you for a ride and they're gonna *ruin* you."

Jonathon spat on the floor and walked away.

"Take it from me, Jonny. She's no good. You want to do something smart for a change? You better bank some place she can't touch the money."

"Screw you, pal."

"No thanks," Burton said. "Your wife already took care of that."

Jonathon broke the glass in the door on his way out of the Imperial Realty office. *Better the glass than that lying grinning face.* He got in the car and drove without knowing where to go.

CHAPTER SIX

Jonathon smiled at the assistant manager, hoping he spoke English. "I'd like to start a new account, please," he said as he sat down at the mahogany and purple-trimmed desk.

"Yes, I can help you with that," the manager replied. His English was accented but fluent and easy. "You're from Canada?"

"Good guess," Jonathon said with a relieved laugh.

"It's your first time in Switzerland?"

"Yes. Beautiful country, what I could see from the airplane."

He smiled coolly. "Welcome to Zurich." He slid the first of the pages across the desk, pointing with the tip of a pen where Jonathon should start filling in the details.

"Thank you."

"You are bringing money for a small deposit, yes?"

Jonathon lifted his briefcase and clicked open the clasps. At the sight of the stacks of Canadian currency, the assistant manager pressed a button to call in a teller. He didn't register any surprise at the cool hundred thousand Jonathon had been carrying around with him. Jonathon had been walking around like he'd been carrying a bomb, and he was relieved to hand it over at last. "I'll be able to access this any time, right?"

"You," said the manager, counting the currency one stack at a time, "and only you. We will take your thumb print."

"Wow," Jonathon said. "So my wife won't be able to touch it, then."

"She has the same thumb print as you?"

Jonathon laughed.

"Then no."

Jonathon swallowed his good humour. It left a bad taste in his mouth. "That's the best news I've had all week."

The assistant manager only grunted by way of sympathetic comment.

Jonathon stepped out of the Air Canada plane feeling lighter and heavier at the same time. His money was safe, well out of Rita's reach, but it was damned shame that he had to go to such measures, just to cover his ass. He'd be damned if he let Rita profit any more from the sale of the Buffalo Narrows Hotel. She'd made enough undeclared income up north.

To his surprise, Rita was waiting for him on the other side of the door of their home.

"Where have you been?" she asked. Her hair was tied back, and she wore no make-up.

He set down his lightened briefcase and his overnight bag, and he continued past her to the bar at the back of the living room.

"You're not going to let me live this down, are you?" Rita asked.

He poured himself a double.

"You're just going to keep beating me over the head with it. How long are you going to keep this up, Jonathon?"

The ice clinked against his teeth.

"What, so we're not even going to try and get past this, are we?"

He set down his glass. "Probably not." He refilled the glass. "You can take the bed tonight. I'll be fine out here."

Her jaw muscles tensed.

The truth of the matter was, he didn't want to sleep in that bed again for a while. He didn't know whose aftershave he'd smell this time.

Global Realty had its office closer to the downtown core, on the ground floor in a high rise. Jonathon straightened his tie and marched in. The secretary smiled, but before she could speak, Bob Myers rose and exclaimed, "By God, if it isn't Davy Crockett himself, returned from the great wide wilderness." Myers was one to talk. Confined to an urbane office like this, the great grizzly bear of a man looked bigger than ever. He roared a laugh and met Jonathon at the door with a thrust-forward hand and a clap against Jonathon's arm. "How the hell are you?"

"I'm all right, Bob," Jonathon said. Myers' smile was infectious. It blew away the sombre clouds hanging over Jonathon's head. "How are you?"

"Fine, just fine. Welcome back home, Jonathon. Come on in – great to see you again."

"Thanks Bob."

"What brings you? Tell me everything went all right with the sale of that hotel."

"It did," Jonathon said, though he didn't sound convincing. "The new management is all settled in, and I am now free and clear."

"Feels good, doesn't it?"

"Yes it does."

"So what brings you?"

"Well…" Jonathon chuckled self-consciously and scratched the back of his head. "It's a long story, but…I'm in the market – "

"For another hotel property?"

"For a job."

Emotions flickered across Myers' face, the last and most lingering of which was curiosity.

"Long story," Jonathon asked. "One that requires a lot of beer to help it along."

"Ah," Myers said. "Well, say no more, not until you're ready. In the meantime, step into my office, Jonathon, and we'll get right down to brass tacks."

During the months that followed, Jonathon sold one property after the other. He'd become the intermediate owner of properties that flipped so quickly he rarely had the time – or the need – to put his name on official notarized paperwork. One after the other, Jonathon bought and sold properties like trading cards, with Myers picking up a percentage of the profits every time. Houses, estates, restaurants, small offices around Regina, he bought and sold them all, leaving each a little sturdier and cleaner than when he'd first purchased them.

And once every two or three weeks, Jonathon would board an Air Canada plane for Zurich, bearing currency by the thousands. He left a healthy cut of his own profits in his home accounts, but he would not be without a nest egg of his own, out of the reach of Rita's dirty hands.

REGINA. WINTER, 1976

"Then sell whatever makes sense. I really want that apartment block. I've been eying it for months."

Rita sat across from him at the table. They'd managed some civil conversations, but they still slept in separate rooms. She was watching a spot between his eyebrows, as if by the force of her own will, she could bore a hole in his forehead.

"Sure," Jonathon said. "Yeah, absolutely. Yeah, even the house, if that's what it takes."

Rita's blushed. She betrayed no other reaction.

"All right. I'll see you in the morning." Jonathon hung up the phone on the wall-base. He breathed and massaged his face.

"You're not selling our house," Rita said.

"Our?" Jonathon asked. She folded her hands into fists. "Listen." He sighed. "If I can get this apartment block at the price I think I can get, and if I give it a quick face-lift, then I can flip it and take in enough profit to buy three or four houses like this one." He ran his gaze around the frosty trap his home had become. "I'm only using the house as collateral."

"And if you don't sell your precious apartment block?"

"It's not a matter of whether I can sell it for profit or not. It's a matter of when, and how much."

She lowered her eyes. She picked at dirt under her nails. "Collateral?"

"Unless I can find an investor."

She pursed her lips and raised her eyebrows, as if struck by an idea worth further consideration.

"What, you know somebody?"

Rita cleaned the nails of her other hand. "I might." She cocked her head to the side. She wasn't making eye contact. Such a look used to mean that she had something to hide; now it meant she was happily excited and didn't want to admit it. "My manager at the hotel introduced me to an investor out of Edmonton. He was interested in buying our hotel at the time."

"So he's well off."

She nodded quickly, still keeping her eyes on her nails. "He would have to be. If he had enough to invest, do you think we could keep the house?"

Jonathon considered it. Finally, he shook his head. She sighed through her nostrils and started up from the kitchen table. "I just don't want another partner," Jonathon said. "Besides, we have enough to cover the investment ourselves. If we're the sole investors, we're the only ones who profit."

"Okay, so sue me for trying to help, Jonathon."

Jonathon sat back from the table, hands over his eyes and his head thrown back. He hated when she was in this mood. It didn't matter what he said. She'd take it the wrong way.

"I just thought, maybe if you would let me help you, you'd know that I…" She paused, then exhaled. "You know what? Never mind."

Jonathon got up and poured himself another drink. He never used to drink so much. He thought about farms, and tractors, and long days out under the sun with nothing but the wind for company. "Who is it?" he asked.

"Why should I tell you? You don't want any more partners."

Jonathon shrugged. "So we put up the house. Okay."

She rolled her eyes. "I don't know how to get in touch with him directly, but I know someone who works for him. I can give him a call, see if we can win him over."

Jonathon turned to the bar and dropped in another cube of ice. He pressed the glass to his forehead.

Her hands slid around his waist. "Please," she said. "Please, Jonathon just let me help you for a change." When he sighed, she added, "I haven't given up on us. But if you don't let me try to make it up to you, I'll know *you* have given up." She kissed him on the shoulder.

Jonathon had had to stick around an extra day to oversee the transfer of a large in-town property, so he would follow Rita out to Edmonton the day after she left. Once that was done, the night before his flight, he stopped in at the Global Realty Office to talk shop with Bob Myers.

Myers peered over the desk at Jonathon. "Do we know who this guy is?"

"The investor?"

"Yeah."

Jonathon said, "Rita said she knows his office manager. Reg Lawrence is his name."

Myers frowned. "Doesn't ring a bell. Who does he work for?"

"She said the guy's full name, but it went in one ear and out the other. She kept calling him 'Fred'. Fred Somebody. But apparently he's big enough an investor to afford the Regina Inn."

Myers nodded, mildly impressed. "That's the hotel Rita works at?"

"Yeah. She was there when this Reg Lawrence and his boss Fred were there negotiating the terms of the sale. And the Regina Inn is doing well these days, so he's probably not hurting for cash. That apartment building should be peanuts for a guy like him."

Myers sucked his teeth. "Well…just be careful who you deal with."

Jonathon nodded. "I'll be handling the negotiations myself."

"Uh huh." Myers cleared his throat. "And uh, you sent Rita on ahead? Without you?"

Jonathon gritted his teeth. "The lawyers asked me to be here for this transfer, and I couldn't get out of it. And I didn't want to cancel that initial meeting with Reg today. It was Rita's idea." He cracked his knuckles and stared at the floor. Myers offered a sympathetic sigh. "I have to trust her," Jonathon muttered. "If you can't trust your own wife, who can you trust?"

Myers shook his head. "Sometimes I remember just how young you really are, Jonny."

Jonathon didn't reply.

Jonathon deposited his briefcase and wardrobe bag at the foot of the telephone table in the lobby of the hotel. He lifted the receiver and called the room. He got a busy signal.

He was determined to give her the benefit of the doubt. He checked his watch. He checked the room number with the front desk. He searched every female face in the lobby and in the bar. No sign of Rita. He tried calling her room again. Another busy signal.

"Damn it," he groaned. He picked up his luggage and entered the elevator, full of dread. He knew something was very wrong. The last time he'd felt this way, his suspicions had been on the money. He wanted to be wrong. With all his heart, he wanted to be wrong.

The elevator bounded to a stop and dinged. He expected to see her standing on the other side of the doors, pleasantly surprised by his arrival, but the corridor was empty. He followed the hall down to his assigned room. From two doors away, he could hear the music. His heart thumped. He was pre-emptively angry. At the very least, she was twenty minutes late for meeting him downstairs. At the very worst –

He stood outside the hotel room, listening through the door. The music was definitely coming from within. He knocked. There was no answer, though someone turned down the volume. He waited, listening for voices. He knocked again, louder this time.

"Who is it?" Rita asked.

"Me," he answered.

He heard a soft, questioning voice. There was a soft reply, followed by a hushed exclamation. Suddenly, motion.

"Gimme a second!" Rita said.

Jonathon's temperature rose. He slid the key into the lock and twisted the knob.

"Wait! I'm not – "

He entered, almost pinning her between the closet and the back of the door.

"I'm so sorry Jonathon," she said. Her hair was wet and tangled, and she wore a towel like a wrap-around robe. "I didn't get much sleep at all last night, and I took a nap – I only woke up not ten minutes ago and I went to take a shower and when I came out and realized what time it was..."

He pushed past her. The bed was a mess. The phone was off the hook. "Restless, were you?" he asked, pointing to the floor and the pile of laundry she'd made of the bedcovers. There was a single wine glass, used, on the nightstand. The bottle beside it was nearly empty.

"I didn't sleep well," she shot back. "Why didn't you call me to tell me you were here?"

"I did call," he answered, pointing at the unhooked phone receiver beside her bed. "Twice."

"I mean from the airport!" she retorted. Her face was red. "You should have woken me up. I would have met you downstairs."

"Why call from the airport?" Jonathon asked, standing between the open bathroom door and the closet. "So you could buy somebody a little time?" Something caught the corner of his eye. He looked in the bathroom. On the counter, there was another wine glass. It was wet, as if it had been recently washed. "Good God, you couldn't wait one damned *day*?"

"Jonathon, how *dare* you!"

"What?" he asked. "Accuse you?" There was a discarded sock poking out from under the closet door. "What the *hell* would I have to accuse you of? Adultery?"

Jonathon flung the closet door along its track. A young, red-headed man stood with his unworn pants balled up and pressed against his naked groin. Jonathon reached in and pulled the stranger out of the closet, shoving him through the open bathroom door. The red-head stumbled on the rug and sat awkwardly on the toilet. "Reg Lawrence, I presume?"

"Oh God," Reg said. "I am so sorry."

"You shut your mouth, asshole, and put your pants on while you still can." Jonathon slammed the bathroom door.

Rita backed further into the hotel room, morose and angry. She said nothing.

"I sent you on ahead to conduct business in my place." He looked her up and down, disgusted, disillusioned. "This is how you conduct business? Which business were you conducting?"

"It's not what it looks like."

Jonathon blinked at her. "It's not…" He laughed in spite of himself. "It's not what it looks like?" He laughed again as he kicked his luggage out into the hall. He laughed in the elevator.

He stopped laughing when he put down the money to rent another room down the hall and out of earshot of Rita's room. He didn't go to bed until well after the bar was closed for the night.

Jonathon snorted awake. He was lying face down on the hotel room bed. His pillow was damp with sweat. His room phone was ringing.

It was eleven in the morning. He didn't want to talk to Rita. Not until he was sober. He clamped his pillows to the back of his head and shouted at the phone. It rang again, insistently. If he didn't answer it, he figured, Rita would come banging on his hotel room door, crying and screaming and begging forgiveness, even if it meant doing it out in the hall where everyone could hear her.

He slapped the night table until he found the receiver. It took two tries to get the handset angled correctly. "Hello?"

"Mr. Parker?" It wasn't Rita.

"Yes?" He rolled over. "That's me."

"Good morning, Mr. Parker. This is the front desk. We have a message for you from your wife."

Great. "Okay."

"She says you're to call a Mr. Anton – Fred Anton. There's a number here too. Would you like me to give it to you?"

Jonathon sat up in bed and hunted for a pen and the hotel stationery. "Yes, give me a second." When he was ready, he asked for the number, and he wrote it down, along with the name Fred Anton. "Thanks. Anything else in the message?"

"Only that she wanted you to know she's checked out already."

He wasn't surprised, but he was mildly relieved.

He didn't expect to see her at home when he got there.

"Thanks," he said, and the desk clerk told him to have a good day. Jonathon sat on the edge of the bed, weighing his options and reliving the last two days – every word, every promise. He didn't know what to make of this turn of events. He didn't know what to do next, or who to believe, or who to trust. But in the end, he decided that Fred Anton hadn't had anything to do with the mess that had become of Jonathon's marriage, and he deserved more than an unreturned phone call. He got up, showered, dressed, and after a quick breakfast downstairs, he called the office of one Fred Anton.

CHAPTER SEVEN

Fred Anton sat at his desk like a quiet conqueror, self-possessed but relaxed and amused. He seemed to wear his office, and to wear it as comfortably as any other man might wear a fine Italian suit. Everything was well-coordinated, from the plush burgundy carpet to the cherry wood desk. Even his tie matched the colours in the art deco mural on the one wall. Like the rest of the Anton Building, the man's office shone with sunshine and chrome, and it was adorned with artificial waterfalls. Anton himself wore a well-tailored suit that flattered him, despite his advancing age and despite the signs of a body accustomed to luxury and excess. Anton was on his feet, pouring himself a drink. "Mr. Parker," he said. He had a deep voice full of good humour. "Welcome." He set down the tumbler and put out his hand. Jonathon approached and shook the offered hand.

"Thanks for seeing me, Mr. Anton."

"Please. Call me Fred." He pointed at the decanter. "I know it's still early, but the sun's over the yard arm somewhere. Can I interest you?"

Jonathon hesitated, but he accepted.

"You're younger than I expected," Anton laughed. "Sure you're old enough to drink this?"

Jonathon offered to show his ID.

"Relax," Anton said. He gave Jonathon a generous glass. "Have a seat. Reg told me about your proposition."

Jonathon forced a smile. "Did he tell you about anything else?"

Anton seemed curious.

"Uh – forget it. He gave you all the details?"

Anton sipped his drink and hummed an 'uh huh' into his glass. After swallowing, he pointed vaguely at Jonathon and said, "It's been a long time since I've been to Regina. You know that's where I'm from?"

59

"No, I didn't know," Jonathon said.

Anton asked about certain nostalgic restaurants and landmarks, and he mentioned the hotel. Jonathon mentioned Rita in passing, and before long, Jonathon was offering the name of the restaurant that served the best souvlaki in town. Anton knew the best Italian restaurants, including, to their surprise, one that Jonathon had never even heard of.

Anton sat on the corner of his desk. "So this apartment building," he said. "You think it'll flip reasonably quickly?"

"Absolutely. Thirty days at the outside."

Anton showed his ready smile. "Ah, the ambition of youth."

"No, I'm serious," Jonathon said. "I have a couple of people already interested in it. All I have to do is give it a quick face-lift, and it's good for sale. Thirty days."

Anton smiled more cautiously this time. "And what is it you propose? The old 'What's in it for me' question."

"I found it," Jonathon explained, "I put the work into fixing it, I find a buyer and negotiate the sale. You finance it. We split the profits fifty-fifty."

Anton finished his drink. He set the sweaty glass carefully on a coaster, twisting it on the cork. He studied Jonathon, and Jonathon wondered – not for the first time – if people mistook his confidence for arrogance. "A long time ago," he said, "I was like you. Quick. Cocksure. But someone gave me a break, and they held me to my word." He smiled and tilted his head. "And now here I am. I was good to my word, and I didn't let my partners down."

"I won't let you down either, Mr. Anton."

Anton squinted.

Jonathon smiled sheepishly. "Fred."

"Good. You'd better not." Anton put out his hand. "Partner."

Jonathon grinned.

Bob Myers was unenthusiastic, much to Jonathon's disappointment.

"You did see the cheque, did you not?" Jonathon asked. "What more could you ask for? This is in the *bag*, Bob."

Myers stabbed his desk with his index fingers. "Jonathon, you lie down with dogs, you get up with fleas. It doesn't matter how rich the dog is."

"What the hell are you talking about?"

"When you said 'Fred Somebody', I'd been worried you were talking about Fred Anton – and now here you come in here with a big fat cheque from the guy."

"You know him," Jonathon said.

"Of course I know him. Everybody knows him." Myers lifted an eyebrow and allowed, "Everybody but you, apparently." He scratched his beard, then sat forward and explained. "I have a few friends who are Mounties, and I hear things, you know?"

Jonathon laughed incredulously.

"Fred Anton is bad news, Jonathon. You don't know him."

"He's an investor, and I know as much about him as I do any other investor. It's just business."

"Fred Anton is more than a businessman, Jonny. You ask him where he got his money from. You ask him who his associates are. His *Italian* associates."

"You've got something against Italians?"

"I've got something against the *mob*, Jonny."

Jonathon stared at him, and when the tension grew too great, he laughed at Myers' poker face. "Oh come on, Bob. A guy like that – what would he be doing hanging around a bunch of wise guys?"

"The guy hasn't worked a day in his life, and he pals around with people who..."

"Bob, you invest a little, you get a little profit; you invest that profit in something bigger, you get a bigger return on investment. Make enough smart decisions, and eventually you get to the same point Fred is." Jonathon laughed again. "Bob, that's no different from what I'm trying to do."

"*You* don't associate with the mob."

Jonathon tired of the gag. "What's your proof?"

Myers closed his mouth.

Jonathon rolled his eyes and sighed, still chuckling at the absurdity of the baseless accusation. "If Fred was up to no good, he would have been caught by now. Isn't that what they say about the Mounties? They always get their man?" He shook his head. "Just because he's Italian and rich, that doesn't mean he's in the mob. Don't judge a book by its cover."

"You can tell a lot about a book by the library it's kept in, Jonathon." Myers shook his woolly head. "You just watch your back, all right? Maybe I'm wrong. I don't know. I just don't want to see you get burned. You've had enough of that for one year."

Jonathon paused by the open office door. He left.

Rita was home. She jumped up from the couch when he came in the front door, but he refused to speak with her. He refused to look at her. He'd only come in long enough to refill his suitcase with clean clothes to last him a week.

"Jonathon," she pleaded through the closed bedroom door. "Will you at least listen to me for thirty seconds?"

He didn't answer. He opened his nightstand to take out some personal items, and he stopped. In the drawer was his wedding picture, turned face down even in the drawer.

"Jonathon, you ignore me," she warned through the door, "and I swear, you will regret it."

He threw socks and clean underwear haphazardly into his suitcase. He zipped up the luggage, and then he heard the slamming of the front door. He teased away the curtain from the window, and he saw Rita's car speeding away with clouds of burnt rubber fouling the air and staining the driveway.

Dr. Vladimir Petrovski adjusted his John Lennon glasses and coughed. Jonathon wasn't sure if it was anxiety, nervous energy or the cold snap that made the small, Eastern European man so twitchy.

"I've had the security system replaced too," Jonathon said. "So now, an alarm goes off if someone tries to prop open the back door for too long. Some of the residents had been keeping the door open day and night, meaning anybody could have just walked in off the street. That new alarm system should help with your insurance rates."

"It's quite a lot of money," Petrovski said. He fidgeted with his tie.

"And it's a great investment," Jonathon reminded him. "The passive income alone should bring you a return on investment in four years or less. More, if you decide to sell it later."

Petrovski nodded. "I came to dis country vit' little more than two pennies to rub together, and now look at me." He blew warm air into his gloved fists. The apartment building rose before him like Everest. "Buying an apartment building. Me, a landlord! Like some kind of big shot."

Jonathon smiled and shook Petrovski's hand.

"And now I have tenants!" Petrovski said. "Who knew this day would come?" Petrovski muttered excitedly to himself as he followed Jonathon to the warm interior of the apartment building lobby, where it was easier to thaw the ink in their pens.

Jonathon stood on the threshold of Anton's office, looking pointedly at the oversized calendar on the wall. Anton chuckled deep within his chest. Twenty-eight days had passed since the last time Jonathon was standing in that Edmonton office. "All right, all right. So you're good."

Jonathon beamed.

"Come in here and gimme my money, you arrogant son of a bitch," Anton laughed. Jonathon had the cashier's cheque already drafted. Anton clapped him on the shoulder. "Not bad. Not bad at all. For a farm boy."

Jonathon shrugged. "Growing corn, growing profits – it's all the same to me. Same basic concept. You sow a little here, you wait for it to mature. When you harvest it, you reinvest some of it, and you bank the rest."

Anton brought out a fine bottle of VSOP to celebrate the close of the venture. "And that calls for a drink."

"I won't turn it down."

"Twenty-eight days," Anton said. "That's a tough act to follow."

Even though he was riding high with the profits from the sale of the apartment building, Jonathon had already been thinking ahead to the next big thing.

"That's the look of a man hungry for more," Anton said. "What are you onto now?"

"A few little deals already in the works," Jonathon confessed. "And one very big one."

"Oh?"

"Do you remember the old SGIO building?"

Anton took a moment to sound it out. "Saskatchewan Government Insurance Office…" His eyes flashed open and he bellowed, "Oh yeah! I remember the place. That's an old landmark."

"Eight stories of architectural heritage," Jonathon said.

"Wait – you mean you're thinking of picking up *that* place?"

"That's what follows a tough act," Jonathon said.

"You're not kidding," Anton laughed.

Jonathon smiled. "You want in on it?" Anton gave him an '*are you serious*' look. "It'll take me some time. Something that big always takes time. But, I'm scheduled to inspect the building and go over the numbers on Monday."

"This Monday," Anton said, as if it was a question.

"I can keep you informed, if you want."

Anton picked up the cheque Jonathon had just given him. "Sow a little magic, farm boy." Jonathon took back the cheque and accepted a refill. They clinked glasses. "You in town for a while?"

"Just overnight."

"Doing anything tonight?"

"Sleeping," Jonathon answered.

Anton shook his head. "Wrong answer. Meet me here at 7:00. I'll take you to a place that serves drinks you've never even *heard* of. Besides, there's somebody I want you to meet."

Jonathon made it as far as the front doors of the Anton Building before he loosed a whoop of triumph and laughed his way outside. He could have clicked his heels, if not for the worry that Fred Anton was watching him from his office window. With long, quick strides, Jonathon made his way back to the parking lot.

There was a dark car parked in the corner of the lot. Jonathon saw two men in the car, talking and moving around. He could have sworn one of them was lowering a pair of binoculars. One of them pointed to a hotel down the block. *Private eyes on a divorce case,* he thought.

When Jonathon backed his rental out of the parking spot, the car started its engines and followed for a couple of blocks, then went north, out of sight.

REGINA. SUMMER, 1978

Jonathon was at his desk reading over a sales contract when Myers tapped on the door frame. "Hey," Jonathon said. "Come on in."

Myers remained in the doorway. It was hard to read the man's expression.

"What's on your mind?" Jonathon asked, genuinely concerned.

"Another deal with Anton?"

"Sure, why not? Without him, there would be no SGIO Building deal."

Myers shook his head. "I'm not sure that's a deal we should be involved in, in the first place. Especially not with Anton."

"Oh what is it with you and Anton? Did you ever meet him in person? Did he insult your mother or something?"

"I've been hearing about..." Myers exhaled. "About things your *friend* has gotten himself involved in. Questionable things."

"We make easy money too. Is what we're doing '*questionable*'? No. It's totally above board. We buy, we renovate, we sell. If we don't feel like doing the renovations ourselves, we hire someone else, and in those cases, we make money without hardly trying. That's how we work, and that's how Fred works. There's nothing illegal in that."

"That's not what the RCMP believes."

"Funny, I thought we lived in a country that believed in 'innocent until proven guilty'. What have they got against him anyhow?"

"He's been seen in association with people who…who don't have the best of reputations."

"So why don't the Mounties go after *them*?" Jonathon shook his head. "Sounds like harassment to me, Bob. And it's none of our concern."

"It's all about optics," Myers said. "Whether he's guilty or not, it doesn't matter. If people – if prospective *clients* – believe that we're in cahoots with a suspected mob boss…"

"Oh, for God's sake."

Myers held up his hand. "If they believe we're complicit with the mob, they're going to avoid us like the plague. And that's not the kind of trouble we can afford."

Jonathon scoffed at the idea.

"Think it over, Jonny. Maybe we should tone it down for a while." He smiled half-heartedly. "We're in a good position right now. And maybe a little downtime is what we need. You especially."

"Me?" Jonathon snorted. "I'm fine."

Myers peered at him with soft but tired eyes.

"I'm fine," Jonathon answered.

Jonathon opened the door, bracing himself for a slew of invectives and threats. "Rita?" he asked.

There was no answer. But his voice carried an unusual echo, a certain blandness that he heard whenever he walked into an unoccupied property.

"Rita?"

He closed the door behind him. There was no place for him to hang his coat, nor was there a rubber mat to place his snowy boots. He shook off his footwear and crept deeper into the house.

"Rita, are you here?"

The living room was bare. The carpet looked darker where a couch had once protected its colour from the south-facing window. The chairs were gone, too, and the coffee table. Only the ugliest of the paintings remained on the wall. She'd even taken the clocks and calendars.

"What the hell?"

He went into the kitchen and found spoiled leftovers in the refrigerator. The plates, the bowls, the glasses, the cutlery, the pots and pans, everything but a broken egg beater was gone from the kitchen. In the bathroom, she'd left nothing more than a dried out crust of soap and some sticky rings where the shampoo bottles had been. If they hadn't been bolted to the floor, Rita would have taken the sink and bathtub too, he was sure of it. In the bedroom, there was only a pile of ripped sheets and a crocheted blanket dumped in the middle of the dusty floor. She'd taken all the wine out of the cellar, all the fine liqueurs – everything but the pool table, presumably because it was too difficult to disassemble and take upstairs.

Jonathon stood in the middle of the basement, his hands on his hips, looking from one empty corner to the other.

"Well, *shit.*"

And then he was struck by a worrisome thought. He ran back upstairs and out the door, scrambled into the Cadillac and drove, posthaste, to the bank.

Behind him, the black car followed at a leisurely pace. It followed Jonathon's car all the way to the Royal Bank, and it parked between two other vehicles of the same make, model and colour.

Jonathon was breathless by the time he reached the teller. He slid his bank books across the counter. "Can I check the balance on my accounts, please?" The teller was happy to help him, but only for a moment. "What is it?" he asked, noting the concern on the teller's face. "What's wrong?"

"Your account shows a zero balance at the moment," she said.

"Which account?"

Blank-faced, she said, "All of them, Mr. Parker."

The blood drained from his face. "All of them? What about my business accounts?" His hands trembled. Shock sucked the breath out of his lungs, leaving him light-headed.

"All of them, sir. Including your business accounts."

He stood before the teller, his teeth clenched, his hands clamped to his sides, his nostrils flaring. He couldn't trust himself to speak.

"Is there anything else I can help you with?"

A cool and distant part of his mind expressed mild surprise at his inability to speak.

"Mr. Parker?" the teller asked.

"Who," Jonathon forced through his teeth.

"Who withdrew the funds?"

He nodded stiffly.

The teller checked. "Your wife, sir. Rita Parker."

Jonathon took his bank books and walked away on legs as stiff as pins. He slammed shoulder to shoulder against an incoming customer, and said, "Sorry." He had no furniture, no money in his Canadian accounts, no *shampoo…*

He was unaware of the two men sitting in a dark car parked facing the bank. One of them had his finger hooked over his chin, lost in thought. The other was folding his newspaper. Both were watching Jonathon as he smiled secretly and bitterly to himself. One asked a question; the other laughed and nodded. The driver started the engine, but he kept the headlights off.

Jonathon muttered under his breath. At least he'd managed to spirit away better than half of his funds to his Swiss bank accounts. *Wouldn't she be surprised if she found me in two days driving around in a new car…*He snorted and jumped into the Cadillac. *Never thought I'd be grateful to that two-timing bastard Burton.* But without Pat Burton, Jonathon would never have gotten the idea to set up his foreign accounts. He considered his legal options as he started the engine and began to drive.

A car followed.

At Global Realty, Jonathon shuffled off his coat and hung it up in the closet. He caught sight of his own reflection, and he remarked how life had begun to leave its mark in his eyes and in the set of his mouth.

The receptionist returned. "You're here! I'm glad you're back." She frowned. "Are you okay?"

"I'll be fine. What's up?"

"Mr. Anton has been calling you since this morning, and I hadn't been able to get a hold of you at home..." She handed him a couple of memos each with a callback number.

"Yeah, sorry about that. My wife took the phones." He turned the memos around so he could make sense of her handwriting.

"I'm sorry, what?"

"Forget it," he said. "Thanks for this." He gave her a tight smile, then retreated to his office to call Fred Anton. Myers sat at his desk the office across the hall from Jonathon. Stretching the phone cord to its snapping point, Jonathon got up and closed his office door. "Fred Anton, please. It's Jonathon Parker returning his call." After a moment, the call rang through.

"Jonny! Thanks for calling me back. I've got some good news."

"I could use some."

"It's my turn to work the magic. I've got a buyer on the hook for the SGIO Building."

Jonathon sat abruptly on the edge of his desk. "Really?" He laughed. "Really! That's great! Wh – when do they want to inspect the building?"

"This coming Tuesday or Wednesday, if you can make it. Book me a room at the Sheraton for me, will you?"

"Sure thing. Let me set it up for Tuesday then."

"Good. Strike while the iron is hot. I like that. I'll let you get to it then. You take care now, Jonny. I'll see you when I get there."

"See you soon, Fred."

"Ciao."

"Ciao."

Jonathon hung up and dumped the air out of his lungs. Three years earlier, Jonathon had been flipping burgers. Two years earlier, he'd been flipping bungalows. Now, his life was flip-flopping from one extreme to the other – from rage to elation. Work would help keep him glued together, focused. He picked up the phone to call the inspectors.

Myers knocked on Jonathon's office door and entered without being officially invited. He dropped a news magazine on Jonathon's desk. It flipped open to a picture of Fred Anton. Jonathon hung up the phone. Myers said nothing. He waited until Jonathon finished reading the article. Jonathon's fingers tingled, as if the magazine had been electrically charged.

Police seize Edmonton developer's weapons cache, said the headline, and below it, the sub headline added: *Businessman accused of Mafia ties.* In one of the pictures, Fred Anton was looking suspicious behind dark glasses and getting into a sports car with tinted windows. Standing on the other side of the car was a similarly dressed man, clean-shaven and dark-haired. In another picture, a pair of plainclothes officers were standing near a pile of weapons worthy of a small platoon in Viet Nam; one of the pictured officers was cycling the action on an AR-10 semi-automatic rifle. Lined up in order of size were more semi-automatic rifles, a brace of shotguns, a couple of Lee-Enfield rifles, and five or six Mauser pistols.

"I had a phone call today," Myers said. "Another client. Said he likes me and everything, but he can't afford to be seen doing business with…with people complicit with the mob. Says his lawyer told him it's in his best interest to cut ties with us."

Jonathon folded the magazine closed.

"That's the third one this week," Myers said. "You didn't think image was important."

"I have an image to protect too," Jonathon countered.

"Then you'll have to do it solo, I'm afraid."

Jonathan frowned. "What are you saying?"

"I'm saying I can't be having you working here under my broker's license. I can't afford to lose any more clients."

Jonathon stood and opened his mouth to tell Myers what had happened not a few hours earlier – how Rita had emptied the house and all his accounts, how he didn't even have a bed to sleep on that night – but Myers turned his back and walked out.

"I'll give you two weeks," Myers said. "Tie up any loose ends, but don't bother taking on any new projects." He shook his head and closed the office door. "You're on your own, Jonathon."

Myers had no idea how right he was.

CHAPTER EIGHT

Regina. Fall, 1978.

Jonathon walked into the bar, feeling hollowed out and tired. Negotiations over the SGIO Building were slow going. But that wasn't
the only deal Jonathon and Anton had on the go. Jonathon was
pulling in enough income to re-equip his house with furniture and
necessities.

Every day, Jonathon waited for divorce papers. Rita was dragging
her heels. If Jonathon slept at all, it wasn't doing him any physical good.

"Jonathon!"

Jonathon looked for a friendly face in the bar. Occupying booths,
tables and stools at the bar were countless half-familiar faces, none of
them he could put a name too. Regulars of the place, but no one who
should know him by name. He heard his name shouted again over the
strains of an electric guitar and a thumping bass drum. Then he saw
the pale hand shoot up. And then he heard the braying laugh, and
Jonathon's stomach turned sour.

"Come on over!" It was Pat Burton, looking a little balder and a
little more pot-bellied since the last time Jonathon had cast eyes on the
pathetic philanderer. Burton was trying too hard to look like Michael
Caine, wearing a beige suit and dark brown turtleneck, putting one foot
up on the seat across from him and draping his wrist over his upraised
knee. "Have a seat! I'll buy."

People were watching Jonathon, who hooked his boot on the brass
rail at the bar so he could avoid sharing a booth with the two timing
lecher. Burton got up and chose a table close to the bar.

The music wasn't so loud that Jonathon could feign ignorance.
"Come on," Burton laughed. "What's a few drinks between old
friends?" Burton sounded like he'd already had a few drinks. His head
wobbled.

The cocktail waitress reached across the bar beside Jonathon.

"Hey, sweetheart," Pat said to the waitress. She rolled her eyes at the sound of Burton's voice, and Jonathon smiled. She returned the smile, though hers was tarnished and rushed.

"Why don't you get me another one of these, and one of whatever my friend there wants. Sky's the limit. Wait..." Pat held a five dollar bill to his forehead and said in his best impression of Carnac the Magnificent: "Scotch, on the rocks."

"May the bird of paradise fly up your nose," Jonathon muttered under his breath. He pulled a chair away from Burton's table and sat down.

"Sir?" the waitress asked.

"Make it a double for me," Jonathon sighed. He took off his tan-coloured, tweed jacket and hung it off the back of his chair. He smiled at the waitress again, and this time, she warmed to him. "Haven't seen you around for a while," he said to Burton, though his eyes were on the rear profile of the waitress as she walked over to the bar. It wasn't a bad view at all. She was athletic, wholesome, and she had a no BS-allowed attitude about her, as if countless gritty eyes had ground her down to hardy bones and self-sufficiency. Burton was watching her too, and he was running his tongue over his teeth. Jonathon could think of a dozen different places he wanted to be, but he couldn't find it in him to leave the waitress alone with the toad that was Pat Burton. "How are you, Pat?" Jonathon asked. The question was flat and desultory. He was too sober to tolerate Burton's cologne.

"Doing *great*! Flippin' everything in sight. Six figures three months in a row now – you can't beat that." Burton laughed. "Or maybe you can – with a baseball bat to the knees!" He snorted, crossed his arms on the table and leaned forward. "Heard you're a made man, now."

A tumbler of Scotch and a smaller glass of water appeared before Jonathon. "Yeah, well we all hear things, don't we?" He thanked the waitress, who was bending slightly to deposit the beer glass in front of Burton. Her blonde hair swung from behind her shoulder to within Burton's greasy reach. Without thinking, Jonathon tucked the girl's hair back where it belonged, so it wouldn't be soiled by Burton's wandering hand. She glanced at Jonathon, eyes wide. He couldn't tell if she was revolted by his touch or if she'd been taken aback by his chivalry. Jonathon wrapped his hands around the tumbler, thinking, *That is the softest hair I've ever touched...* He watched the waitress until she was out of earshot. "Speaking of hearing things." Jonathon's voice was taut. "Heard anything recently about Rita?"

Burton snorted. "You still married?" He chugged his beer.

"Not for long." He drank his Scotch faster than he ought to have. Between the burn of alcohol and the sickening leer on Burton's face, Jonathon bared his teeth and shuddered.

"She's shacking up with a guy I know at the Hyatt. Management likes to keep a close eye on its own, if you know what I mean. A really, really close eye."

While Burton mumbled on about the latest in Rita's string of use-'em-and-lose-'em conquests, Jonathon signalled the waitress over. Burton didn't even notice when Jonathon asked the waitress her name. *Jennifer*, she answered softly, while Burton was describing one of Rita's favourite positions in bed. Jonathon gave the waitress enough to cover two more rounds of drinks, plus a generous tip. "You want to get out of here?" he asked her.

She smiled, but now she looked tired. *So many different smiles, and hair as soft as corn silk.* "I'm busy."

"After your shift," he said.

"Yeah," said Burton, feigning sobriety. "Jonny and I, we've been aggravating each other up to now, and we're having a little trouble making up. We might need a..." His fingertips brushed against the hem of jeans, tracing her hip. "A go-between, if you know what I mean." She slapped his hand away.

"Do that again," she warned, "and I'll have to ask you to leave."

The ambient conversation had hushed. Burton laughed loudly and humourlessly. In the background, the sound system was playing Carly Simon's *You're So Vain*. Jonathon stood up, taking his coat with him. "I'll take my drink at another table."

"Sure." The waitress left without another word.

"Hey," Burton said to Jonathon. "I just saved your ass. You should be grateful to me."

"Saved my..."

"You never learn, Jonny-boy," Burton drawled. "You never learn. You wanna be happy for the rest of your life, never make a pretty woman your wife. That's what they say." Burton rolled his eyes. "Jonny, they're all the same. If anybody should know that by now, it's you, jackass. They're all the same. The first smile's free. After that, you've gotta buy in advance, over, and over, and over again. Before you know it, they'll be draining you dry."

"Oh, piss off."

Burton lobbed his lecture over his shoulder without watching where Jonathon was re-camping. "What, you think they like you because of your charm? You flash a little cash, and they're on you like piranhas on a shaving cut." He snorted into his beer and started singing "*If you wanna be happy...*"

Jennifer found Jonathon at the new booth near the back door. She left a fresh glass of Scotch in front of him. This time, she offered an uncomfortable but grateful smile. He winked and lifted his glass to her health. But as soon as she went off, flashing a brilliant smile at a double-dating table, he thought of Rita, and of his empty house. He'd replaced all the necessary furniture, but it wasn't the same. His home was as empty as the day she left, and emptier than the day he took possession of the place.

Weeks later, standing in the cold November wind, handshakes were exchanged all around. Anton joked with the older businessman who had agreed to purchase the austere Gothic Revival-style SGIO Building. The older man smiled and nodded, then retreated to a waiting limousine, where a driver held open a rear door for him.

Anton clapped Jonathon on the back. "What are you doing tonight?"

"Sleeping," Jonathon said.

"Where?"

"At home."

Anton shook his head. "Wrong answer. In Calgary, there's a place where you can get a steak as big as your thigh, and the wine's the best anywhere." He nodded. "Let's go."

"What, now?"

"Life's for the living, Jonny," Anton said as he led the way to Jonathon's Cadillac. "Especially when we've got cause to celebrate!"

Less than five hours later, Anton was cuddling close to an attractive young brunette, who laughed openly and squirmed away from Anton's tickles. Anton let her go, but she stayed close, running her fingers over the back of Anton's hairy hand.

"What's next?" Anton asked, refilling Jonathon's flute with champagne. They were on their second magnum.

Jonathon glanced at his hand as if reading from an invisible calendar. "Friday, we finish the paperwork on the apartment complex on Alport Crescent."

"Right, right…"

"Monday, the Prairie Rose Motel, and on Wednesday…"

"Too far ahead," Anton announced. "Jonny, you have to learn to live one day at a time! Besides, if you can remember all that off the top of your head, you haven't drunk enough." He slapped the table and wagged his finger at Jonathon. Jonathon grinned and obliged. Anton's girlfriend whispered something in Anton's ear, and his face went slack. "What, now?" She smiled and took Anton by the hand, leading him to the dance floor. They looked like a pair of refugees from the Ritz who'd been stranded in a colony of cowboys. Anton eased off the tension in his bowtie, and Jonathon laughed. In five minutes, Anton was whooping it up with the best of them.

REGINA. SPRING, 1979

Jonathon was dead to the world when his phone rang. He rolled onto his side and clicked on the light. According to his watch, it was a little after midnight. The phone rang again. He answered it. "Hello?"

"Jonny!" It was Anton, and there was noise in the background. "What are you doing, farm boy?"

"Sleeping," Jonathon replied.

"Where?"

"In bed."

"You're an old granny, Jonathon. Get your ass on a plane."

Jonathon laughed. "No."

"Come on, you don't have to be anywhere until Thursday. Live a little."

"A plane to where?"

"Vancouver. You'll get an extra two hours back in your day when you travel west."

"Fred."

"Sleep on the plane. Wait – What?" Anton was shouting the question at someone in the same noisy room with him. "Yeah, all right." To Jonathon, he said, "Harvey here says you're a weak-kneed bastard if you stay home. You've got to see this place, Jonathon. There's a three to one ratio – favouring the women! All you have to do is pick the height, the weight, the hair and the eyes."

"It's almost one in the morning!"

"Not here it isn't. Get on the plane. I'll have someone meet you at the airport. Besides, I picked up a new deal, and I want you to meet the guy who's selling the place."

Laughing, Jonathon said he was getting up and he'd be there in a couple of hours.

A black car followed him to the airport. Its driver and passenger chartered a private flight, scheduled to arrive only minutes after Jonathon landed in Vancouver.

A few days later, Jonathon and Anton were standing poolside in Los Angeles, California, both wearing sunglasses and seersucker suits. On three sides, new and well-maintained apartment complexes rose around them, shading them from the morning and afternoon sun. An elderly woman took the papers from Jonathon, and she signed her name wherever he told her to put the pen.

I'm in Los Angeles, Jonathon thought. *And I've just made another million dollar sale.* He was in L.A. He was hitting the big time.

He and Anton were momentarily distracted by a six foot tall, fully articulated Barbie doll wearing nothing but a bikini, a sunhat and a wink.

The elderly woman returned his pen, and Anton shook her hand with genteel grace. Jonathon thanked her and wished her a good day.

On their way out, Anton asked, "Ever been to Vegas?"

"Isn't that a little out of our way?"

Anton gave him a patronising smile.

"Well, I've always wanted to try my hand at baccarat," Jonathon said.

"That's the spirit."

All sense of "night is for sleeping, day is for work" was gone. Two a.m. was just a number on a clock. Jonathon slept when he could, wherever he could, and in the morning, he showered, ate and stepped into the whirlwind of luxury and adventure that had become his life.

Anton met him in the lobby of the hotel, dressed to the nines. Even in a tux and black tie, Jonathon still felt under-dressed compared to Anton, who had the look and carriage of a man born to wealth. They walked together outside. In L.A., there was never a shortage of limousines. There was one waiting for them near the main doors of the hotel.

"Are you at least going to give me a hint where we're going, all dolled up like penguins?" Jonathon asked, once they were in the car.

"No." Anton gave the address to the driver, who looked in his rear view mirror at his well-heeled passengers. Anton folded his arms across his chest and smiled knowingly at the driver, who blew a low whistle and put the limo in drive.

"Just a hint," Jonathon pleaded.

"No."

They drove for about half an hour, with both the driver and Anton pointing out various must-see attractions along the way. They passed through Beverly Hills, past the sprawling mansions of one celebrity after another. They were still in Beverly Hills among the mansions when the limousine pulled over to the curb and let them out. Anton adjusted his tie and dinner jacket. "Nice place, huh?"

Through the wrought iron fence, past the tuxedoed body guards at the gate, beyond the fountains, the palm trees and the manicured lawn, Jonathon could see an enormous house, with a garage adjacent that was at least as big as Jonathon's own house back in flat, dull, pedestrian Regina. The sound of merriment and music floated over the California opulence. Women in sequins walked arm in arm with gentlemen of the upper crust. Outside the gates, a cameraman and a reporter presented their IDs to the bodyguards.

"I need you along as legal advisor," Anton said.

"Legal advisor!" Jonathon stopped suddenly, when somebody half-familiar walked by; the stranger was the spitting image of Billy Crystal. "What kind of law?"

"Hoping to negotiate the rights to the Canadian book release and maybe a film or two."

"For – "

Anton hushed him as they approached the gates. Anton dug out the invitation folder from inside his dinner jacket and tendered it over to one of the gatemen. "He's with me," Anton said, pointing to Jonathon. The guards gave them warning looks, then passed them through. "Relax. You look like a walking coronary."

"Fred!"

"And there he is now, the man of the hour."

Anton pointed at the porch, where a Black man was entertaining questions in front of a camera. Suddenly, the assembled crowd laughed, all but the man standing in front of the camera.

"No…way…" Jonathon whispered.

"I'm friends with his agent. It's how I got these invitations. So live it up, mingle a little."

"Is that *really* Muhammad Ali?"

Anton laughed and slapped Jonathon on the back. "Close your mouth, you hick. You're staring."

Jonathon gaped just the same.

REGINA. SUMMER, 1979

Jonathon had criss-crossed the continent, unaware that every departure and arrival, every hotel room, every restaurant dinner was being carefully documented and scrutinized. By late fall that year, he'd become aware of a strangely familiar car turning corners after him, then disappearing in thicker traffic. More often than not, he'd laugh at himself, thinking maybe he was being followed by the paparazzi. After all, he was hitting the big time now, and he was being seen with big players. He was making money hand over fist, and he wore it well, in good company and in public. He could forgive a little idle curiosity in the papers; after all, in Saskatchewan, a rags-to-riches farm boy was suitable antidote for the slowest news day. He never let it bother him.

He'd recently returned from another trip to Switzerland, feeling drowsy but secure. Even though he could afford a couple of losses, he still forged on, selling what he could, where and when he could, in partnership with Fred Anton. He was operating out of his own private offices, now – labelled outside as Antonino's Enterprises Ltd., J. Parker, Licensed Realtor – and he was as independent an operator as he had ever been. He was no one's employee. He was a free agent, working in partnership with Fred Anton. He was a businessman. He'd reinvented himself, and for the first time in his life, he felt like he had both feet firmly planted on solid ground.

He opened his door and exited with Ivan Petrovski, who was mopping his forehead. He was a nervous man who carried his anxiety around in his belly, but he was good-humoured.

"A year ago, I never thought I would be the man buying an apartment building like some kind of big shot landlord, and now here I am, buying another one!"

Jonathon nodded. "Yeah, but this one's in a unique location. With those zoning changes, it should *double* in value."

"Oh, ho ho, I hope you're right. So many more tenants, all paying rent and saying 'Fix this! Fix that! Something's leaking.' All the time, trouble. It's good we keep the same superintendent. My poor heart, it's not so good now," he laughed. He turned and shook Jonathon's hand. "But I'm glad to being working with you again."

"The pleasure's mine, Mr. Petrovski. And thank you!"

Petrovski flashed his twitchy smile, wiped his brow and replaced his hat.

Jonathon watched the little man leave. He had no more appointments that week, he'd given Laura, his secretary, the day off, and Anton was away in Italy on vacation with his wife. For the first time in a long time, he could sit back and reflect on the delirious mayhem of the last few months. He needed time to catch up and make sense of this new reality: Jonathon Parker, nearly a millionaire. A real Cinderella story.

And his house was still empty. He had no one but his own reflection to talk to.

He wondered what shift Jennifer was working this week at the pub. He smiled, reached behind the door and plucked his tan jacket off the hook, and he locked up the office for the weekend.

Jonathon was steps away from his car when a dark sedan shot ahead and made a hard right onto the sidewalk, cutting Jonathon off. "What the hell?"

The passenger's door opened, and an auburn-haired man jumped out. Jonathon froze. The stranger had an arresting look on his face, frighteningly similar to the one Jonathon had worn the day he pulled Rita's lover out of a hotel closet. Jonathon half-raised his hands. "What do you want?"

The passenger caught Jonathon by the shoulder, pulling him toward the revving car.

"What the hell do you want?" Jonathon asked, rolling clear of the man's grip. But the stranger was determined, and he was fast. He wrapped Jonathon in a martial artist's hold, and when they struggled, Jonathon spied the butt of a gun dangling from an underarm holster.

"That's right," the stranger said in Jonathon's ear. "You get the picture."

Jonathon stopped resisting, but his feet were reluctant to move. He needed time to think his way out of trouble. "All right," he said. "Whatever you want – my wallet's in my right pants pocket."

"Get in the goddamned car," the stranger said, "that's what I want." He kicked the back of Jonathon's knee, weakening his leg, and he pushed Jonathon into the car.

The black-haired driver turned, pointing a gun at Jonathon's face. He said nothing. He didn't move until his companion sat in the front passenger's seat and told Jonathon to move over and sit in the middle of the backseat. Jonathon complied, and the passenger drew his gun, cocked the hammer and flicked the safety off. He nodded at his friend the driver, who put away his own gun and put the car in drive. Jonathon looked around the car. The backseat doors had no handles on the inside.

"What are you looking at?" asked his fellow passenger.

"Nothing," Jonathon answered.

"Good. Then shut up and enjoy the ride."

CHAPTER NINE

They'd driven well outside the city limits.

"What's this all about?" Jonathon asked. He spoke to them as if they were rabid dogs.

"All in good time," said the red-head. He'd put down the gun, but it wasn't far from his reach, and Jonathon hadn't come up with an effective escape plan yet. They had the upper hand.

They drove through farmland for better than half an hour. The late afternoon sun shone through road dust. They drove through the junk yard gates, unnoticed and unmolested.

Oh hell, Jonathon thought. *This is the perfect place to dump a dead body.*

He regarded his captors in a new light. The dark-headed one had a vaguely Roman side profile. *Mobsters,* Jonathon thought. But that didn't explain the red-head. He'd never heard of a red-headed mobster before. *Irish, maybe? A friend of the Family?*

The car rolled across crunching gravel and came to a stop beside the hollowed out remains of a car. Trash was piled shoulder high in categorical piles all around them.

The red-head got out of the car first, and he pulled open one of the rear doors. "Out," he said. Jonathon obeyed. The dark-haired one took his time getting out of the vehicle, pausing to light a cigarette before checking the ammunition in his pistol. The red-head smiled.

"What do you want from me?" Jonathon asked.

The black-haired one shook out his match and squinted against the cigarette smoke that blew up into his eyes. He didn't answer.

"You like our office away from the office?" the red-head asked.

The red-head was turning white at the temples, and he had one yellowish-brown tooth. He had few wrinkles or scars, so it was hard to estimate the man's age, but he may have been in his mid-to-late forties. He had freckles across his cheeks. He seemed to be lean, athletic and in good shape, like a swimmer or an Olympic acrobat, and over this physique, he wore a sheepskin jacket and a knitted scarf. He was well-dressed but forced-informal at the same time, like a catalogue model pretending to be down to earth. The black-haired one was broader across the chest, and he walked like a man whose larger mass had been compacted into muscle and bone; when he moved, the leather of his jacket creaked, and his jeans were one size too small. Like his partner, he may have been middle-aged, more than forty and less than fifty; he looked like he was in the prime of his life, physically, mentally and socially. The skinnier one cocked his head, as if he still expected an answer to his question.

"It's a little draughty," Jonathon said, straight-faced. "And I didn't get to read your shingle on the way in."

"Doesn't matter who we are," said the man in the leather jacket. He exhaled smoke. "In fact, it's better for you if you don't know."

"Are you at least going to tell me why you kidnapped me?"

The red-head said, "Don't get smart-mouthed. My partner's liable to get in a pissy mood. You won't like him when he's in a pissy mood." He drew his weapon and switched the safety off. "Matter of fact, you won't like *me* when I'm in a pissy mood."

"You know the game," the black-haired one said. "You cooperate, and life is good. You play around with us, you play dumb, and we make your life a living nightmare."

Jonathon winced and shook his head. "What the hell are you talking about?"

Neither of them spoke, but the red-head kept shooting eager glances at his friend, as if to ask if he could pull the trigger now.

"Tell us about Anton," the darker one said.

Jonathon was more confused than ever. "Who, Fred?"

"Who, Fred?" the red-head echoed, mocking him.

"He's a real estate developer, like me," Jonathon said. "He's a good guy. What do you..."

The man in the leather jacket drew his gun and stepped forward, pressing the barrel against Jonathon's forehead. Jonathon forgot to breathe. *What the hell is going on?* He peered out the corners of his eyes for hidden cameras. He'd thought he'd left Hollywood behind.

"I think you've failed to recognize the seriousness of your plight," said the red-head. "And I told you he'd get in a pissy mood if you jerked us around."

"I'm answering your questions!" Jonathon half-laughed. "Put the gun down, and we can talk."

The dark-haired one cocked the hammer of his pistol. The barrel left a cold kiss-print between Jonathon's eyebrows.

"Jesus!" Jonathon exclaimed.

"You've gotten yourself mixed up in some bad business," said the red-head. "Work with us instead of against us, play it straight and keep your smart-ass mouth shut, and we can get you out of it."

Jonathon was about to plead his obedience, but the dark-haired one stared him into silence.

"You know he's hooked up with the Mafia," said the red-head. "And we can't have them playing around, not here, not in our own backyard."

"And we don't appreciate you holding the gate open for them," said the dark-haired one.

"Fred Anton is not involved in the Mafia. I would know."

"Oh," said the red-head, "so you're as chummy as that, are you?"

"We're business partners," Jonathon answered. "He's helped me by financing a few real-estate deals, that's it!"

"We wish we could believe you," said the red-head. He'd put away his gun, and now he was picking loose threads from the patches on Jonathon's jacket elbows. "But you make a hell of a lot of money for a real-estate agent."

"Too much," said the darker one.

"What Fred does on his own time is his own business," Jonathon muttered. "But whatever it is, it's legal."

They didn't seem to have heard him. "How much are you worth these days now, Parker?" asked the red-head.

"That's none of your business." There was so much pressure behind the gun that the barrel pushed Jonathon's head back. He closed his eyes and said, "I don't know. Just under a million?" He wished he hadn't said it.

"Good," said the red-head, nodding. "Then you can afford our services after all."

Jonathon risked turning his head. "What?"

"Consider us your life insurance brokers," said the red-head. He nodded at his partner, who eased forward the hammer and lowered his gun. "Five grand a month."

"*What?*"

"For life," said the red-head, and his partner nodded solemnly. "You've got yourself mixed up with some bad people, Jon-boy. We're here to protect you from them."

"To protect you from yourself," said the other.

"Five grand a month, for life, or," said the red-head, contemplatively, "you decide you're willing to tell us what we want to know. You cooperate."

"I *am* cooperating," Jonathon said.

The ginger shook his head. "You tell us where Anton fits in the ranks. You tell us who's above him. You tell us what he does. You tell us where goes, what he does on the side, everything. Then we'll renegotiate the premiums. Cut down your payments. Until then..."

"Until then, five grand a month," said his partner.

"I'm not paying you guys jack *shit*," Jonathon said. "You don't have anything on me but a gun!"

Jonathon heard the creak of leather. Light exploded behind his eyes. Jonathon stumbled to the left, and then his legs gave out. He tumbled at their feet, dazed. He touched his temple, and he was amazed to see blood on his fingertips.

"You're right," said the dark-haired one. "But we can fix that."

Jonathon struggled to his feet, but the red-head drove his foot against the back of Jonathon's leg, forcing him to the dirt again. Once Jonathon was bent over double, the red-head kicked him in the ribs, knocking Jonathon clean off his knees onto his side. He kicked Jonathon again, and blood-stained breath burst from Jonathon's lips.

"Don't worry about trying to find us," said the dark-haired one. "We'll find you. Be ready for us early next week for our first installment."

The two thugs went back to their car. The red-head said, "Oh, and don't bother calling anybody. For one, no one's going to believe you. For another, we'll know." He smiled. "And we'll kill you."

"There's no place you can go that we can't find you," said the linebacker in the leather jacket. "Sweet dreams, Jon-boy."

They left him there, struggling against vertigo and the cold. Jonathon brushed the dirt off his elbow patches, fixed his coat and followed the tire tracks to the front gate.

"What the *hell* was that all about?"

That night, Jonathon discovered there *was* something worse than driving through the prairies. Walking through the prairies was far, far worse. For almost three hours, he marched on the spot. Only until he entered the city limits did he feel like he was making any geographical progress. His house was on the far side of town. But stumbling around downtown Regina after dark with a bleeding face and bruised ribs was a good way to get himself arrested for drunk and disorderly. He needed to find a bathroom and a sink where he could get himself cleaned up. Fortunately, the Neighbour's Pub was between Jonathon and his home, and they were open late. He fell in through the door and walked straight for the bathroom, ordering a Scotch on the rocks as he went.

Jennifer was on shift. She glanced at him once and smiled. Then she saw the state of his face and excused herself from the table she was serving. She intercepted him on the way to the bathroom. "My God, Jonathon – what happened to your face?"

"It's no big deal."

"Your face covered in blood and it's no big deal?"

"It's stupid," Jonathon said. "I wanted to go for a walk to clear my mind, and I ended up outside city limits, and it was dark – it's embarrassing, and I don't want to talk about it."

"What, you fell and hurt yourself?"

"I told you it was embarrassing."

"Oh God," she said. But she looked like she was about to laugh. "You sure you're all right?"

"I'll be fine." He showed his warmest smile to prove it. "Just as soon as I wash up."

"Scotch on the rocks?" she asked. "A double."

"Yes *please.*"

Jonathon sat in his office, drumming his fingers on the desk. He'd been doing that for hours on end over the last two days, and it was driving Laura crazy. He'd avoided answering his phone, and that was driving his secretary crazy, too. He'd had dreams overnight of the mob storming his bedroom and suffocating him with a pillow on suspicion that he'd ratted on Anton to a rival family or another gang. *Gangs in Regina,* he thought. He wished he could laugh it off. But it was hard to imagine otherwise. He'd been abducted at gunpoint, pistol-whipped, beaten into the dirt, and was now anticipating the first collection of extortion money. *What else could it be but gangs?*

Shortly after Laura went on her coffee break, Jonathon picked up the phone.

He hung up the phone, thinking better of it. *No sense in making Anton panic.*

He picked up the phone again, this time dialing locally instead of calling out long distance. "Yes, Bob Myers please. Yes, Jonathon Parker. Yes, I'll hold."

There wasn't anyone else he could trust. He didn't want to worry his parents. They were getting on in years, and they were already lecturing him about his free-wheeling lifestyle. He had no one else he could trust, not with something like this. Rita was a lost cause; Jonathon had remained good friends with his brother-in-law, but he didn't want anything getting back to Rita accidentally. And who else could he turn to, Pat Burton?

"Hello?" asked the voice on the other end.

"Bob, it's Jonathon. How are you?"

"...Fine."

"Listen, Bob, I..." He sighed and massaged his face. "I'm not saying that you were right and I was wrong. But I had some interesting... things...happen the other day, and I uh... "

Bob coughed into the receiver. "Listen, Jonathon, I'm gonna have to call you back."

Jonathon felt his temperature rise. "Are you all right?"

"Yeah, I'm fine. I've just uh…got a client who walked into my office."

"Okay, but could you – "

"I'll have to call you later. Bye now."

The line went dead.

Jonathon grunted and hung up the phone. "Love you too, Bob." It wasn't at all like him. Myers either agreed with you or he disagreed with you; he never ignored you. He always had time for Jonathon, even when their opinions clashed. This was completely unlike Myers.

Jonathon's office door opened. His first thought was, *Why are there porno actors in my office?* One of them was wearing a very bad wig and a fake mustache. But he hadn't taken any time to hide the freckles on the apples of his cheeks. It was the red-head. The man beside him, the dark-haired guy, wore a fake beard. Jonathon smothered a laugh behind his hand.

"You're kidding me, right?" Jonathon asked. "With the disguises and everything?"

The red-head put a briefcase on Jonathon's desk and opened the latch.

"You've got something for us today," said the man with the fake beard. "Names, addresses, phone numbers, pictures?" The stiff beard bobbed whenever he wagged his chin.

Jonathon opened his desk drawer. Inside, he kept a fat, unmarked envelope. Under it was a mini-cassette recorder, which he sometimes used to record business conversations conducted over the phone. He powered on the device and quietly but quickly pressed the record button. He left the desk drawer open, with the recorder out of sight. "This is extortion," he said. "And that's illegal, you know." The red head laughed. He placed the envelope inside the open maw of the empty briefcase. "Five thousand, just like you asked." The red-head quickly closed up the briefcase and removed it from the desk. "Aren't you going to count it?"

"If we find out you've gypped us," the red-head said with a shrug, "we'll find you."

"I'm an honest businessman," Jonathon said. "Even around people I don't trust."

"Your honesty would be put to better use," the red-head said, for once ditching his tough-guy act, "if you told us what we needed to know."

Jonathon swallowed, but his mouth and throat were dry. "And if I do get you something you can use against Fred Anton?" He looked from one to the other. "How do I contact you? I don't even know your names."

"We'll find you," the red-head assured him.

"We can cancel this policy at any time," interrupted the man with the black hair and the fake beard. "This is a strictly confidential arrangement. You breach confidentiality..."

"And we breach you," said the red-head.

Jonathon gave them a sarcastic look. "Seriously? The dialogue, too? And why the disguises? Are you ashamed of something? Or are wigs and fake beards in fashion these days?"

The dark one was in no mood for jokes. "You breach confidentiality, and you're no longer under our protection. We surrender everything we know about you. Everything. And then we make your life a living hell, you get me?" He pointed at Jonathon's nose. "You make another attempt to contact somebody through that pal of yours, Myers, and we take another ride out to the country for a quiet heart-to-heart."

"We'll be seeing you around," said the red-head from the door.

They left, closing the door gently behind them.

"What...the...*hell*," Jonathon shouted.

The phone rang. He caught it mid-ring.

"Antonino's Enterprises," Jonathon said, clapping his hand to his brow. "Jonathon speaking."

"Jonathon, it's me." It was Bob Myers again. "Sorry I couldn't speak just then."

"No problem," Jonathon said. "I had someone walk into my office around the same time."

"You have time for a drink tonight?"

Jonathon breathed a sigh of relief. "Yeah. Actually, that's a good idea. This isn't something I want to discuss over the phone."

"You okay?"

"I will be. What time do you want to get together?"

"Seven. You want to go to Neighbour's' Pub?"

"You bet. I'll be there." They said their goodbyes and hung up.

Jonathon was breathing easy. A weight had been lifted from his shoulders. Myers had been in a forgiving mood, and they were both doing well. They were competitors now, but they rarely dealt in the same class of properties, so they didn't horn in on each other's niche. They shared round after round, so by eleven or so, they were rosy-cheeked and laughing it up over exploits past.

Jennifer came over with her serving tray and two more drinks. "I hope neither of you intends to drive tonight," she said, chuckling at their exaggerated gestures.

"You kidding?" Myers snorted. "You seen how many cops are out there tonight? It's like a Shriner's convention, only instead funny cars, they're all driving around in unmarked vee-hick-les."

Jonathon laughed at the image and at Myers' pronunciation. "And if you believe any of them, they *always* get their man."

Myers smiled and gazed into his refilled beer glass. Jennifer cleared away the empties, saying nothing. Jonathon watched her walk away.

"I haven't been this drunk since…" Jonathon couldn't remember precisely, so he said, "Vegas."

"With Anton?"

"Yeah, we went," Jonathon said. "Swear, that man has a different girlfriend in twenty cities between Canada and the U.S. And a wife!"

"So maybe he can fix you up with somebody," Myers said. "For the right price."

Jonathon came down from the beer-induced giggles. They locked eyes. Myers lost the staring contest. He drank. "What are you saying, Bob?" Jonathon asked.

"Nothing," Myers said, wiping foam from his lips.

"You saying he's some kind of pimp?"

Myers shrugged. "What do I know about the guy? I only know what I hear. Money laundering. Weapons dealing. Drugs. Is it so much of a stretch to think he might have access to working girls too. You said yourself, he's got so many girlfriends…"

"It's bullshit. It's all bullshit, Bob, and you know it. He's a real estate speculator, same as you and me, only better at it than you and me combined."

"Nobody's that good. Not Fred-Anton-good, not for the kind of money he brings in."

"Oh, give me a break, Bob. The guy owns like…" He searched for the words. "Eleven shoe stores, a couple of car washes, a gravel pit, some kind of industrial plant – concrete or whatever – and he owns practically half of Edmonton, all right? Since when was that illegal?"

"Jonathon."

"What, you want the receipts to go with it? Proof of revenue? God, who died and made you the Revenue Agency, huh?"

"I'm sorry, Jonathon, I didn't mean anything by it," Myers said. "But come on, how do you explain away his guns, huh?"

"He's a collector. He collects military stuff. My *grandfather* collects military stuff. He's got like three rifles of his own – does that make him some kind of mobster too? Seventy-year old man holding up bars and gas stations?"

"Jonathon, lower your voice."

"Why should I? You won't listen to me otherwise."

Myers sighed and waited for Jonathon's steam to blow off. "You done?"

Jonathon leaned forward. "You go back and read that article again, the one you showed me the other day. All that was taken from his house were a couple of antiques, some ball and powder muskets from the 1800s. And those were part of his registered antique collection! What's he gonna do, fly down to Cuba and sell Fidel Castro a couple of flintlock rifles and a powder horn?"

Myers snorted a laugh.

"Most of those guns were decommissioned – even said so right there in the article. Had the firing pins removed – and you can't get them restored without somebody noticing. And on the other page in that spread? It was an article written by somebody else altogether, and *that* was about Edmonton police efforts to locate and seize illegal firearms. Totally unrelated."

"Yes, but that article about Fred – "

" – Even said that Fred had no criminal record. That article is all headline and no story."

"That doesn't mean *anything* Jonathon. Lots of people go around with no criminal record. It only means they haven't been caught yet."

"Bob, did you actually *read* the article, or do you only buy the magazine for the pictures?"

Myers' colour rose above his beard.

"The article said that because of the crackdown on guns, guys like Fred were having a hard time building and keeping a perfectly legitimate and *legal* collection in their homes. They never accused him of anything – they used him as the poster boy for *responsible* firearms ownership, goddammit! The headline was deliberately misleading. Headlines sell newspapers, the truth doesn't."

Myers's voice was barely audible. "So tell me why he's been seen hanging out with mobsters."

"Mobsters? What mobsters?"

"I was hoping you could tell me," Myers slurred.

Jonathon sat back, exasperated, and he spread his hands. "Does he even *know* they're mobsters? Hell, Bob, I've been seen hanging out with a couple thousand people this year, and any one of *them* could be mobsters, and I wouldn't know it. Does that make me a mobster? God, Bob, if I knew somebody was a member of any organized crime, I'd avoid him like the plague! So would Fred! End of discussion."

Myers nodded. "End of discussion."

They drank in silence for a while.

"What's this sudden obsession with Fred about, anyhow?" Jonathon asked.

Myers finished his beer and made like he was about to leave. "It's not an obsession. Just innocent curiosity."

"Why?"

"I care, Jonathon, all right?" Myers put on his coat. "I care about *you*. So sue me."

Jonathon rolled the beer around the bottom of his glass.

"I gotta get back before the wife kills me. I didn't realize it was so late." Myers left money on the table to cover his half, plus a tip. "Let's do this again sometime." He dropped his wide hand on Jonathon's shoulder. Jonathon put his hand over Bob's. Jonathon knew: this was probably the last time they'd drink together. "Take care."

"Take it easy," Jonathon said. Once Bob was out the door, Jonathon crossed his arms on the table and dumped his head into the cradle they'd made.

He smelled her perfume before he saw her standing beside him. "Can I get you anything else, Jonathon? One more for the road?"

"No," he said. He dug in his upper coat pocket for his wallet and money. "No, I think I'm finished for the night." He tugged a bill from the fold, and it tore. "Whoops."

"That's all right. We can tape it up."

He collected the money Bob had left on the table, added his own to it, and gave it to Jennifer with both hands. He laughed at the sight, and she smiled. "Keep the change," he said. She folded everything together and promised that she'd be right back.

"I was hoping you could tell me," Bob had said.

"Shit," Jonathon spat. "Son of a bitch!" Bob – his trusted friend and colleague – had been pumping Jonathon for information. Bob was a good friend of a couple of RCMP officers. It wouldn't take much to make an informant of a good friend. "That bastard…"

Jennifer returned, and Jonathon toned it down.

"Sorry," she began.

"I didn't give you enough?"

"No – you gave me too much!" She showed him the torn bill. "It's a hundred dollars."

Jonathon shrugged and finished his beer. "So? Like I said, keep the change."

"I can't." She put the bill on the table in front of him. "I'm sorry, I can't accept it. I don't want to be accused of something, once you sober up."

Jonathon allowed the point. "All right." He picked up the torn halves of the hundred dollar bill and said, "How about if I use this to buy you dinner on your next night off?"

"How about you sleep this off, okay?" She collected two more empty beer glasses from his table and swiped her dish cloth over the rings they'd left behind.

"I'm not so drunk that I'll forget," Jonathon said. "But all right. If you want me to ask you when I'm sober, you're just going to have to give me your number."

"You don't know what you're getting yourself into," Jennifer said. "Besides, I have to give the babysitter a night off at least once a week."

"I'm sure the parents can find another babysitter for one night."

"I am the parent," she said.

Jonathon tilted his head. She didn't have a mother's figure. He nodded once. "Single mom?"

She continued to clean his table. "Yeah."

"All the more reason to have someone give you a decent night out. No expectations, no pressure. Just dinner. You and me, high class restaurant, some place quiet enough where you can have an adult conversation without shouting over the music. What do you say?"

Jennifer turned away, taking her serving tray with her.

Jonathon sighed and rubbed his face.

Jennifer returned and laid a napkin between his hands on the table. On it, she'd written her number. She walked away again, smiling over her shoulder. He smiled back, folded the napkin into his upper shirt pocket, and left the pub.

Outside, he noticed two black four-door sedans, both unoccupied, and he thought about Bob's comment, how Regina was swarming with unmarked cars tonight.

"*I was hoping you could tell me,*" Bob had said.

"Son of a bitch," Jonathon sighed.

An idea began to form in his head, and it turned his stomach. His two "insurance brokers" had driven a black sedan, too, one like the unmarked car in the parking lot.

"No," he breathed.

He thought about the car that had followed him in and out of traffic for weeks, and about the car that had screeched to halt, cutting him off on the sidewalk. He wondered what an unmarked cop car looked like. Would it have handles on the inside of the rear passenger doors? Or would handles be a standing invitation for an arrested suspect to open the door and run away?

Not possible. Not damned possible – God, tell me I'm wrong. He walked home, scuffing his heels the whole way.

CHAPTER TEN

Jonathon breezed into his office and said only a brief hello to Laura. "Listen, I'm going to go out to the Langstaff property, and I want you to..."

She was holding out a stiff envelope. It was sent by registered mail.

He clapped his hands together and said, "Please Lord, let these be my divorce papers."

"I don't think so," she said. "Take a look at the address."

He noted the gravity of her expression, and, now worried, he took the envelope from her. He ripped open the seal and slid out the folded legal documents from within. "Laura," he said as he read on, "get Anton on the line and transfer the call to my desk. Now."

She nodded and got to work. He read on; it was nothing but bad news. She had Fred on the line before Jonathon was comfortably seated.

"Fred," Jonathon said, "we've got a problem."

"All right," Fred said. "Whatever it is, we can handle it. What's the matter?"

"I just got a registered letter in the mail. It's from the Government's chief counsel."

Fred was quiet for a moment. "It's about the SGIO Building?"

"Yeah. It's a formal notice that they're rescinding on their contract to sell us the building."

Jonathon barely had the words out of his mouth before Fred cursed. "They can't just back out of a deal like that!" Fred said.

"I know."

"No, the contract is legally binding! Shit, we've already sold it to someone else!"

"Can we get Harvey to look into this?"

"That goes without saying," Anton said. Harvey was one of Anton's long-time friends, a lawyer and a member of Mensa. If anyone could get the matter straightened out, it would be Harvey. "Did they say why they're backing out?"

"You sitting down?"

"Tell me."

"They're saying they won't honour a contract that binds them to dealing with a firm that's 'known to be linked to organized criminal elements.' Word for word, Fred."

"Sheeyit," Anton replied. "Shit, damn it, *maledetti bastardi!* Jonathon, you listen to me, and you believe me. I have no more links to organized crime than you do."

"I know that."

"Jesus H. Christ," Anton sighed. "They're doing it again."

Jonathon leaned back in his chair. "Again?"

"Fax me a copy of that letter. Fax a copy to Harvey too. I'll call ahead. Damn it! I'll sue their asses for damages and for defamation of character. *Figli di puttane!*"

"Sue who? The government council?"

"Let me handle this, Jonathon. This is old business I should have dealt with once and for all, before I ever left Regina. I'll call you back with our next steps. Don't you worry about this one. This is mine, and it's personal." Anton said a quick goodbye and hung up before Jonathon could say another word. He sat stunned at his desk with the letter between his hands.

"Laura?" Jonathon held up the letter. "Do me a favour and fax this to Edmonton? Send a copy to Harvey while you're at it."

Don't think about it, Jonathon told himself. *Don't think about it. Make it look like you're enjoying yourself. Think about something else.*

"Kent, for the last time, *please.*" Jennifer pointed down, firmly. "On your seat."

The seven-year-old plopped down on his chair as if his strings had been cut. He kicked his feet under the table.

"First time in a fancy restaurant, hey buddy?" Jonathon asked of the boy.

Kent swung his head from left to right in a definite 'no' fashion. He lashed out his hands and grabbed his plastic glass, pulling it forward so he could blow bubbles in his chocolate milk. His mother was unimpressed.

"Kent!"

Jonathon said, aside, "It's all right, he's having fun."

Gus Minos, the owner of the restaurant, announced his arrival with a bellowed hello. He popped the cork of a new bottle of Dom Perignon. "Good evening, my friend. You bring company this time, and any friend of Jonny is a friend of ours. And I see our young gentleman friend here is having some bubbly of his own making. How is the young miss?"

Jennifer's five year old daughter was being exceptionally well behaved, even if her mannerisms were wooden, formal and shy. She didn't make eye contact with anyone at the table, except for her older brother.

"Gus," Jonathon said, "this is Jennifer, and her two children Kent and Lisa."

Gus was pouring champagne into one of the two flutes he held in his other hand. "A pleasure to meet you." He gave the first glass to Jennifer. "You be good to this guy. He's been good to us." He gave the other filled glass to Jonathon. "To a long and happy friendship. And maybe some romance, eh?" He indicated that they should clink glasses.

Jennifer giggled awkwardly and clinked her glass against Jonathon's. The kids snickered.

"You need anything, you call for me," Gus said. He left the rest of the bottle in a bucket of ice beside the table, and he went off to roar joyfully at other regulars of the restaurant.

"What are you doing? Did you order this?" Jennifer asked. "This is expensive stuff!"

Jonathon shrugged. "You're worth it. Besides, he always brings me one whenever I come here."

"Wow. He must really like you."

"I did him a little favour a couple of years ago, and he says he owes me."

"It must have been an expensive favour."

Jonathon shook his head. "He needed a little help putting some money together to open the place. It meant a lot to him, but I was happy to help." He explained, "Somebody helped me out in a big way, once upon a time, and I can never repay him. The least I can do is follow his example and give someone else the break they need."

Jennifer regarded him as if in a new light. She clinked her glass against his again.

Bad business awaited him in the morning. Outside these walls, there was extortion, and assault. He wondered if he was being watched.

He touched her hair. It was as soft as ever.

Anton arrived by airport limousine just as Laura was leaving for her morning coffee break. Anton smiled and kissed her on both cheeks. "Nice to see you again, Fred," she said. "I'm just headed out for coffee, do you want anything?"

"Not yet, but thank you for the offer. You enjoy yourself. We won't be long."

Laura left behind Jonathon, Anton, and a long, painful silence.

"I don't like that look," Jonathon said. "I've never seen you upset."

"My…friends…got to the government council, and to our buyer."

"What, now the buyer's backing out too?"

Anton rocked on his heels.

"Well shit," Jonathon said.

"It's frustrating as all hell. This has been going on for years, but for a while there…" Anton shook his head. "Ah, well maybe I should never have come back here, Jonny. Not back to Regina. They chased me out of here years ago, and maybe I should have stayed gone." Sagely, he inclined his head and said, "The world's a big place for a man like me. But for guys like *them*…a small city is the whole world, and they want to rule it. Big fish in a small pond."

Jonathon thought of the two thugs in costume, who hit hard and played for keeps. "Who are they, these friends of yours?"

Anton slowly paced the floor, until he bent wearily into a chair and sat. "Two men by the names of Ryder and Callaghan." He ran his hand over his mouth. "RCMP."

Jonathon closed his eyes. "And they believe you've done something illegal."

"That's what they say," Anton said. "But this goes way back. A couple of goons."

Jonathon sat in another guest chair. "Does one of them have red hair? Kinda going grey at the temples?"

Anton raised a bushy eyebrow.

"Both of them just under six feet tall. One with dark hair and broad shoulders?"

"Good God," Anton groaned. "They got to you?"

"They've been trying to." Jonathon didn't want to make the man worry any more than he had to. Jonathon could look after himself.

"No shit."

"No shit whatsoever," Jonathon said. "They're trying to blackmail me."

"For doing what?"

"Maybe blackmail's the wrong word. Protection money, more like it. But I'm already covering my ass." He opened the drawer and showed Anton the mini-cassette recorder.

Anton was smiling and shaking his head.

"They're not the sharpest tacks in the box," Jonathon said, replacing the recorder.

"They never were."

"I've already caught them implicating themselves in a protection racket."

"Jonny, you be careful."

"I'm always careful. But I'm not going to let them get away with this, Fred. Especially not cops. No one should be above the law. And I'm going to take them down a peg."

"You don't know who you're playing with. These are *cops*."

"So what if they are? They're crooked cops, and with enough evidence, I'll put them away for good. They've got no right going around accusing people of being members of the mob – they have no proof, but they're making life…difficult."

"Miserable," Anton said.

"For the both of us," Jonathon agreed. "Are they trying to shake you down too?"

Anton didn't answer directly. "I'm sorry I got you mixed up in this, Jonny."

"It's not your fault. It's because you're Italian, isn't it?"

"My family is Italian, but I was raised here. I don't even remember the old country – I was too young to remember. I'm as Canadian as you are, Jonny."

"I believe it."

"But it's not about that. Not entirely. And I'm not a crook," Anton added. "I never have been. But some people, like Ryder and Callaghan, they just can't stand to see good guys win, you know? After a while, the job gets to them. They see crooks everywhere. They'd plant evidence on their own grandmothers if they suspected them of tax evasion."

ß"We're not going to let them win," Jonathon said.

Anton spread his hands. He looked like he was out of options and out of optimism. "How can I help you to nail the bastards?"

Jonathon said, "If I give them enough rope, they'll hang themselves. I know we're innocent – they haven't got anything on us. For the better part of the last eighteen months, I've been at your side, here, in Edmonton, half a dozen places across Canada and the US. The only thing criminal about you is your sense of humour."

Anton chuckled.

Jonathon added, "And the cruelest thing you ever did was wake me up in the middle of the night, haul me out to Vancouver, get me drunk, then wake me up for breakfast in Corpus Christi, Texas."

Anton laughed. Then he sighed. "Thanks, buddy."

"For getting drunk and letting you spirit me away?"

"For backing me up."

"I told you I wouldn't let you down."

"Swear to God, Jonny, I've never had any criminal dealings, organized or otherwise. I don't need to! Sure as hell I don't have any so-called Mafia connections either. If I did, Ryder and Callaghan would no longer be a problem."

Jonathon gave him a warning look, which Anton acknowledged with a subtle nod of his head. "Besides, it's too easy to make money legitimately. We're living proof of that."

"I'll drink to that," Anton said. His smile soon faded. "Jonny, I gotta tell you. If Ryder and Callaghan are behind this, I'm afraid this is gonna get worse before it gets better. Don't underestimate them, Jonny, even if they are as dumb as they look. They're detectives now, last I heard, and they're in either Special Investigations or NCIS."

"NCIS?"

"National Crime Intelligence. The Special Branch for Organized Crime."

"How?" Jonathon laughed. "As stupid as they are?"

"Don't underestimate them," he said again. "If they are with NCIS, then either they're good at their job, or they've got lots of faithful friends. Either way, that spells bad news for us. You be careful. And trust no one."

REGINA. SPRING, 1980

A new wife, two step-children, a new baby on the way, and a lot of furniture in a brand new house all made for a full and happy home, for the first time in years. Aside from finalizing the divorce with Rita, marrying Jennifer was proving to be the wisest decision Jonathon ever made. It limited his gallivanting about with Anton, but under the circumstances, that was probably for the best. Besides, with Jennifer, there was humour at the dinner table, and homework, and life lessons. There were giggles and Band-Aids, Saturday morning cartoons with Cocoa Puffs and Lucky Charms, Sundays with children shooting imaginary guns in the backyard while Jonathon mowed the lawn, or raked the leaves, or watered the dead grass to make a skating rink for the kids to play on. There were long, blustery evenings with the fire going, *Charlie's Angels* on TV, and Jennifer sitting on the couch beside him, her feet on his legs, and a new crochet project spread out over her knees. There was peace in the household, and a sense of stability, something Jonathon hadn't sensed since he left the farm in Ontario. His life was back on track.

Despite the refreshing changes in Jonathon's life – and in Jennifer's – there was always a vague sense of gloom that clouded Jonathon's joy. Jonathon had regular visits from his two extortionists, more or less a month between each payment. A year ago, five thousand a month would have been nothing but pin money out of Jonathon's budget. Now, with a full family to support and with fewer prospects on the horizon – thanks in part to whispers in the industry about Jonathon's collaboration with a mob boss – five grand a month had evolved from a pinprick to a full force pain in the ass.

And they weren't cooperating with his "investigation" any more than he was complying with theirs. They never let slip their names or their involvement with the RCMP. They only took the money, renewed their threats and left before Jonathon could record anything more damning.

Of late, they seemed tired of the game. Though they were more creative in their dialogue, their threats didn't seem as sincere. He didn't take them seriously. No one could take two grown man in fake beards and a wig seriously.

He trusted they would get tired of pushing around an immovable object, and that they would go pick on someone a little easier to intimidate.

Anton's omen hung over Jonathon's head like something out of *The Pit and the Pendulum*. It would get worse before it got better, he'd said. Jonathon spent months holding his breath, waiting for the other shoe to drop.

One morning, the shoe dropped, and though Jonathon had been anticipating the worst, it still came as a shock. They may have been dumb and melodramatic, but Ryder and Callaghan were resourceful. Far more resourceful than either Jonathon or Anton would have expected.

Jonathon returned to work one morning with his head full of things he had to do and people he had to call, all of it normal Monday stuff. Laura met him at the door with the mail and messages.

"How was your weekend?" Jonathon asked, shrugging off his jacket.

"It was great. Still liking the new house? All unpacked yet?"

"Almost. Still a bunch of boxes down in the basement." He looked at a thick envelope in the pile that Laura had given him. "What's this?"

"It came from the Real Estate Board this morning," Laura said.

He opened it where he stood. His blood drained from his face to pool in his feet.

"What is it?" Laura asked. "Are you all right?"

"They revoked my real estate license."

"*What*?"

"Dear sir, blah blah blah…pains us to revoke your real estate license under regulation blah blah blah – due to your suspected associations with organized crime."

Laura was speechless.

"The *hell* – suspected associations with – good *God*."

"Can they do that?" Laura asked.

"*They* seem to think so."

They shared glances. Jonathon needed to sit down and think. Laura sat her desk, her eyes red-lined and misty.

"It's all right," he said. "We'll get to the bottom of this." He smiled softly. "You wait and see. We'll get this straightened out in no time." He checked his Rolodex and stopped at Harvey's number. What he needed was some sound legal advice.

Ralph Mackenzie was a bespectacled, potbellied bureaucrat from the Regina Real Estate Board. He waved off everything Jonathon said.

"You know these accusations are unfounded," Jonathon said. "Prove that I have any connection to any criminal element, here in Regina or anywhere else in the world."

"Mr. Parker…"

"You can't, because it doesn't exist!"

Slowly, Mackenzie said, "The RCMP have informed us that your partner, Mr. Fred Albertino – "

"Anton," Jonathon said. "Fred Anton. And he doesn't have so much as an outstanding parking ticket, let alone a criminal record."

"I'm sorry, Mr. Parker. My hands are tied!"

"You're the head of the Board!"

"And I'm acting on orders from the Attorney General's office. Perhaps you should take the matter up with him."

"The Attorney General."

"Ask my secretary for his number," Mackenzie said, "as you leave. I'm sorry, Mr. Parker, but I'm not in a position to reinstate your license until such time as you can prove that you and your partner have no association with the criminal element."

Jonathon opened his mouth, astounded and unable to form a logical retort. He made a few aghast noises, he laughed once, incredulously, and finally he managed to say, "So much for innocent until proven guilty, huh? And due process in a court of law?"

"Until then, I wish you a good day."

"Who made you judge and jury?" Jonathon spat. "Never mind. Forget I asked. I already know."

Jonathon jammed his hands in his pockets and stormed across the parking lot, swearing left and right, even using a few phrases he'd learned from Anton. It had been hours since he left the Board's office, and he'd been scrambling to find another agent to help him through the last details of outstanding sales.

"Man alive! Until you can *prove* you're not doing anything illegal, Mr. Parker," Jonathon muttered as he got into the Cadillac and slid the key into the ignition. "The onus of proof is on you, Mr. Parker. There's nothing I can do about it, Mr. Parker. Bullshit." The engine wouldn't turn over. "Bullshit!" He tried again, and this time, the car started.

Headlights flooded the passenger's side. A car was stopped perpendicular to the Cadillac. "Damn it!" Jonathon checked his pockets, the glove compartment, and finally, under the driver's seat. "Why now, damn it?" He fumbled with the power button the mini-cassette recorder. He'd been out of the office all day, though he'd known they were due to come by while Laura was out on her coffee break. Since he'd played hooky from the office, he'd forced them to come looking for him. He hoped they wasted a lot of gas.

He'd had the wherewithal to keep the bank envelope in his brief-case, and that he'd brought the briefcase with him everywhere he'd gone. He slipped the recording device into his jacket pocket, turned off the engine and exited the vehicle with his briefcase. He walked around the back of the car, making a note of the license plate number. It was a government plate, but blobs of mud conveniently obscured half the letters and numbers.

The red-head opened the rear door of the car, letting Jonathon in first. The dark-haired guy sat in the driver's seat with his gun visible. The red-head sat in the backseat with Jonathon. Jonathon sat with his back against the door, and he was relieved to discover interior door handles. It wasn't the same car as before. "Tell me," Jonathon said as he released the clasps of his briefcase. "Do you two split this fifty-fifty? Supplement your meagre policeman's salaries?"

Both men were startled to the point of aiming their guns.

"Relax," Jonathon said. "I'm just shooting in the dark." He turned over the bank envelope. "It's all there, all five thousand. I'm good to my end of the bargain."

The red-head examined it quickly, paying special attention to the corners of the bills and to the serial numbers. "Hey, the Lord loves a cheerful giver." He regarded Jonathon. "Say, you want your real estate license back?"

"Well, that makes good business sense, doesn't it? I can't pay you if I'm not making any money, and I can't make money until I get my license back."

"Just answer the question," the driver said.

Jonathon tried not to roll his eyes, but fortunately, the car's interior was dark enough that they couldn't see him do it. "Yes."

"Say please," said the red-head.

"What do you want this time?"

"Intel," said the driver. "You cough up what you know about Fred Anton, and you get your license back. We may even cut down your premiums, if you ask nicely."

"You want intel?" Jonathon said. "As in intelligence?" His cheeks burned. There were two guns close at hand, and his 'friends' seemed more bitter and impatient than usual. "I can't blame you for wishing you had some."

"Watch…your mouth…" said the red-head.

"I mean, after all, 'intelligence' is the 'I' in NCIS, isn't it?"

"Shoot in the dark once too often, Parker, and you're liable to shoot yourself in the head," said the driver.

"Who else would want information on a suspected mob boss? One you've been hunting for years. Who else but the Special Branch on Organized Crime?"

The red-head clapped the driver on the shoulder. "Put it in gear. We need to take a drive into the country."

"Not tonight, boys," Jonathon said, reaching behind him. "Prior engagement, sorry!" He pulled the door handle and tumbled out onto the pavement. Before either of the two extortionists could get their feet or car in gear, Jonathon was in a full sprint. He hurdled a concrete parking barricade and ran in an arc toward the nearest alley, then out onto a cross-street, across the road and down the block. He walked into a late night Tim Horton's and went straight to the washroom without anyone behind the counter noticing he'd come in. He panted over the sink, and on second thought, he reached over and locked the bathroom door. He washed his face with trembling hands.

He'd just run from the cops.

He checked his mini-cassette recorder. He stopped the recording and rewound the tape. He exhaled so loudly it sounded like a groan of ecstasy. He'd captured the whole conversation.

Twenty minutes later, he emerged from the washroom to a crowd of impatient stares. He apologized and explained he hadn't been feeling well. He ordered a cup of coffee, and asked where he could find a telephone in order to call for a taxi.

He couldn't help but feel like he'd just advanced the game to a new level, and like Anton said, it was going to get worse before it got better.

CHAPTER ELEVEN

Regina. Summer, 1980

Ryder and Callaghan weren't the only ones with resources. Jonathon continued to collect revenue from rental units and businesses who leased space from him. He'd earned enough in sales commissions over the last two years to keep his house in order for up to five years on his savings alone. And just because he couldn't act as a sales representative, having his license revoked had no impact on his ability to buy and sell his own properties. The loss of his real estate license was an inconvenience, but it wasn't going to impoverish him. And, aside from the money he kept in a safe, which was hidden in a panel in the dining room wall, Jonathon still had cash in his Zurich account. He was gloomy, but he was neither broke nor out of options.

But what pissed him off was that two men – police officers, no less – were forcing him out of business simply because he had befriended a man they didn't like. He was determined to bring them down. The problem was that cops protected their own. Jonathon needed to build an irrefutable case against them, and he needed to protect himself, as well as his own family.

All that, and they were bleeding him dry with their repeated demands for money.

And worse, Jonathon had had to make a pact with the devil himself. Because he couldn't negotiate his own sales anymore, and because Bob Myers refused to have any further contact with him, Jonathon had had to turn to Lucifer in a leisure suit: Pat Burton. Fortunately, Burton could be business-like when a commission was on the line. With Burton's services, Jonathon sold the house he'd owned with Rita, and with the proceeds from the sale, he set about buying a new business: a flower shop in the same building where he worked.

They were on the way to the flower shop on a hot summer's day. Burton was in the front passenger's seat complaining about the heat and the leather seats. Having the windows down offered no relief at all. Burton was saying something about frying eggs on the sidewalk. Jonathon signalled to reverse into a parking spot, and a VW Rabbit appeared suddenly in his rear view mirror.

"What the hell!" Jonathon leaned on the horn. No sound came out. The VW turned into Jonathon's spot. Jonathon tried the horn again. The mechanism clicked, but there was no sound. The Rabbit's driver got out, oblivious and carefree. "Thanks a lot, you jerk!" Jonathon shouted out the driver's side window. The driver walked on.

"What's wrong with the horn?" Burton asked. "I thought you just got this car serviced."

"I did!" Jonathon tried the horn again. No sounds. "Jeez, just one more thing to worry about." Burton reached over and tried the horn himself, as if he had some secret and fail proof way of activating it. "Look," Jonathon said, "why don't you go on in and catch the vendors before they close up shop for the night? I'll drop this thing off at a garage and see what's wrong with it."

"Sounds like a plan. Meet me back here."

"Sure. I won't take long."

Burton exited and groaned about the heat and humidity. As soon as he'd closed the door, Jonathon drove on.

Business was slow at the garage, so one of the mechanics waved him straight through into one of the bays for immediate service.

"And what can I do for you today?" asked the mechanic.

Jonathon demonstrated. He leaned on the mute horn. "It was working just fine the last time I used it."

"How long ago?"

"A couple of days."

"Pop the hood for me, and I'll take a quick look. You had any work on the car since the last time the horn worked?"

"No, not so much as an oil change." Jonathon turned off the engine, popped the hood and got out to watch over the mechanic's shoulder. "I mean, it's no big deal, but with the crazies on the road today, you know…"

The mechanic had pulled a screwdriver from the pocket of his overalls. He touched the metal end to a couple of contacts, and the horn made them both jump. "It's probably a fuse or rust on the contacts somewhere. I'll need to dig in. You got about fifteen, twenty minutes?"

"Sure," Jonathon said. The mechanic directed him to the greasy-smelling office for a cup of coffee from the coin-operated machine while he waited. He'd barely had the cup in hand when the mechanic came in and hooked his finger at Jonathon, signalling him to join him outside. The mechanic had the driver's side door open, and he'd pulled off the fuse panel flap. The mechanic pointed to a small, simple looking device plugged into one of the fuse slots. He took Jonathon around the back of the car and pointed out a long, horizontal device magnetically attached to the underside of his rear bumper. Jonathon's heart was in his mouth. "Do you know what that is?" Jonathon asked.

"No idea. But it was wired to your horn circuit. Whoever did it must have been in a hurry. It wasn't fully plugged into the slot. Vibrations musta shook it loose, I guess."

Jonathon stood watching the mechanic, his coffee forgotten in one hand. Someone had tampered with his car. Someone had broken into his car, and Jonathon hadn't even noticed it. Did they do it overnight, when the car was parked in front of his house, while he, his wife and his step-kids slept? While he was at the office? While he was at a buyer's house? The mechanic replaced the fuse and tested the horn, jarring Jonathon out of his thoughts.

"Well…at least now the horn works," the mechanic said. "What do you want me to do with the…the thingamabob here?"

"I don't know. I'm not even sure what it is. Do you know?"

The mechanic took back the wires and components, inspecting them and turning them this way and that. "Seen something like it."

"Oh?"

"Yeah, but only in the movies, you know? Just didn't know it had so many parts. Never thought you had to plug it into the fuse box, but I guess that makes a bit of sense. You need to power it somehow, right?"

"Power what?"

"Listening device. Or maybe some kind of tracker. You know, like the FBI use when they're following somebody."

Jonathon hoped he wasn't blushing visibly, but his face and ears burned. "I thought that was just a simple box they attached to the bottom of the car..."

As they discussed its components and functionality, two unmarked cars and one RCMP cruiser bounced over the curb and parked at awkward angles, blocking all the garage bay doors. The cruiser had its lights flashing. The baggy eyes of the mechanic were startled. He kept his mouth shut and his hands very still as the driver of the cruiser exited his vehicle and marched toward him.

"I'll take that," the constable said. He grabbed the device in an overhand grip, bobbed the brim of his Smokey Bear hat, and retreated to his car. A moment later, the cruiser left, followed by the two unmarked cars, leaving Jonathon and the mechanic behind in a cloud of churned sand, exhaust fumes and dumbfounded wonderment.

The mechanic lifted and eyebrow and regarded Jonathon.

Jonathon grinned and shrugged. "Training exercise?" The mechanic shrugged too. "How much do I owe you?"

"Nothin'," the mechanic said. "The entertainment was payment enough for me!"

Jonathon's pulse thumped in his throat. The problem wasn't just that somebody had bugged his car; the problem was that Ryder and Callaghan were conspicuous by their absence. They might have been in one of the two unmarked sedans, but they brought at least four friends along.

Fred Anton had been right: Ryder and Callaghan had friends on the force. The game was getting complicated, and Jonathon was just beginning to understand how badly outnumbered he was.

REGINA. WINTER, 1980.

Jonathon had been thinking about Christmas presents for his parents and which stores he wanted to hit that afternoon. He should have been paying more attention to his surroundings.

Jonathon got out of his car and locked the doors, then headed toward the strip mall, shivering against the wind. It looked like more snow was on the way.

He heard the tires and the engine, long before he saw the car. He knew it was them. He just knew. He picked up the pace.

Over his shoulder, he saw the sedan revving toward him, oblivious to a car backing out of a spot.

Jonathon turned to run, but the car was that much faster. The red-head swung open the passenger's door as the driver slammed on the brakes, barricading Jonathon from running any further. Jonathon turned to run the other direction, but he had no traction, and the red-head had the advantage of surprise. Jonathon fell face first to the slush, with the red-head leaning on his back.

"Move and I swear, I'll put a bullet in the back of your skull."

Jonathon wheezed against the pressure crushing him against the pavement, making it difficult for his lungs to expand. All his weight – and that of the red-head – was on his lower ribs. Cold steel cracked on the bone of his wrist. The icy grip and the ratcheting sound grated against Jonathon's anxious nerves. He'd never been handcuffed before.

"Get up," said the red-head. He held a firm grip on Jonathon's elbow. "Move along," he shouted at a passerby. "Police business – nothing to see here." He escorted Jonathon into the backseat. The interior door handles had been removed again. This time, the red-head rode in back with Jonathon, keeping a gun trained on him the whole time. Slush spewed out from under the rear tires as the car fishtailed out of the parking lot, onto the street and into traffic.

Snow had softened the contours of the junk yard, and it had fallen through the missing windows of abandoned cars. The driver threw the transmission into park and left the engine running. He jerked open the rear passenger door on the red-head's side. Both officers pulled on Jonathon's legs and arms to get him out of the car and to dump him in the snow outside. The driver kicked Jonathon in the kidneys, flattening him. He kicked Jonathon in the lower back twice more.

"The hell are you doing, running from us? Huh?" the red-head shouted. "How far did you think you could run, you son of a bitch?"

Another kick, this time to the ribs. With his arms pinioned behind him, he couldn't defend his face when a black boot swung up and cracked against his cheekbone.

"Answer him!" shouted the other. Before Jonathon could respond, a boot cracked one of his ribs. He couldn't catch his breath. "Answer him!"

"I don't know what you want!" Jonathon managed. Pain radiated up into his arm pits and down to his hip.

One of them grabbed a fistful of Jonathon's hair, pulling him to a sloppy sitting position on one hip. A photograph was thrust in his face, so close he couldn't get his eyes to focus.

"You know this man?"

"Who are you?" Jonathon asked. The question earned him a slap across the face. "Which one of you – " The red-head backhanded him, leaving bruises where knuckles had connected with bone.

"Do you know this guy?" the dark-haired one enunciated. "Yes or no?"

"And don't lie to us," said the other. "We'll know when you're lying."

Jonathon leaned back from the photograph so he could get his eyes to focus.

"Answer him!" screamed the red-head. Jonathon hesitated, but began to nod. The driver balled up his fist and was about to drive it into Jonathon's nose, but the red-head snapped, "Ryder – wait."

The driver – the man with the dark-hair – Ryder was his name. By process of elimination, that meant the red-head was Callaghan.

"Yes," Jonathon said.

"What?" asked Callaghan. "What did you say?"

"Yes, I know him," Jonathon replied.

Callaghan smiled. "Who is it?"

It had been years since he'd seen the guy. He'd spent that time wiping the name from his memory, and now, between two ringing ears, his memory was foggier than ever.

"Who?" Callaghan shouted.

"Reg," Jonathon shouted back. "Reg Lawrence."

"Good boy," Callaghan said. "You told the truth for a change!" He held up the picture, baring his teeth at it in a mockery of a smile. "You caught him in the act, didn't you? Porking your old lady. Must have pissed you right off, catching him in her hotel room like that."

They waited for Jonathon to respond.

"Isn't that right?" Ryder asked. "Answer him!"

"Yes, I was upset," Jonathon said. "Anybody would be!"

"Enough to push him around?" Callaghan asked. "Throw him into the bathroom and threaten him? And don't try to lie about it."

"I pulled him out of the closet and I threw him into the bathroom, that's it. I didn't lay a hand on him!" Jonathon protested. "That was years ago. I've grown up and moved on."

"Oh, but you don't forget things like that," Callaghan said. "No self-respecting husband lets another man get away with something like that. He keeps his anger inside, and it grows and it grows, and it gets so big that it *explodes*." He slapped Jonathon again. "And he can't contain himself anymore, can he?"

Jonathon asked, "Is that what this is about? Reg Lawrence?" He snorted, and to his surprise, his mouth dribbled blood. He spat and asked, "What, is he a boyfriend of yours?"

It was the wrong thing to say.

Jonathon lay on his side, eyes unable to focus on any one object at a time. He wasn't sure which one had hit him, or how many times he'd been struck.

"Be nice," Callaghan warned. "It's a long walk home."

"I didn't lay a hand on him," Jonathon insisted. His voice was thin and watery.

"We didn't say you did," Ryder replied. "But you know who did." He pulled another picture out of a manila envelope. "You know who did this to him."

It was another picture of Reg Lawrence. Only this time, he was lying stretched out on a metal table, and his face was grotesquely bloated. Callaghan pulled Jonathon to a sitting position again.

"He…he's dead?" Jonathon asked. Reg hadn't been much older than Jonathon.

"You know who killed him," Ryder said. "And because you're such a good citizen, you're gonna help us put the bad guy behind bars."

"Aren't you?" Callaghan cooed. He tapped Jonathon's face and pinched his cheek. "Do this one little thing for us, and you get your life back."

"Do what?" Jonathon asked. "I didn't even know he was dead!"

Callaghan looked at Ryder and remarked, "He's such a good actor, ain't he? Acting all surprised…"

"I don't know what you're talking about," Jonathon said.

Ryder slid a type-written document out of the envelope. The words Witness Statement were typed across the top. Five or six paragraphs, written in the first person, explained that Jonathon had had several conversations with Fred Anton, wherein Anton had issued threats against Reg Lawrence. Jonathon had only time enough to catch a glimpse of the occasional word or phrase per paragraph, but two lines he managed to read in full. Jonathon was supposed to have received a phone call from Anton, who'd allegedly said, "It's done. He's not a problem for us anymore."

"I'm not signing this," Jonathon said. "I can't!"

Callaghan drew his gun and pressed the gun against Jonathon's temple. "You think we're playing games here?"

Jonathon gritted his teeth. The barrel was cold. "I can't sign this!"

"Oh," Callaghan laughed. "He needs a pen, that's why."

"Oh right!" Ryder said. He offered a pen.

"I won't sign my name," Jonathon began, seething against the pain in his scalp when Callaghan dug his fingers in and pulled Jonathon's head back. "I won't sign my name to a pack of lies."

"Idiot," Ryder snapped.

Callaghan flung Jonathon's head forward, forcing him off balance. "Oh, you will sign it."

"I didn't even know he was dead! I never had that conversation. We never even talked about Reg after Fred fired him! And that was years ago!"

"I think we get it," Ryder said. He stood up from his squatting position, and he drew his gun too. "You care more about Freddie boy than you do about your business. About your house. About your wife and kids."

"You leave my family out of this," Jonathon said. "You leave them the hell alone – this is between me and you two. You leave them the hell alone, or I'll..."

They stood beside him, grinning, waiting for the incriminating threats. When they weren't forthcoming, Ryder sighed and said, "You know, I'm tired of you dragging your heels. You don't want to take us seriously, fine. Either you're with us or you're against us, and if you're against us..."

"Say goodbye to your sweet life," Callaghan finished.

"Your business," Ryder counted off. "All your investments. Your freedom. Your family. "

"Leave them out of this!"

"And then you're going to have to sign it anyhow," Callaghan said. "You do it the easy way, or we do it the hard way. It's your choice."

They waited. Jonathon hawked and spat blood on the snow.

"Going once," Callaghan said.

"No," Jonathon answered. "I won't sign it."

"Going twice," Callaghan warned.

Jonathon braced himself and shook his head.

"Sold," Ryder said. He tossed his gun up in the air, caught it by the barrel and brought it crashing down on the top of Jonathon's head. Callaghan followed it up with a kick to Jonathon's head. A foot in Jonathon's crotch doubled him over, screaming in pain. Another kick to the rib and the shoulder knocked him over. He tried to protect his gut and chest with his knees, but he had no defence against the kicks and blows that pummeled his head, his back and his sides. Something hit him in the temple, and all he could see were painfully bright sparkles on a field of black. He heard a rhythmic whooshing sound in his head, and his body felt pinned to the ground by an enormous atmospheric pressure that simultaneously weighed him down and sapped the strength from his limbs.

Everything hurt. Every bruise throbbed. He couldn't breathe without coughing, and every cough felt like an explosion that was ripping open his chest from the inside.

He hadn't realized he'd passed out until he came to again. Gobs of gritty, wet snow hit his ear; Ryder and Callaghan were driving away, spinning their tires on a patch of ice.

Jonathon struggled to roll over, off his face. He brushed the snow out of his eyes and mouth, and when he spied the blood on his fingers, he realized they'd at least had the decency to remove the handcuffs before leaving him to die. He struggled to his hands and knees, and then from his knees to his feet. He'd gotten up too quickly. He fell to his knees again. He stayed on all fours until the vertigo and nausea passed. His limbs gave out.

CHAPTER TWELVE

The road turned, and as Jonathon stumbled on the edge of the hidden ditch, he quickened his pace. He could see the city far in the distance, glowing against the falling snow like a dome of soft, yellow light. He had no idea what time it was. His watch had either fallen off or had been taken. He had a vague idea where he was. It was cold, and he was sick to his stomach; only the threat of pain in his ribs prevented him from retching. Shivering made all the bruises light up. He knew at least one rib was cracked.

He heard the sound of an old diesel engine driving up from behind him. He turned and stuck out his thumb. It was an old blue Ford farm truck. When the truck didn't slow down, he leaned further into the lane, waving his arms. The headlights stabbed through to the back of his head, and he raised his forearm to shield his eyes. The truck passed him by. No blowing heater, no warm seat, no quick trip back into town.

A bang burst, rupturing the winter silence. Jonathon ducked and shouted in pain.

Something made a comical flopping sound, and the truck pulled over to the side of the road. Jonathon picked up his pace, running like Quasimodo toward the truck. By the time he got there, the farmer was out, using a long handled wrench to free the last lug nut on a flat tire.

"Please," Jonathon wheezed.

The farmer jumped up, clutching his chest. "Jaysus Murphy!" Then he saw Jonathon's state. "What the hell happened to you?"

"Please," Jonathon said. "I could really use a ride back into town."

The farmer stared. "Yer gonna have to wait 'til I get the tire changed."

The doctor slid the X ray picture onto the glowing white viewer. "A fall, you said?" he asked. He tucked one hand into his white lab coat. "What did you do, fall off a cliff?"

Jonathon roused. He couldn't make his mouth-sounds to line up into a coherent question, but the doctor seemed fluent in mumbles.

"Welcome back. Do you know where you are?" the doctor asked.

Jonathon faintly remembered being pulled out of the truck and being seated in a wheelchair. He remembered being at the nurse's station and trying to answer questions, but he didn't remember actually entering the hospital or coming into the examination room. He was lying on an examination table. He didn't remember getting out of the wheelchair, either. He wondered how many orderlies it had taken to get him stretched out. "Hospital?"

"You were dropped off about an hour ago," the doctor said.

Jonathon mumbled something about being late and about Jennifer being worried about him.

"Just relax," the doctor said. "We're just running a little busy tonight, but we'll get you patched up in no time. In the meantime, you need your rest. And drink your fluids."

"How bad is it?" Jonathon asked.

The doctor frowned and shook his head. "Severe bruising of the abdominal area, possible kidney damage, hairline fraction of the eighth and ninth ribs on your left side. Probable concussion. You're going to have to take it easy for the next couple of days, and no hockey for the next six weeks." He was quite close to the examination table now, frowning as if disappointed in Jonathon. "You're sure it was a fall?" he asked, pointing to the cuts and bruises around Jonathon's face.

"Hm…? Yeah. Fell. Down some stairs. Hit my head. It's slippery out."

"That it is," the doctor said. "But most people, when they fall down, they conk their heads only once. They don't fall on the back of their head *and* on their face at the same time."

Jonathon understood the implications. "I fell," he said.

The doctor closed the clipboard. "We have a police officer stationed just outside the triage area," he said, "in case you want to press charges."

Jonathon shook his head, but his brain felt loose in his skull, and the motion made him feel sick to his stomach. "What time is it?"

The doctor checked the clock on the wall. "Just about 10:35."

Jonathon grunted. "Funny, I thought it was later than that." He set his head gently against the hard cushion of the examination table, and he watched the dots in the ceiling wheel around and around.

Jennifer had the front door open the moment he pulled into the driveway. Despite the blowing snow, she stood in the open doorway with Michael in her arms. Michael was asleep. Jonathon took great care on the driveway. He walked slowly, so he wouldn't provoke a flinch reflex and shout in pain. Someone had put salt down, but it was loose and it rolled under his heel. At the hospital, the nurses had cleaned up his face pretty well; aside from a couple of stitches in his left eyebrow, he seemed none the worse for wear. He'd never bruised badly before, and he was glad of it now. His ribs, however, had already turned all shades of red and purple, and promised to change colours over the next few days.

"Where the hell have you been?" For the sake of their sleeping son, Jennifer had kept her voice level and quiet. "Do you have any idea what time it is?"

"I got caught up in work," Jonathon said. As he came closer, Jennifer's eyes widened.

"What happened to you?" Then she blurted, "Are those *stitches*?"

"I was at the office late," Jonathon said, squeezing through the door, "and I left the office and it was dark, and I slipped on the front steps in all this snow and ice." He pointed to his eyebrow. "Hit my head on the way down, tumbled ass over teakettle the whole way down."

"Oh God," Jennifer said. She closed the door. "But those are stitches! You went to the hospital? Why didn't you call me?"

He kicked off his boots and went directly to the kitchen for a drink without taking his coat off first. "I didn't want to worry you."

"You didn't want to me to worry?" She watched him pour a glass of Scotch. "What the hell do you think I've been doing for the last seven hours?"

"Jennifer – please…honey…stop shouting."

"I'm not shouting."

Jonathon pointed to Michael, who was fussing in his sleep. Jennifer pursed her lips, then went to put Michael back in his crib. When she came back, she had her finger raised and pointed at his face.

"I know what this is about," Jennifer said. "It's Laura, isn't it?"

"What?"

"I've seen how she looks at you."

Jonathon gaped. "She's married!" he laughed.

"What's that got to do with anything?"

"I fall down stairs and break open my face, and you assume it's because I'm having an affair?" He laughed, and he regretted it.

"You spend all day with her – and I've seen how you two pal around when I'm at home stuck with the kids."

Jonathon caught her by the shoulders. "Jen. I've been on the receiving end when somebody else fooled around behind my back. It's not something I would wish on my worst enemy. Well, maybe I would wish it on Pat Burton, but that's it. Sure as hell I wouldn't wish it on my own wife, especially when *she's* been hurt the same way in the past."

Jennifer lowered her eyes, but her face was red.

"I wouldn't do that to you," Jonathon said. He pulled her closer and hugged her. Her hands brushed across his ribs and he yelped.

"Oh God, I'm sorry – are you okay?"

Jonathon groaned through his nostrils. "Two cracked ribs." He forced a laugh. "She likes it rough, I guess."

"That's not even funny, Jonathon," she retorted. She lifted the hem of his shirt and inspected the bandages. "You should sue the property managers for negligence. I mean look at you!" She ran her fingers across his bruised forehead and lips. "You should have called me from the hospital."

"Why, so you could pack three frightened kids into a car and freak out in the waiting room?" He kissed her lips. "I'm sorry I didn't call."

"Well, you should have."

"I know." He kissed her again. "If I gave you your Christmas present a couple of days early, would that make it up to you?"

"I don't know, Jonny. It would have to be one hell of a Christmas present."

"Oh good! Because it is."

"What is it?"

"I'll show you in the morning." He kissed her on the nose.

Jennifer pushed the stroller through and over patches of snow that had been poorly cleared, and where the going was trickiest, he stooped, wincing, and lifted the front wheels. They stopped outside the building where Jonathon had his office.

"I'll wait here for you," Jennifer said.

"No," Jonathon laughed. He pointed to his immediate left. "We're here. Read the sign."

The sign over the ground floor shop said "JP's Flower Basket". A sign on the window said "Under New Management".

"Wha…" Jennifer's mouth hung open. "What did you *do*?"

"I bought the place," he said. "For you. Merry Christmas."

She managed one incredulous laugh.

"Do you like it?"

"Like it? Jonathon, I can't believe it! It's fantastic!" She grabbed him by the shoulders and pressed a messy, giggling kiss on his lips. When she released him, it was with a delicious sigh. She stood back, her hands on her hips, nodding at her brand new flower shop. She was so excited, she jumped up and squeezed her husband around the busted ribs. She let him go with a quick and profound apology. But she couldn't contain her joy. She kissed him again and again.

CORPUS CHRISTI, TEXAS. CHRISTMAS SEASON, 1980.

Jonathon decided he would rather be damned than let Ryder and Callaghan ruin this Christmas. He'd called up Rita's brother and wished him a Merry Christmas – they bore no ill will toward each other, and in fact, had remained pretty good friends, even after the divorce.

He'd splurged on presents for his children. He bought champagne and wine for his fellow businessmen around the block – men with whom he'd had more than a few beers from time to time. He'd written cheques to charities in Regina and around the province. He'd been blessed with an easy fortune, despite his troubles with Ryder and Callaghan, and he got a kind of spiritual high from putting that money to good use.

He decided this was the year he would pay it back to the people who helped him to become the man he was. He couldn't crow about his own successes while his parents managed the affairs of someone else's farm and sat around watching TV in some claustrophobic little house on the edge of town. He would do something for them that would leave them in ecstatic wonder for years to come. That meant thanking them in the best way he knew how. And that meant taking his parents down to Corpus Christi.

Jonathon's mother Norma nodded noncommittally. "Well, it is nice." She looked from the luxury resort to Jonathon, and back to the resort again. Sun shone off the umbrellas and palm trees planted around one of the swimming pools. Tanned tourists of every shape, size and nationality walked between spacious cabins, wearing their shorts, breezy shirts and sun visors. "Jonathon," she laughed. "This is a lovely Christmas present! I've always wanted to vacation in a place like this, but I never thought…"

Jonathon shared a secret smile with Edward.

But Edward shook his head. "Son, it sure is nice, but you know your mother and I could never afford this."

Jonathon raised his hand. "You put up only what you want, whatever you feel comfortable with. I'll put up the rest. It won't be a problem."

Norma's eyebrows pulled together. "How expensive *is* this place?"

"About nine hundred and fifty thousand dollars," he answered.

"Wha – *what*?"

"We could never you pay that back to you," Edward said.

"You mean you're going to…" Norma's mouth twitched. "You're going to *buy* the whole place?"

"We," Jonathon said. "Don't worry about it, Dad. I'll come in as an investor. I'll make my money back through a return on investment.

The income's more than enough to live on and to pay me back over time."

"Jonathon, listen to me," Edward said. "I'm not sure about this."

"Then why don't we meet the owners? We can go over his numbers, take a look at the books, and then we'll work out the math. If you're not comfortable, we won't go through with it. But think of it, Dad… You said yourself you weren't ready to retire, but the winters and your arthritis…" Jonathon smiled at his mother. "The Gulf Coast is just a couple of miles down the road. And you know, you can rent horses and ride along the beach for hours…"

Norma shrugged. "Ed, it won't hurt us to at least take a look at the papers." She pushed him toward the main office, where Jonathon was headed.

When business was done, Jonathon checked them into the resort for a week, and went back home to spend Christmas with his wife, his two step-children, and Michael, the baby of the family.

For what felt like the first time in years, Jonathon breathed deeply and slept well, carefree and content. He'd done what he was supposed to do. He was doing the right things for a change, and looking after others.

REGINA. JANUARY, 1981.

Jonathon had "Saturday Night's All Right for Fighting" stuck in his head. He was mouthing the words when he walked into the office. He figured anything was better than more Christmas carols. It would take weeks to wash them out of his mind, and if anyone was up to the job, it was Elton John.

"Good morning Laura," he announced. "How were your Christmas holidays?" He took off his coat, and when he didn't get a response right away, he turned, forgetting the song stuck in his head.

"Uh, just great," she said. "Your father just called from Texas."

"Great. How's he enjoying himself?"

Laura instead looked down at the hand written memo. "He said your last fifty thousand hasn't arrived there yet."

"What do you mean?"

"Their resort deal? It was supposed to close today."

"That's weird. I thought we wired that money over two weeks ago," Jonathon said.

"Well," she said, "your father says it's definitely not there."

"He's gotten the last few installments with no problem, right?"

"Right," she answered. Her shoulders relaxed and she exhaled. "You know, the only thing I can think of is that maybe something got screwed up at the bank because of the holidays. I'll give the bank a call, once they open."

He tried to smile and agree with her, but something was irritating the back of his mind, making him painfully anxious. He checked the time. "Twenty minutes," he said. "Do that. And let me know if I need to – " He shook his head. "No, you know what? If there's a mix-up at the bank, they're going to need to speak with me in person anyhow. I'll head over there. They'll be open by the time I get there."

Rita, he thought. *Damn you – you'd better not be up to your usual tricks.*

The bank manager met Jonathon and ushered him into his office. "Have a seat." Jonathon did so. "I'd wondered when you would be coming in to see me."

Jonathon frowned. The manager had narrowed his eyes and lips, as if he was scrutinizing Jonathon's face for signs of a lie. "You were expecting me."

"Your business account is seriously overdrawn."

Jonathon shook his head. *Not again.*

"Now, you've got an excellent record with us, Mr. Parker, so I've been giving you the benefit of the doubt. But I'm glad you finally came in for a chat."

"My account can't be overdrawn," he said. Not only was it a new business account in a different bank, but as a divorcee, Rita wasn't authorized to access his account information. "No, my accounting skills are a hell of a lot better than that." He handled the ledgers himself, not only for his personal and business accounts in Canada, but abroad as well. He'd been generous, but not without budgeting for it first. He laughed and added, "I just deposited two hundred and twenty thousand dollars in that account. I just sold another apartment block, and I put the proceeds directly into the business account."

Then it hit him: if his account had been overdrawn, then hundreds of thousands of dollars had just been withdrawn, and unless he got that money back ASAP, he'd be in default of the sale of the Corpus Christi motel. Everything they'd already spent on its purchase – including his parents' entire life savings – would be lost to the buyer.

"My account can't be overdrawn," he said. "Where does that kind of money go without being noticed? Especially over Christmas?"

The manager handed across an account statement for Antonino's Enterprises Ltd. The balance was written in red ink: -$22,354.67.

"There are at least thirty N.S.F. charges on here," Jonathon said.

"Fifty-two of them, actually. Most of them came about when your month-end bills came due."

Meaning whoever took that money must have taken it out sometime over Christmas week or the week before… "And you reversed the wire to Texas. No wonder my parents are so worried." He muttered under his breath, "That's the first thing to get fixed." Another line jumped off the page. "What's this?" He pointed. "A transfer made on the 17th? For four hundred and fifty thousand dollars? Good God – that's almost half a million dollars! Which account did it go to?"

The manager scouted through the various documents and file folders on his desk. He found what he was looking for, and he handed it over. "Here's the wire transfer authorization right here. You signed for it yourself." It was dated the 17th.

Jonathon laughed angrily. "I signed no such thing."

"The transfer was sent just after ten that morning. Next morning, your secretary Laura phoned in the wire transfer instructions, but by afternoon, when we found your account was already overdrawn, we reversed the instructions."

"I didn't sign this."

"After that, since we didn't hear anything from you or from your secretary, we started returning your cheques the next day."

"Our offices were closed for Christmas after the 18th, and I'm telling you, I didn't...*sign*...this," Jonathon said. "It's impossible."

"It matches your signature."

Jonathon allowed, "It's a good likeness."

"Mr. Parker, I'm in no mood for this, this morning." He threw three more withdrawal slips across the desk. "These were all done on the same day. All with the same signature."

"On the 17th of December."

"Yes!" The manager was exasperated.

"Sir," Jonathon said, levelling his voice, "on December 17th, I was in Corpus Christi. Texas. From the 15th to the 19th, I was in Texas. I wasn't even in the country when I was supposedly standing around in line signing these withdrawal slips. Now try again!"

Now the manager was paying closer attention to Jonathon's side of the story. He looked over the slips again.

"I've got plane tickets," Jonathon said, "boarding passes, motel receipts, and if you need them, I'm sure I could get signed witness statements."

The manager grunted and laid out each of the slips side by side. "These were all done by one teller." He rubbed his stubbly cheek. "She was a temp."

"Fantastic," Jonathon snapped. "You believe me then. Now what are we going to do about it?"

The manager was still musing to himself. "We'll have to call her up and find out who signed these slips." At least the manager no longer believed Jonathon had signed the transfer or withdrawal chits. "She only worked the one day, replacing someone else who had called in sick. Our usual fill-in is on maternity leave." He was thinking out loud. "I'll have to get personnel to track her down."

"And when is that going to happen?"

"Well, I'll have to wait until the personnel office opens, and they'll have to contact the temp agency...temp agency will have to track down that teller..."

"And what am I supposed to do in the meantime?"

The manager extended his hand, flat, palm down. "We'll get to the bottom of this."

"Yeah, but in the meantime, not only am I twenty-two grand in the hole, but I've got month end bills not paid, I've got kids to feed, I've got two parents worried *sick* about their life savings, and damn it, I've got a near million-dollar deal about to default. How can we get this money back?"

The manager's hand drifted down to the top of his desk. "I should have told you this right from the beginning."

"Told me what?"

"You tell me these funds were withdrawn without your consent. And in my heart, I believe you. But a bank does not conduct business by hearts and feelings, especially when there's close to a half-million dollars on the line."

"I can get you the proof you need."

"I know, but we can't conduct that investigation until the first one is closed."

"Wha...what other investigation?"

"You didn't get those messages either, I see."

"What *investigation*?"

The manager sighed and said, "The RCMP has not yet completed its ongoing investigation of your account."

"RCMP..." Jonathon's voice trailed off. "What are they accusing me of?"

"Money laundering."

Jonathon clacked his teeth together to keep from shouting a curse. He sat back hard in the chair, pressing his fist against the chair's arm.

"Apparently the Regina City Police have also launched an investigation into your accounts."

"Money laundering?"

"Cheque fraud," the manager said.

Jonathon laughed in spite of himself. "They really get around, don't they?"

The manager didn't seem to understand the question.

"So there's nothing you're going to do about it," Jonathon said with a sigh. He was getting tired of the same old refrain. '*My hands are tied. I'm powerless to act. I'd like to help you, but...*'

"I wish there was something I could do," the manager said. "But I'm sorry. I can't interfere with an ongoing police investigation. Not a municipal police investigation, and sure as hell not an RCMP investigation." He bobbed his head from one side to the other. "I can, however, make a more thorough investigation of my own. Your accounts might not be the only ones affected." He rose, and Jonathon did too. The manager offered his hand. "I'll make some inquiries of my own. It's the least I can do."

Jonathon shook his hand, thinking bitterly, *Yes, it really is the least you can do. God help you if you tried to do more.*

Jonathon called Texas from his office. Edward Parker was beside himself.

"No, Dad, listen to me for a second."

"A 'hassle'? Define 'hassle!'"

"Dad. I need you to get them to extend the closing date until the fifteenth. I'll get the money to you before that."

"We have our life savings tied up in this, Jonathon."

"You think I don't know that?"

"You'd better not disappoint us, Jonathon."

"There won't be a problem. Tell them it was because of a miscommunication at the bank, and we couldn't get it fixed before now because of the holidays."

"Jonathon..."

"I love you both," he said into the receiver. "And I'll call you again as soon as I have more news. Let me know how it goes with the extension."

"This was your idea," Edward reminded him. "Now you fix this." Edward hung up.

Jonathon replaced the receiver onto the hooks. Laura came in a moment later. She'd brought him a cup of coffee, and without a word, she put it on his desk in front of him. He thanked her for it. But before he opened the lid, he had another call to make. It didn't take long to make the connection.

"Hi Fred."

"Jonny."

"Listen, you remember that deal I was talking to you about, the one in Texas?"

Anton sounded distracted. "The motel, resort, whatever that thing was?"

"That one."

"What about it?" Fred asked.

Jonathon had a headache coming on. "It's about to close, and I'm four hundred grand short."

There was a long pause on the other end of the line. "What happened?"

"My bank screwed up, and they transferred some money out of my account into somebody else's account by mistake."

"That's a hell of a mistake."

"You're not kidding. They're trying to get it straightened out right now, but it's going to take a couple of weeks."

Fred muttered something in Italian.

"I was hoping you could maybe help me out," Jonathon said.

Fred sighed. He hardly had to say "no" out loud. Jonathon detected the same old refrain, this time from the least likely singer. "Jonny, I've been getting a lot of heat lately. I'm getting it from all directions, but most of it's because of that damned SGIO deal of ours."

"Still?"

"Harvey's advised me to lay low for a while. Maybe even close down the business for a while, at least until things settle down."

Jonathon's bowels had turned to water. "Fred," he said, "I have to tell you. I'm in a real need here. Can you make me a…a personal loan or something? You know I'm good for it."

"I'm sorry, Jonny. No can do right now." His voice was unusually soft and slow. "Everything I own is tied up right now. Besides, I promised Harvey, no more deals until this all blows over." Anton sighed heavily, as if groaning with indigestion. "I'm sorry."

"It's all right, Fred. I understand." He lifted his chin and said, "Besides, I've got one more option open to me."

"That's good, Jonny. That's real good. I hope it works out for you, and I hope this all gets straightened out quick."

They lapsed again into silence.

Ryder and Callaghan, Jonathon thought. *Ryder and Callaghan. Why...?* "All right. I guess I'll talk to you soon, Fred."

"Keep in touch."

They said their goodbyes and hung up. He opened his coffee and took a moment to steel his nerves. *This is not how I expected my day to go*, he thought.

"Laura?" he called.

"Yeah boss?"

"Do me a favour and book a flight to Zurich for me?" He'd start re-organizing his calendar and rehearse what he was going to tell Jennifer, why he was going to be gone for a couple of days. He'd have to figure out some way of buying American souvenirs for the kids...

Ryder and Callaghan, he thought. *What the hell did I ever do to you...?*

Laura's voice cut through his reverie. "Yes, hello, I'd like to make a reservation on – "

"Laura!" Jonathon shot to his feet and said, "Hang up the phone!" Sweat beaded on his forehead. It had occurred to him that they could be monitoring his phone line. If they were, they now knew he was on the move. "I'll call from another line."

Laura gently hung up the phone without saying goodbye to the travel agent. She stared in wonder. "Is everything okay..."

"It will be," he said as he threw on his coat. He took his coffee and briefcase, and he left.

The flight attendant smiled and said, "Passport please, Mr. Parker?"

He turned it over.

The attendant's smile broke as she keyed in the information. She betrayed little when she said, "I'm sorry, Mr. Parker, but there's a travel restriction on your passport."

"A what?"

"A travel restriction. I'm afraid I'm not allowed to sell you a flight pass today."

"What kind of restriction?"

She studied the readout on her computer terminal. "Customs and Immigrations have flagged your passport for 'no international travel.'"

"What for?"

"It says it has something to do with an RCMP investigation? I'm sorry, there's really nothing more specific than that." She turned the monitor around to prove her point.

Jonathon read every line twice. He took his money and stormed out of the terminal, sensing airport security close at his heels the whole way.

Stupid or not, connected or not, menacing or full of a cruel sense of humour – either way, Ryder and Callaghan had officially pissed him off.

CHAPTER THIRTEEN

Jonathon was once again in league with the devil.

He crumpled the newspaper in his lap and sighed loudly. *Police investigate local realtor for cheque fraud, money laundering.* His name was all over the article. His picture, his company name, the failed SGIO sale, everything was there. Fred Anton's name appeared a few times, too. It was the third day in a row he'd hit the front pages. He couldn't go into a coffee shop without having people point at his face. They weren't even being subtle about it. Regina had spoiled. One minute he was everyone's friend, the next, he was a byword and typecast as a sleazy villain, the unspeakable name passed behind hands from mouth to ear. He'd never felt so exposed, nor so reviled. All that stood between Jonathon and a raving mob, it seemed, was a lack of torches and crucifixes. There was no shortage of pitchforks. No shortage of rope, either. Even Kent was getting teased – bullied – about it at school, because his rich step-dad, of whom he'd once bragged, had been outed as a fraud and a crook.

And now Jonathon was back in Pat Burton's office, because he had no one else to turn to. If Pat Burton was the only one left to trust, Jonathon was in a sore spot indeed. He didn't need aspirin. He needed Pepto-Bismol and a fifth of Scotch. And a miracle.

It was a relief to get away from his own office, at least. For now, Jonathon had left the burden of media relations and customer care to Laura. He was tired of saying "I'm sorry you feel that way" and "I have no comment." Laura was much better at it; and she could always weasel her way out of a long conversation by taking down the phone number and convincing the caller that Jonathon would call back as soon as he had returned to the office.

He had to get that money back to Edward Parker. A loving son wouldn't leave his father in a lurch like that. He'd pull out all the stops, if it meant protecting his father's life savings, or at least covering the deficit until the investigations were handled and all four hundred fifty grand were returned. And Jonathon had the money to do it, that wasn't a problem. He had more than enough in his foreign accounts to cover what was missing and to save the Corpus Christi deal. It was his money, legally, safe and clean. It was his by rights. All he had to do was go and collect it. No one else could do it for him, and it certainly wasn't something that could be done over the phone. All he had to do was go overseas. Then everything would be all right – at least until he had everything sorted out.

The question was: how to get from here to there?

Burton returned to his office with a glass of water and a bottle of aspirin. He offered them both to Jonathon. "You're asking a hell of a thing," Burton said. He showed his lopsided, greasy grin. He ogled Jonathon as if estimating his value at a cattle auction.

"I figured, if anyone knows somebody who could help me, it would be you," Jonathon said.

"What kind of social circles do you think I run in?" Burton laughed, this time with a hearty dose of irony. "Besides, if I knew anybody who ran around with that kind of crowd, it would be you." He pointed at the crumpled newspaper in Jonathon's lap. "I thought you knew people who knew people, if you know what I'm saying."

"Not funny, Pat."

"Always knew you were a wise guy," Burton said.

"Enough. Look, if you don't want to help me..."

"Relax!" Burton had his hands up, and he'd pulled a saucy, nonchalant smile to one side of his face. "I didn't say no." He shrugged and made a grinding, creaking noise with his voice. "I might know a guy who can help."

"Where can I find him?"

"He hangs out a lot at Neighbour's Pub."

Jonathon nodded and rose from the borrowed chair, leaving the discarded newspaper behind. As Fred Anton used to say, the sun was over the yard arm somewhere. He unhooked Burton's coat from the stand and tossed it to him. "Care to make the introductions?"

Cory Carter was a decent looking fellow with a year-round tan, a chiselled face, a lean build, and every eye of every woman in the place. He'd combed back his jet black hair and slicked it into place with gel. He looked like the brooding, evil twin of the Fonz. He was a modern-day greaser, one more likely to carry a silenced pistol than a switchblade. When he looked up and spotted Pat Burton and Jonathon, though, his brittle temper seemed to melt into good humour. He leaned against the booth cushions, leaving only a loose hand on the table to toy with his pack of cigarettes. He sat with his feet extended under the table and his knees wide apart.

"Hey," Burton said. "Like you to meet a good friend of mine."

Cory extended his hand with casual grace.

"Cory Carter," Burton said as the two men shook hands, "Jonathon Parker. Jonny, Cory."

"Have a seat," Cory said, pointing to the opposite seat. He sat up and withdrew his feet. "What are you two drinking?"

Burton's head was set on a swivel. His lips twitched. "Oh, no. I'm not sticking around." He licked his lips and added, "I'll uh…I'll let you two talk it out. I'll be seeing you, Jonny."

The silence was awkward. A waitress eased the tension by asking for their orders. Cory was good with the half-glass of beer that he still had. Jonathon ordered his usual double Scotch.

"I think I seen your picture in the newspapers," Cory said.

"Hard to find someone in this town who hasn't," Jonathon said, scanning the faces and heads in the bar. He ran his hand under the table. He found countless sticky buttons of used gum, but no signs of a listening device. "I need a set of ID," he said. He tried hard not to move his lips while he spoke. "But I didn't know who I could talk to about it."

Cory smirked. "And this has nothing to do with the…the *stuff* in the papers?"

"Actually, no. Not really. I just need to make one trip. An overnight trip. Urgent business." They stared at each other, as if they were locked in some battle of wits. "Pat says you're resourceful."

Cory didn't answer straight away. He waited until the waitress had returned with Jonathon's drink. "He says I'm resourceful, huh?"

"And that you're…subtle," Jonathon said. "Confidential."

"By moving about, do you mean, out of the city, or out of the country?"

"I need to make a legal, financial transaction," Jonathon said. "But not with a domestic bank."

Cory caught onto his meaning right away. His smirk faded. "How soon do you need it?"

"As soon as possible."

"There's a premium on 'as soon as possible.'"

"I can pay you up front," Jonathon assured him.

"You have any pictures? An old passport maybe?"

Jonathon pulled out an envelope prepared for just this purpose. He passed it under the table and left it on Cory's knee. Cory left it there for a moment. Someone had caught his eye.

"I think that should be everything you need. Old passport, new photos," Jonathon said.

"How serious are you about all this?" Cory asked. "This stuff doesn't come cheap. It's five up front, ten more later, just so you know."

"Thousand?"

"Yeah."

"Then make it happen," Jonathon said.

"I heard they froze your assets," Cory said.

Jonathon finished his drink and got up to leave. "You're not the only resourceful man in these parts, my friend." He may not have been making any new deals, but he still had passive income coming in from rentals and from businesses he either owned or had financed on the side. Jonathon said, "My number's in that envelope. Give me a call when it's ready, and I'll bring the first five in cash. Once I get back from overseas, I'll have the other ten for you. It won't be a problem."

"Tens, twenties and fifties," Cory said. "Nothing bigger."

"Done," Jonathon said. He left a five dollar bill for his drink and for Cory's.

Jonathon stopped in at the dealership.

"Always a pleasure doing business with you, Jonathon," said the dealer. "And I don't give a damn what the papers say."

"I appreciate that, I really do."

"You've been nothing but honest with me, and you've brought me a lot of good business." He dangled the new keys from the otherwise empty key ring. "Too bad you had to give up that old Caddy though. She's a beaut. She treated you all right?"

"Yeah, she ran like a charm," Jonathon said. "I just needed to trade for something a bit smaller, you know?"

What he needed was a car that Ryder and Callaghan wouldn't recognize. He only needed it for a couple of hours, long enough to get to the airport unmolested.

"What with this economy, I've had to cut back some bills," Jonathon explained.

"Yeah, recession's killing us all."

"Between the gas prices and the insurance…"

The dealer dropped the keys into Jonathon's hand. "Don't worry about it. I'm hearing the same thing from a lot of other businessmen, and they're not in as tight a position as you are right now." He handed over the handwritten receipt and temporary registration. "Don't forget these."

Jonathon laughed. "I remember."

"Get caught without those, and you'll be in a world of hurt," the dealer said. "And I wouldn't wish that on you – not now, not ever. But especially not now."

Jonathon nodded. "Boy, do I know it. Thanks again for the trade."

"My pleasure. Here's hoping business picks up for you again real soon."

"And yours too," Jonathon said. They shook on it and wished each other good luck.

"Say, you want a hand transferring stuff out of the trunk into the new car?"

"Naw. It's all good."

Besides, all he had in the back was a wardrobe bag and a small travel case.

He had one more stop to make before hitting the airport. Cory Carter had called his office first thing that morning, saying that he had a package waiting for delivery at the usual place. Jonathon would hit the Neighbour's Pub before driving to the terminal. And as far as Jennifer knew, Jonathon was headed south to check in on his parents in Corpus Christi.

Cory passed him an envelope under the table, as Jonathon had done a few days earlier. Taking Cory's example, Jonathon didn't immediately reach for the envelope or open it up. They chatted about sports, the local businesses and about mutual friends, until the waitress came by to ask for their orders. Cory ordered another beer. Jonathon asked for a plate of fries.

Once she was gone, and while Cory kept a weather eye open for undercover cops, Jonathon opened the envelope without lifting it above the height of his navel. He tilted the passport to the brassy light and read his new name: James Richard McConnell. It was the same name on the new driver's license. Jonathon exhaled. Never in a million years had he dreamed of playing a real-life James Bond, skulking out of the country and sneaking back in again without anyone noticing.

"And the other ten?" Cory asked.

"In an overseas account." Jonathon pointed to the envelope with the passport inside. Cory nodded his immediate understanding. "As soon as I'm back on home soil with the money in hand, I'll contact you."

They made small conversation while waiting for the waitress. Cory made some passing warnings about who to trust and what not to say. He had an uncanny knack for pointing out who was likely an off-duty cop, and which one was still on the clock. He explained what he saw to Jonathon, telling him what tells to look for, what body posture, what kind of walk, and he detailed what to look for if checking someone for a concealed weapon.

Jonathon took it all to heart, saying little and listening a lot, while splitting the plate of fries with his unlikely ally. *My accomplice*, he thought abruptly. "And what kind of a cop wears a wig and a fake beard?" he asked, not realizing at first that he'd spoken out loud.

Cory snorted a laugh. "A dumb one. Why, have you seen one around?"

"A pair of them," Jonathon said. "Once, a couple of years ago," he added, seeing Cory looking moodier and more tense than ever. "It was a prank."

Jonathon ate a few more fries, but he left before he lost his nerve.

Jonathon was listening to an Eddy Rabbit tape on the car stereo, and he was thinking about Jennifer, about his parents, about the snowy conditions, and about how well he'd sleep once he'd cashed out his accounts in Zurich. He hadn't been paying attention to his driving.

A police siren whooped behind him.

He checked the speedometer. He'd been driving about ninety kilometres an hour. The posted limit was one hundred. He frowned and slowed down, easing over toward the curb. The police car followed him, its lights whirling. *Tail lights,* he thought. *Temporary plate must have fallen off. Maybe it's the muffler.* They both parked. Jonathon turned off his engine. The last thing he needed to do was to make the officers suspicious.

Oh shit, he thought. *My ID.*

The cruiser was about a car length behind him, parked on the soft shoulder. The two officers in the patrol unit stayed in their vehicle, their heads bowed slightly together as if they were listening to their radio. Jonathon opened the glove box and took out his spare wallet, where he'd kept his authentic driver's license. He dumped his other wallet, the one with the false ID, under the driver's seat along with the new passport. For good measure, he took out the temporary registration papers and his proof of insurance from the glove box too, having them all prepared for the officer, who was now approaching on the driver's side. His partner crept up alongside the passenger's side of the car. Both cops kept their hands on their guns. Jonathon rolled down his window. "Good evening," he said.

"Hi," said the officer on Jonathon's left. "Can I see your license and registration please?"

Jonathon held them out the window. "Is there a problem? I know I wasn't speeding."

The officer took the papers and examined them with a flashlight. "All right. I'll have to ask you to step out of the car, please." He gave the papers back.

"Is it really necessary?" Jonathon asked.

"Out of the car," the officer said.

"If I was speeding, can't you just give me the ticket? I'm sorry, I'm running a little late, and I know you're just trying to do your jobs."

"Now."

"Please – I need to catch a plane."

"Step out of the car *now*, sir."

Jonathon pulled the door latch and let himself out. The officer took a step backward, hand firmly on the butt of his holstered side arm. His partner opened the front passenger's door and rummaged through the glove compartment.

"Is that really necessary?" Jonathon asked. He was especially glad he'd only had the fries, and had forgone his usual Scotch.

"Step back toward the rear of the vehicle please," the first officer said. "Stand behind the trunk and keep your hands visible."

Jonathon held his hands stiffly at his sides, and on rigid legs, he walked to the back of the car. Traffic passed them on the highway. There was no sight of Ryder and Callaghan, but he could feel their presence. When the second cop leaned across the gear shifter to check under the driver's seat, Jonathon felt his temperature and blood pressure rise. *Why else would I get pulled over, doing ninety in a hundred zone?* He clenched his jaw. *Damn it – how did they know what to look for? How'd they know which car to follow?* Then he thought of Cory and of the trouble *he'd* be in, if Ryder and Callaghan knew too much.

The second officer called his partner over, and they compared the ID that Jonathon had presented to the ID that had been found under the seat. The first came back looking confident and convinced of a decision he'd just made.

"It's my friend's ID," Jonathon said.

"Hell of a resemblance," the officer said. "Turn around."

"They say everybody's got a twin," Jonathon replied. *Damn it, damn it, no! Damn it!*

"Turn around and put your hands behind your back. I'm placing you under arrest for possession of a stolen vehicle."

Jonathon cursed under his breath and turned. "But it's my car."

The first officer took Jonathon's right wrist and put a cold metal cuff around it. "That's debatable, now isn't it?" He cuffed Jonathon's left wrist. "The car's registered to Jonathon Parker. Here we find you with one driver's license for Jonathon Parker, and one for James McConnell. Now either that means you're James McConnell and you've stolen Jonathon's car, or you're Jonathon Parker and you're carrying around false identification. So which one is it?"

The second officer assisted in escorting Jonathon to the back of their cruiser, tightening his grip on Jonathon's elbow whenever he tensed his muscles.

He was being arrested. He was going to go to jail, and Jennifer was going to find out. That was the last thing he wanted. He'd been so close to the easy solution. No one would have gotten hurt. He could have pulled the Corpus Christi deal out of the fire, his parents would be set up for life, and no one would have been the wiser.

But they'd stopped him. Ryder and Callaghan. They'd found out, and they'd set him up. They'd been lying in wait for him, lulling him into a false sense of security, and then, just a few kilometres from airport, they caught him doing ninety in a hundred zone. His blood boiled.

"For that matter," said the second officer, "for all we know, the registration's a fake."

"It's not. The receipt's in the car. Check for yourself. Go back to the dealership, ask for Eric, he'll vouch for me. It's my car."

The first officer said, "Then you'll be charged with possession of forged identification. Your choice. We're good either way." While his partner opened the cruiser's rear door, the officer pushed Jonathon's head down and sat him in the back seat.

Damn it. Shit! Damn it. Damn it!

CHAPTER FOURTEEN

REGINA. JANUARY, 1981.

Jonathon and Jennifer sat knee to knee. Jennifer was red in the face. Jonathon couldn't help but glance over his shoulder at the policeman guarding the interview room door. They had only five minutes.

"Please tell me," Jennifer said, "what on earth is going on."

"It's not as bad as you think."

"They told me you stole a car from the dealership and that you were using fake ID!" She kept her voice down, but she was desperate for answers.

"They're trying to charge me with stealing my own car," Jonathon said. "I don't know how, and I don't know why. But when we get a statement from the dealer, they won't have a leg to stand on."

"And the ID?"

"I wasn't using any fake ID. I mean, I did have some with me." He regretted it as soon as he'd said it. "I wasn't using any fake ID, Jennifer. You know me better than that."

"You had some *with* you?" Her voice was quieter but harsher than before.

"Listen, the ID is no big deal, and they can't charge me with anything. I wasn't trying to pass myself off as whoever was on the ID. For all they know, that ID was a…a…a film prop or something, and those aren't illegal unless you try to pass yourself off as somebody else in order to commit a fraud."

The tension eased from her shoulders, but she wasn't appeased by any stretch of the imagination. "Well…when can you get out of here? Aren't they supposed to release you on bail or something?"

"That's the thing," Jonathon said with a sigh. He rubbed his eyebrows. "This is Friday night."

"I know. We'd made plans."

"I can only get out after my lawyer sees a Justice of the Peace, which can't happen until Monday morning, because the JP's already gone for the weekend."

"Oh, you're *kidding* me," Jennifer snapped.

Jonathon nodded. "I think they delayed processing me for that very reason."

"What, so they could hold you here over the weekend?"

Jonathon didn't answer.

"Who's 'they'?" She asked. She held his hands. "Jonathon, what's this all about? Really."

"I wish I could tell you. Listen..."

"You wish you could tell me," she echoed out of the corner of her mouth.

"Listen," Jonathon insisted. "On Monday morning, I'll be home, right after we see the JP. My lawyer says that all the charges will be dismissed as soon as they're presented. Until then, this is nothing but a pain in the ass."

"A weekend-long pain in the ass. The kids were really looking for-ward..."

"I know."

She shook her head. "Jonathon, I don't understand any of this. Why are they charging you with anything? Why are they holding you here, if they know the charges aren't going to stick anyhow?"

The officer behind them cleared his throat and opened the door. "Let's go, Mr. Parker."

"But my five minutes aren't up yet," Jonathon said.

"Yes they are."

"We got in here at five to the hour. We've still got two more minutes."

"Not by my watch," the officer said.

"But..."

"I'm sorry, Parker, are you being uncooperative with an officer of the law?"

Jonathon stared at him. *They got to you too, did they?* He shook his head and got up to leave.

"Jonathon," Jennifer whispered.

"Monday," Jonathon said. "I'll be fine. Don't let the kids drive you crazy."

"And what am I going to tell them?" Jennifer asked.

The officer closed the door between them before Jonathon could answer.

Both dressed in decent, grey suits, Jonathon and his lawyer Dan Jenkins jogged down the crowded front steps of the Provincial Courthouse. "Thanks for all your help, Dan."

"Not a problem, Jon. Hell of a thing though, holding you over the weekend on trumped up charges of fraud and auto theft."

Jonathon hummed in disappointed agreement.

"You still think it's because of those two Mounties?"

"Positive," Jonathon said. "Beyond the shadow of a doubt."

"Then you'd better let me know the moment anything else happens. We're going to need a lot more concrete evidence if we're going to make any case against them. Get their names on tape, at least. Confirming their names and their intentions on a single tape recording?" Jenkins laughed bitterly. "That's nearly as good as a confession in a court of law."

"You bet, Dan." He chucked his thumb over his shoulder, indicating the court house behind them. "Because this is a waste of everybody's time."

They stopped on the snowy sidewalk, shook hands, wished each other a good morning and marched off in separate directions. Jonathon took a cab to the flower shop he'd bought for his wife; she had driven herself to work after dropping Michael off at the daycare.

The bell jingled over the door, and Jennifer looked up from the ribbon she was curling with an edge of a scissors blade. "Hey. Good morning. It went well?"

"Yeah, no problem at all." He closed the door behind him, shutting out the bitter cold and sealing himself in with the cloying scent of flowers. "Dan's a great lawyer."

"Your parents are back from Texas."

Jonathon said, "Oh."

"They keep calling, wanting to talk to you, and telling me how upset they are at losing everything."

Jonathon groaned. "Did you tell them where I was over the weekend?"

"No."

Jonathon stepped behind the counter and they hugged. "I love you."

"I love you too," she said. "But I wish you would tell me what's really going on."

"I wish I could," Jonathon said. "If I could understand it or believe it, honey, you know I'd tell you everything. But for right now…" He sighed. "For right now, I've gotta call my parents."

"Jonathon." She handed him a freshly trimmed long stem rose. "Don't call them. I think they'd rather hear it from you face to face."

"They're at home now?"

She nodded. They kissed, she gave him the car keys from her purse, and he left with the rose in hand.

Jonathon told his parents – and his grandfather – as many of the details as he could. After all, most of it had been in the papers already; he told them little more than they'd already read or heard about on the news. He told them about the unfounded charges of money laundering and cheque fraud, about the theft of all his money out of his accounts, about being pulled over doing ninety in a hundred zone and being thrown in jail over the weekend for something he didn't do.

If Edward heard one word of it, he made no sign.

"Dad, I can't blame you for being angry," Jonathon said. "That's a lot of money, and I realize that." Edward averted his gaze; he stared out the living room window. "But it's not like I'm doing this on purpose! Dad, I'm your son. You know I wouldn't get involved in criminal activities. Up to now, have you ever known me to…to…to do so much as throw trash on the ground, or cross against the lights?" Edward didn't answer. "You're right for being upset. But don't be angry at me, please! I'm doing everything I can to fix this."

Edward suddenly got up from the couch and went into the kitchen. After a moment of anguished silence, torn between husband and son, Norma got up and joined her husband in the kitchen.

Jake, Jonathon's grandfather, sat in his favourite La-Z-Boy, picking his teeth. Jonathon sat on the couch nearest his grandfather's chair. "You're how old now?" Jake asked.

"Twenty-five. Why?"

Jake shifted positions and coughed into his fist. "I envy you, in a way."

Jonathon laughed.

"Most people go their whole lives without flying around to places like New York, and Vegas, and Beverly Hills and all that. Most people, they never make more than a couple of hundred grand in their whole lives, and here you are, you've made what, half a million every year the last three years?"

Jonathon smirked.

"You b'n married. Divorced. Married again. Three kids, a couple of houses, an office building, a flower shop – hell, I lost count. You've been all the way up, and now you're all the way down. Lots of people been all the way up and all the way down, and not many of them are still so young that they can recover, like you. When you're young, you invest big, take greater risks, 'cause you know, you have time to recover from your losses."

Jonathon nodded slowly.

"And Jonny." Jake sat forward, his fingers steepled between his knees. "You're only twenty-five." Jonathon laughed. "So get over yourself. You're only twenty-five, and you've already got more experience behind you than most men have at fifty. That's a hell of an advantage. And imagine how much more you'll have by the time you get to your father's age. Or mine." Jake sat back again. "Yeah, you've had your ass kicked and you're not as rich as you were a little while ago, but maybe you just got too damned big for your own britches. Ever think of that?" He dug his cigarettes out of his pocket. "You're young. You got your health. Get over it."

Jonathon smiled and said, "Or you could have said, 'Stop crying over spilled milk.'"

Jake puffed his cigarette to light and blew out the match. "Yeah."

"But thanks. I needed that."

"I never turned down an opportunity to kick you in the ass. It was a pleasure."

Norma was standing in the living room doorway, almost smiling. Edward was behind her. Jonathon faced them and said, "I know this is going to sound stupid, but…You have to trust me, just a little while longer. I will fix this." He looked around the hallway, the living room and the kitchen, and he commented, "Just glad we never mortgaged this place."

CHAPTER FIFTEEN

REGINA. FALL, 1981.

Jonathon and the dealer exchanged keys; Jonathon gave away the keys to the Cadillac, and in exchange, he took the keys for a used Pontiac. The dealer wrapped his hands around the Pontiac keys, before Jonathon could pocket them. This time, the exchange was driven by economics, more than secrecy.

"If I could give you one piece of advice?" the dealer asked.

"Sure…"

The dealer's smile was more wince than humour. "Don't drive the damned thing around until you get the permanent registration papers in the mail?"

Jonathon grinned and took the keys away.

Jonathon finished his last call for the day and sat back, staring out the window. Any place was better than his office. The only expensive thing left in the place was the name plate on the door. Antonino's Enterprises had sold off most of the business machines, laid off Laura and sold her desk the next day. He'd left his desk nearest the window, leaving nothing but a gulf of faded carpet and one potted plant between him and the door.

He decided he wouldn't wait any longer. He had no other appointments, no other deals lined up, and since it was Friday, Jennifer had let her staff run the store while she stayed home with Michael. There was no good reason why he should stay at the office and not be with his wife and son for a pleasant Friday afternoon. He gave a passing thought to some of his business friends up and down the block; often they'd get together at one shop or the other to have a couple of beers before closing up for the weekend, but none of them would be ready to close up their stores so soon, and he didn't want to sit around waiting for them to finish. He just wanted to be home, with his tie undone and his shoes off.

As he went driving up his street, he saw a small flotilla of cars and vans, not far from his house. *Block party*, he thought at first. It was a little late in the season for one more backyard barbeque, but, he decided, maybe it was a shower for the daughter of one his neighbours, or maybe a family reunion.

As he approached, he wondered, *Do we know this many people? Did Jennifer invite them all over?* Then he noticed all the people standing about in their coats and boots, watching some strange activity, the way people all seemed to flock to a burning house while wearing their pyjamas and slippers. *Oh God – don't tell me my house is on fire!* There were police cars, but no fire trucks.

His driveway was crowded with people, vehicles, boxes and equipment. Through his closed car windows, he heard sounds of construction. Then he saw Jennifer standing outside the house, with Michael in her arms. She was shouting at someone.

There was a bang on the hood of his car, and Jonathon jolted in his seat. It was a police officer. He rolled down the window. "Are you blind?" the officer asked. He looked like he'd been signalling for Jonathon to pull over to the side of the road instead of parking on his driveway.

Jonathon got out of the car and brushed past the officer. There was a man on his front lawn, and he was breaking up the concrete of his patio with a jackhammer. "What the *hell* is going on?"

A man in a dark suit approached him. He wore a clip-on badge. Jonathon didn't recognize the emblem any more than he recognized the name. "Are you Jonathon Parker?"

"Yes – who are you? What are all these people doing here? What's going on?"

A pair of officers walked out of his house with bankers boxes. They wore gloves.

"What the hell is going on here?" Jonathon asked.

The dark suited official held up a piece of paper, which also bore an official-looking seal on official-looking letterhead. With a level voice, the man said, "Mr. Parker, this is a search warrant, authorizing us to search the premises for gold, jewellery, precious gems and other valuable items that we suspect have been brought into this country by clandestine and illegal means."

Jonathon's mouth hung open. "Clandest…are you accusing me of *smuggling*? Who are you people?"

"Canada Customs. We've been notified that you've been travelling frequently back and forth to the United States, and that you've brought back undeclared goods to be sold on the black market."

Jonathon said, "I've been to the States. That's no secret."

"And the gold and other items?"

"Gifts," Jonathon said. "For my wife! And I declared them each and every time! I haven't done anything illegal."

To his monotone voice, the official added a bland smile. "We've already found a number of items inside, Mr. Parker. That's why we've extended our search to the exterior of the property." He pointed at the man with the jackhammer.

Jennifer was watching him. As soon as Jonathon made eye contact with her, she voiced her disgust, rolled her eyes and returned indoors. Jonathon followed her. The flat-toned official followed Jonathon inside.

The ruined patio was less of a mess than the kitchen was. Floor boards had been torn up. Cupboard doors had been opened and pulled off hinges. Dishes, clean and dirty, were scattered everywhere, on the counters, on the floor, in the sink, on the stove. The refrigerator had been disconnected and pulled away from the wall. Food was thawing on the kitchen table, soaking the opened mail and eviscerated toy animals from the kids' rooms. There was dust, dry wall, potting soil and peeled paint all over the floor. The hall carpet was gritty with muddy boot prints and all the detritus tracked out from the kitchen.

"Who's going to clean all this?" Jonathon asked.

They'd placed in the middle of the hallway floor all manner of home electronic devices to be boxed and carted away: a portable radio, a hair dryer, their TV sets, a blender, their toaster and their microwave oven.

Jennifer cried blue murder when someone took a monogramed box out of the bedroom. It was an heirloom from her great-grandmother.

"It's your mess," the official said. "We're not going to add your clean-up to the taxpayers bill. We're here to protect the interest of innocent citizens, Mr. Parker, not to impoverish them."

"And where are you taking all this stuff?"

The official looked at him as if Jonathon had suddenly spoken in Chinese. "We're confiscating it. Until you can prove you purchased this legally and declared it at the border, we consider it smuggled goods." At Jonathon's swelling bluster, the official said calmly, "This is all of foreign manufacture, Mr. Parker. How else do you expect us to protect the interest of honest, domestic manufacturers? I assure you, everything we're doing here is well within the parameters of the search warrant – if you'd like to read it again, here it is – and we apologize for the inconvenience. But if you impede this investigation any further, it'll only waste time, and I'll have to assume you have something to hide."

Jennifer cursed and took Michael into the bedroom. They were both crying.

"Get it over with," Jonathon said. He chased after Jennifer, calling her name. "I swear to God, Jennifer, I don't know *what*'s going on here."

"Well, you'd better damned well find out. Whatever it is you're up to, remember, this affects your family too. It affects our *children*."

"You think I don't know that?" Jonathon asked.

Michael was crying too loudly for sensible conversation. They took turns carrying him and calming him down. When the officials started hammering on the walls, Michael screamed and wailed against the side of his father's neck. Michael reached for his mother, leaving Jonathon's shirt cold from sweat, tears and drool.

"Jennifer, you have to believe me," Jonathon said. "I kept the receipts."

"I don't have a receipt for that necklace," she said. "If I never get that back, I swear to God, Jonathon, I'll..." She sniffed and ran her hand under her nose. "I don't know what I'll do."

He reached for her shoulders. The phone rang.

"Answer it," she said.

Jonathon caught it on the second ring. He kept his hand over the mouthpiece. He listened for any indication that someone was listening in on an extension. "Hello?"

"Your house is a disaster area."

It was Ryder.

"If you need some help with the clean-up, meet us in the parking lot near the shopping centre, where we met up last. You remember it?"

"I know the place," Jonathon said.

"Good. Ten minutes. Get here."

The line went dead.

Jennifer was patting Michael on the back. "Who was it?" she asked.

"I swear, I'll explain everything as soon as I get back."

"What? Where are you going? Jonathon, you can't leave now, not with all this happening!"

"It's somebody who can *stop* this from happening," Jonathon insisted. She followed him out of the bedroom, down the hall, past the banker's boxes and confiscated electronics. "Do you remember the day I came into the Neighbour's Pub, and I looked like I'd fallen into a gravel pit?"

"I can't forget it."

"And you remember the time I told you I fell down the stairs at work?"

"Oh God, Jonathon – you mean..."

He held up both hands and reassured her. "It's not what you think. But these guys, I..." She sighed. "I have to meet up with them, or we'll never see the end of this."

He'd pointed out the open door toward the broken concrete of his front patio. His voice failed him when he realized what else he was pointing at. His Pontiac looked like the punch line of a sight-gag. The tires were off and placed on both sides of the chassis; the doors were off, the hood was up, the trunk was open, and there was someone lying on the driveway, shining a light under the propped-up car. Jennifer swore under her breath.

"These guys that you're going to meet," she whispered in his ear. "Are they the mob?"

He recoiled from her. "What? No!" He shook his head and said again, "No, they're not the mob." He frowned and said, helplessly, "They're cops."

Twenty-five minutes later, the taxi dropped him off at the shopping centre. He walked around the outside to the main parking lot, which was crowded with parked cars, piled snow, and drivers impatient to find an empty spot close to the doors. At the back of the lot, Ryder and Callaghan were leaning backwards against their car, arms crossed, trying too hard to look like Starsky and Hutch.

"You're late," said Ryder.

"I had to take a cab," Jonathon answered. He thumbed the buttons on the mini-cassette recorder in his coat pocket. Once it was powered on and had started recording, Jonathon held it upright in his pocket, careful to keep the microphone end clear of obstructions. He would get these two by the short hairs. He'd hang them in a rope of their own making.

"Something wrong with his car?" Callaghan asked Ryder.

"Maybe he had a flat," Ryder commented. "Come on, Jon-boy. We'll give you a ride. Our car's still warm."

Callaghan had moved his left arm slightly. Under Callaghan's right elbow, Jonathon could see the distinct, grey muzzle of his gun, but the rest of the firearm was hidden from the sight of passersby. Ryder opened the back door, and as before, Callaghan rode beside Jonathon. The door handles had been removed again.

No one spoke until they reached city limits. "This place we're going," Jonathon asked. "Is it a full service junk yard?" They didn't answer. "Because after today, I'm probably going to need some spare parts for the car. Thought I could call ahead next time and see if they have what I need."

"It's private property," Ryder answered.

Jonathon made a special note of the roads they passed through, calling out landmarks as they went. When Callaghan told him to shut up, Jonathon said, "Can you at least tell me what kind of 'help' you're offering?"

"Patience," Callaghan said.

"I'm in an unmarked car driving what, 130 km an hour, you both have guns on me – what am I going to do, make a run for it? How can I, if you've taken the door handles off? So tell me! I'm a captive audience."

"All in good time, Parker." Callaghan laughed and added, "You've got to learn to relax."

They didn't say anything else until Ryder pulled through the open gates and past a few of the brittle, jagged snow moguls of the junk yard. Ryder parked the car, and he turned in the seat so he could point his gun as well. They waited for Jonathon to talk.

"Customs?" Jonathon asked. "Really?"

Callaghan smiled, showing off his one brown tooth. "You should have seen the look on your wife's face when they knocked on her door."

Jonathon cracked a knuckle. "And my parents losing all their money?"

Callaghan shrugged. "An unfortunate by-product of you pissing us off."

"Really sad," Ryder added. "And completely unforeseen." He wasn't convincing.

"But it could have been prevented, you know," Callaghan said. "Really, when you get down to it, you're the one who's in control here. You tell us when to stop."

"Okay," Jonathon said, "stop!"

"Oh, but you gotta say it the right way," Callaghan said.

"Please," Jonathon answered.

"Look, asshole," Ryder said, "let's cut the comedy act. All you have to do is cooperate with us."

"And do what?" Jonathon sighed. They didn't answer. "Look, if it's about that witness statement you want me to sign – the one implicating Fred Anton in the death of Reg Lawrence – I've told you before, I can't sign it!"

"It's easy," Ryder said. "You pick up the pen, you spell out your name. We'll even fill in the date for you."

"I can't swear to something that didn't happen," Jonathon said. "They'd tear me apart under cross-examination! Besides, you don't need me. You guys are the detectives – you find some proof that Anton did it. Find a real, actual witness – that's what NCIS is supposed to be good at!"

Callaghan suddenly sat forward. The hammer of his gun was already cocked, and the safety was off. "Listen, asshole. You think today was fun? We're just getting warmed up."

"I'm not signing that statement."

"You've got a hard head," Ryder said. He smiled. "Allow us to tenderize it for you."

Callaghan reached across and punched Jonathon once in the temple and once in the eye. Punches came from left and right, and with so little space to manoeuvre, Jonathon could only throw up his hands in a weak defence. The door opened, and he fell out. As soon as his shoulders were on the ground, Ryder kicked him in the head, in the ribs and in the groin. Jonathon tried to roll under the car for protection, but someone grabbed him by the ankle and pulled him across the snow. A blow sharper than the rest blinded and deafened him. He didn't hurt so much, then.

His body was moving. Jonathon rolled over to protect his abdomen, and vertigo sent his brain and eyes spiralling out of control. He gripped the sides of his head to keep it from exploding.

"...glass *jaw*," Ryder was saying. They both laughed. Callaghan made a comment Jonathon didn't understand, and the two of them laughed like sniggering bullies in an empty locker room.

"Don't you think," Jonathon groaned, "that the more you hit me in the head..." He breathed, and his sides seized. "...The less likely...I'll be able to hold a pen...?" He rolled onto his hands and knees, soaking his jeans in the melting snow, and when he could trust himself to do it, he sat back on his heels.

"Hey, look at that. Nancy boy's awake." Ryder squatted in front of him. "Jonny, you're awful dull. And sometimes, when we deal with dull people, we have to explain things in small and basic terms. So, allow us to introduce the carrot and the stick."

Jonathon's right eye had swollen shut, and it was bleeding.

"You help us," Callaghan began. He was standing somewhere behind Jonathon. "And we relocate you and your family to some place nice. Witness protection program, we'll say. To help you settle into your new lives, we offer you two hundred and fifty thousand dollars." Reluctantly, he added, "And maybe we'll add in the value of your house and properties."

Ryder held Jonathon's chin. "Means you won't fall apart under cross-examination," he said. "Because you won't have to attend trial."

"...Without evidence, you won't have anything but witness testimony," Jonathon whispered.

"You let us worry about that," Ryder said. "We're pretty damned good at playing the court."

"You take me all the way out here," Jonathon murmured. "You don't tell me your names. You don't tell me where you come from, or why you're after Fred Anton. You don't tell me anything. When they drag me into court to testify, what am I going to say? Huh? 'Oh no, Your Honour, I don't have to testify, because these two guys in Halloween costumes told me I didn't have to.' How am I supposed to believe any of your promises, if I don't even know who the hell you are?"

"And we thought he was a smart guy," Callaghan said to Ryder. "You already claim we're cops."

"From NCIS no less," Ryder said. "Now how would you come by that information, unless you talked to Freddie about us? Huh?"

"Does that make you Ryder?" Jonathon asked the man before him. "And he's Callaghan?"

"Does it matter if we are?" Ryder grunted.

"I just need to know who to call," Jonathon said, "when I'm ready to sign that statement."

Callaghan's boots thumped on the trampled ground. He hit Jonathon on the back of the head with the butt of his gun – not enough to knock him out, but more than enough to leave a goose egg. "Did you enjoy your weekend in lock-up, asshole?"

"We've got your calendar filled up but good, dickhead," Ryder said. "We can arrange it with the municipal cops. Every Friday night, like clockwork. Every Monday morning at the courthouse. They'll print your name in every Saturday newspaper."

"And eventually, people are going to be calling out for justice, stronger punishments – lock him away, they'll say. He's nothing but a crook, they'll say. No one will want to do business with you, no one will want to be seen with you, your wife..."

"You leave my family the hell *out* of this," Jonathon said.

"And then," Ryder said, "we'll give the people what they want. A nice, solid charge. And they'll lock you up for *years*."

"At least five," Callaghan added.

"Only five?" Ryder asked.

"I'm feeling generous. Besides, five's a good start. As soon as he's out..."

"Just leave me alone," Jonathon sighed.

Ryder nodded at Callaghan and said, "You're right. Once they've gone through the system, most crooks end up right back in jail again. Some people are just too stubborn to respond positively to correction." He threw Jonathon's chin aside.

"Are you getting the picture, Jonathon?" Callaghan asked. "You give us what we need, you cooperate like a nice, prosperous, law-abiding citizen, and we move you some place nice, like Australia, for a nice second chance at life."

"But if you don't," Ryder began.

"Don't cooperate," Callaghan said, "and we see how many ways we can make your life miserable. We'll lock you up, time and time again. We'll take *everything* from you. All your friends, everything you own, all your business, and everything you love. And then we throw *you* away." Callaghan shifted his feet in the snow. "So what do you say?"

"Callaghan?" Jonathon asked.

"What?"

"I say you can take your proposition and shove it up your Mountie ass."

Callaghan hit first. He liked to pistol whip. Ryder liked to kick.

Either it was too cold, or they were tired, or they could only punch and kick as long as Jonathon grunted and screamed in pain; when Jonathon bit his tongue, lay in the fetal position and stopped moving, they gave up and left him in the snow. He waited until he couldn't hear the car anymore. He struggled to sit up. Something was squeaking, like a hamster wheel. He put his hand in his pocket and pulled out the mini-cassette recorder. The tape approached the end, and the machine clicked off. Jonathon smiled, though he had a fat lip.

"Hell of a way to do an interrogation," Jonathon mused. He rewound the tape, clicked stop, then clicked play.

"...*everything you love. And then we throw you away.*" "*Callaghan?*" "*What?*"

Jonathon clicked stop, then pressed rewind. It continued to rewind as Jonathon got to his feet and stumbled toward the front gates of the junkyard. His face didn't hurt so much when he smiled.

He had the bastards by the balls, now.

CHAPTER SIXTEEN

REGINA. FALL, 1981.

Ryder and Callaghan had been mostly right about one thing: it was getting harder and harder to find someone willing to do business with him. The bills were starting to pile up, and Jonathon needed a boost to his income. He'd already cancelled Christmas. Unfortunately, he couldn't cancel his mortgage and other loan repayments, not without grave consequences; on top of that, if he continued paying his two extortionists, the twenty grand he had left in the safe would be gone before the new year. There wasn't an hour in the day he didn't curse the names of Ryder and Callaghan.

He found Cory in his favourite booth at the back of Neighbour's Pub.

"You look like shit," Cory said. "How does the other guy look?"

"Guys," Jonathon said. "Plural. There were two of them." He slid into the booth and sat down. "Seriously, I still look like shit?"

"If shit was yellow, green and purple, yeah." Cory pointed to Jonathon's face. "Good thing they took your picture *before* that happened."

"What picture?"

"You didn't see it? You're all over the news."

"Again?"

"Again. Made the evening news this time. Rousted by Customs, huh?"

Jonathon picked at a scab. "God, what a mess."

"Looked like your house got hit by a tornado," Cory scoffed. He was looking around the pub. "They said you're hooked up with some big-time players now."

"Really."

"Organized crime all that. They say you're either a smuggler or a fence. Jewelry, electronics, small appliances, that kind of shit."

163

"They say I'm involved with criminals, eh?"

"That's what they say."

Jonathon eyed him. "Then what the hell am I doing here, sitting with you?"

Cory paled. He squinted at him.

The waitress came to take their orders. Jonathon ordered a double-Scotch, and when he sensed eyes looking him over from afar, he turned and regarded two clean-shaven men at the bar. Jonathon cocked his head sideways, and Cory looked. Cory nodded, looking grave and glum.

"And get a round for those two guys at the end of the bar," Jonathon said. "Put it on my bill."

"Friends of yours?" the waitress asked, smiling.

"Friends of a couple of friends of mine," Jonathon said. She promised she'd add their next drinks to his bill.

Cory looked suddenly constipated.

"I'm getting better at this game," Jonathon said.

"Did you uh…use what I gave you a couple of weeks ago?" Cory asked.

Jonathon frowned. "Why do you ask?"

"Did it work?"

Jonathon leaned forward, folding his hands together. "You know, funny thing about that. Not twenty minutes after I left with that *package* you gave me, I was pulled over and it was confiscated."

Cory was pale. "Shit. You didn't tell them I gave it to you, did you?"

"Only one of us spent the weekend in jail," Jonathon said. "You tell *me* if I said anything."

"Kee-roist." Cory drank better than half of what was left in his beer glass. "Don't look at me, man. I didn't alert anybody. That'd be a death sentence. You think I'd admit to forgery or whatever?"

Jonathon shook his head. "Forget it."

For a while, they sat in silence; both kept their eyes on the crowd and on the exits. "I heard you're something of an investor, yourself," Jonathon said.

"That depends on your definition of investing."

"Burton says that you can take twenty dollars and turn it into fifty in two days."

Cory finished his beer. "I try to keep it pretty low key."

Jonathon lowered his voice and faced the wall, so the guys at the bar couldn't read his lips. "What could you do with a thousand dollars?"

"Party," Cory answered with a half-hearted laugh. "Why?"

"Can you invest it? Double it, maybe, inside a week?"

"Hypothetically," Cory remarked. "I've been known to triple the initial investment, if the timing is right. But inside a week? No."

"Could you – hypothetically – double an investment of twenty?"

"Bucks?"

"Grand."

Cory lifted his glass, then remembered it was empty. "One of my biggest competitors got busted this week."

"Hooray for the good guys," Jonathon muttered.

"You have it with you?"

Jonathon put his hand inside his coat. Cory kicked him in the shin.

"Jesus, I don't think you were serious," Cory whispered.

"Can you do it?"

"I don't know if I can."

The waitress returned with their drinks. She set the Scotch before Jonathon and a fresh glass of beer in front of Cory. Jonathon raised his glass and turned toward the bar. The two obvious undercover cops were watching their table. Jonathon raised his glass higher, as if toasting their good health. The two cops turned quickly and minded their own business. Jonathon slid his hand into his coat pocket and pulled out a fat envelope. Cory reached across the table and snatched it from his fingers, making it disappear as quickly as Jonathon had made it appear.

"Do whatever you have to," Jonathon said out of the corner of his mouth.

"When?"

"I want forty back two weeks from next Wednesday. I won't ask any questions."

"What's my cut?"

"I only want forty back," Jonathon said. "I won't ask how much you actually make on the initial investment."

Cory sipped his beer.

Jonathon sighed. "Give it back, then, and we'll forget this conversation ever happened."

"You'll get your money back," Cory said, clacking his glass against the one Jonathon held. "Two weeks from Wednesday."

Jonathon finished his drink and smiled once more at the cops who had turned to watch them. He waved at them, paid his bill, and left.

———

Having no functional car, Jonathon had called a taxi to take him back to the office after a meeting with his lawyer, Dan Jenkins. The reticent driver was content to let the a.m. news do all the talking. Jonathon leaned forward and tapped the driver, asking him to turn up the volume.

"An Edmonton businessman, Mr. Fred Anton, president of Antonino's Enterprises, says he intends to pursue his lawsuit against the Saskatchewan Government Insurance Corporation, owners of the Heritage building in downtown Regina, for failing to honour their contract to sell the building, and over allegations linking his company to people suspected of having criminal backgrounds. RCMP confirm that Mr. Anton does not have a criminal record, but refused to comment further."

The driver glanced in the rear view mirror. Jonathon sat back, his collar up and his chin down. Exhausted and irritable, Jonathon watched the blocks go by. The driver turned down the volume.

"This is the place?" the driver asked, after the news was done. "You sure?"

Jonathon lifted his gaze. "Aw hell." Reporters and news cameramen were waiting for him. Behind them, Jonathon saw Jennifer watching through the picture window. She looked distressed. She looked trapped. Jonathon paid the driver and apologized under his breath for all the unwanted attention. The driver didn't reply. As soon as Jonathon had the rear passenger's door open, the news crews converged on him, making it difficult to exit the cab. He excused himself several times, but they were persistent and barely moved.

A man tilted a microphone toward his own mouth, saying, "Following the accusation of Mafia influences in the Legislature, we've come to find Jonathon Parker, known associate of suspected mob boss, Fred Anton. Mr. Parker! Did you know about Fred Anton's links to organized crime before you went into business with him?" He tilted the microphone toward Jonathon.

"No comment," Jonathon said.

Another journalist spoke into a mini-cassette recorder, asking, "How has your association with the Mafia affected your – "

"No comment," Jonathon answered. He excused himself again; a cameraman stood squinting behind his burden, aiming the great abyss of a lens at Jonathon's face. Jonathon stuck out his arm and grabbed the door handle of the flower shop, and in opening the door, he pushed the cameraman aside, out of his way. Once he was inside, he turned only long enough to bow his head and lock the door. He turned the sign to 'Closed' and drew the curtain.

Jennifer was at the back of the store, hugging herself.

"Jennifer, please. I don't know what to say – but I swear, I will fix this."

"How can you fix it?" She pointed at the front door. "You did it. You and your buddy Fred have been all over the TV and radio news and – and..." She clapped her hand to her forehead. "And there's a picture in the newspaper with picture of our house, with the address and everything. The place is so crowded I can hardly get to my own front door. Jonathon, I'm scared for the *kids*."

Jonathon closed in on her, holding her elbows. "Shush. It's going to be okay."

"How?" she pleaded.

"I have evidence," Jonathon told her. "I've got lots of evidence against these guys. All we have to do is ride this out a little longer, and we'll have the last laugh, believe me." He hugged her, and she slid her arms around his waist. "Dan's very confident we'll come out on top."

Sheltered behind stands and buckets of flowers, they stood out of sight of the prying eyes of the press, and they swayed in an embrace. She pressed her cheek against his shoulder.

"My friends came over and helped to get most of the house cleaned up and repaired. We still have some work to do, but at least it's livable."

"Thank God," he breathed.

"The backyard, that's a different story. It's still a disaster zone."

He smoothed her hair back from her face.

Jennifer said, "I can't believe that Customs are immune from paying for any of the damage they did. It just makes no sense to me. It's not *fair*. They made the mess. They didn't find anything. The least they owe is an apology."

"I know," Jonathon whispered.

"Oh," she added, "and a tow truck came over from my brother's service station. They towed your car and put it all back together again."

He squeezed her. "I love you."

"You'd better," she answered.

He chuckled. "I have to get upstairs. Lots to do. I need to start writing out a statement, start putting all this evidence together."

"Good."

"Hey, what do you say? It's Friday, we get a babysitter, and we go out to dinner and celebrate."

"Celebrate *what*?" she asked with an incredulous laugh.

"The beginning of the end of all this chaos."

She nodded. "I'll drink to that. But what about your friends?"

"Which ones?"

"The usual crowd," she said. "Richard and the guys?"

Richard was one of the shop owners with whom Jonathon often had drinks on Friday afternoon. Jonathon shrugged off the idea. "Not this weekend. Just you and me. I'll call Richard and tell him I won't be coming this week. I'll tell him I have a hot date."

They kissed, and Jonathon swore he heard the click of a camera pressed up against the glass outside. He left by the back door and went upstairs by the exterior stairs. He entered, closed the door behind him, and went directly to the windows. The press circled the pavement like piranhas, talking and gesturing while looping microphone wires. Before anyone looked up, he released the tension on the cord, dropping the blinds. He turned at the sound of his office door closing.

There, standing just inside Jonathon's office was a young punk, complete with wide dog collar, a hooded sweater under his jacket, gelled spikes in his hair, and a tattoo on his neck. He jammed his hands deep in the pockets of his leather jacket. The punk kept his baggy eyes on the carpet between them, though he looked up before he spoke, and quickly shifted his gaze again, as if he was shy.

"Can I help you?" Jonathon asked.

"I want to join, man." The punk barely moved his lips.

Jonathon gave his head a shake. "What?"

The kid pulled his hand out of his jacket pocket. He stuck out his fist. It was full of crumpled money. He nodded once, and he angled his head, squinting. "I said, I want to join."

"Join what?" Jonathon asked.

"The Mafia, man. I've been trying to get hooked up for years." He shrugged. "I've got lots of – "

Jonathon jabbed his forefinger in the direction of the door and shouted, "Get the *hell* out of here." When the punk sneered and laughed, Jonathon rushed at him, hands open to grab the kid by the lapels of his torn jacket. The punk's eyes flashed open, and he turned for the door. Jonathon had his foot raised to propel the punk faster, but the kid was quick, and he slid through the door faster than Jonathon could catch him. Jonathon followed him out into the hall and down the stairs. The punk leaped down the last six stairs, landing in a crouch at the bottom; he sprang up and hit the door, more falling out into the street than running out. Jonathon marched down the rest of the way and locked the bottom door. Whether anyone from the press had noticed or not, Jonathon didn't know. But he'd find out, he was sure, on the six o'clock news.

He wouldn't get a chance to watch the six o'clock news.

The babysitter had arrived and settled in. Jonathon and Jennifer left by the front door, well-dressed for a night on the town. Jennifer had just asked some unimportant question, when Jonathon reached for the driver's side door handle. Headlights shone from behind the Pontiac. His stomach fell. Car doors opened.

"Don't say anything," Jonathon said to Jennifer, as two police officers approached from the end of the driveway. They had their hands on their holstered weapons.

"Jonathon Parker?" asked the senior partner. He held a piece of paper in his left hand, and he presented this to Jonathon.

"Yes, what do you want?"

"This is a warrant for your arrest," the officer said, "charging you with fifty-two counts of cheque fraud and three counts of wire fraud."

Jennifer and Jonathon exchanged glances, neither betraying more than frustration.

"Turn around," said the officer, "and place your hands behind your back. Ma'am, you're welcome to go back in the house. Now."

Jennifer's eyes narrowed at Jonathon. Words failed him. He turned, his hands behind his back. "The beginning of the end of what-now?" Jennifer asked.

It was Friday night.

Ryder and Callaghan.

Jonathon was in a cell with a number of detainees, most of them drunk, some of them miserable, all of them bored. Jonathon stood in the corner, because he needed to pace and didn't have enough room for it. He leaned against the cell wall.

An officer came, jangling his keys and rousing everyone in the holding cell. "Parker," he said. "Jonathon Parker, step forward." Jonathon pushed off from the wall and waited for the door to open. The officer closed it behind him, promptly, to prevent a rush on the door. "You've got a visitor," the officer said. A second officer put Jonathon in cuffs, and he was escorted between the two of them to a private cell, where Jennifer was waiting. They locked them in together, and they kept Jonathon in cuffs.

"Jonathon, this is ridiculous," Jennifer said. She spared a glance at the officers who stood by, watching them. "You're all over the news.

They're saying you're involved in some type of organized crime, and now here you are, in jail – again!"

"I know," Jonathon said.

"What's with all these fraud charges, anyway?"

Jonathon sat and leaned forward, beckoning Jennifer closer. She sat, bent forward, as he did. "You remember I told you about these cops I had to see?"

"Yes. They were supposed to help you out of this mess."

Jonathon shook his head. "No, they're the ones who got me into this mess. You remember when my parent's land deal in Texas went south – so to speak?"

"Kinda hard to forget, Jonathon."

"It's because those two officers stole money from my bank account." He'd said it so softly, he wasn't sure Jennifer heard him correctly. "RCMP officers. I've got their names on tape and everything."

She was shaking her head. "Wait – you're trying to tell me that a couple of RCMP officers...stole money...from your bank account."

"I know it's hard to understand. I don't get it either, but I know it, and I have everything but a word-for-word confession on tape."

"Wha...what are they doing? Why?"

"They're trying to strong arm me into signing something," he said. "A witness statement."

"Against who – against Fred?"

"Yes," he answered.

She sat back, stunned by the news.

"It's the truth, Jennifer, I swear to God."

She rubbed her forehead. "I don't know what to believe."

"We have evidence," Jonathon said again. "It's just not quite enough, not yet, but it's a start."

"Who's 'we'? You and Fred?"

"No, Dan and I. My lawyer."

"So...the trumped up charges, the theft, the Customs thing – that's all because of these two guys?" Jennifer asked. "All because they want you to sign a false confession?"

"A falsified witness statement," Jonathon said, "accusing Fred Anton of murder."

She laughed helplessly. "And all along, I thought the soaps were interesting. Who knew I was living in one? Do you have an evil twin, too? Any enemies who've come back from the dead after facial reconstructive surgery?" She shook her head. "Are you sure they're really police?"

"Positive. Fred dealt with them in the past, too."

"And they know you're on to them?"

"Maybe. But to them, it doesn't matter if I know or not. To them, it's all part of the game, because they think I can't get back at them, that they're protected by their badges. And that's why I'm here again. But they can't charge me with cheque fraud – they don't have a leg to stand on. This is an even flimsier charge than the false identification thing. But, unfortunately, they waited until Friday night to charge me."

"And you're not going to be able to get out until you see a Justice of the Peace," Jennifer said, as if reciting by rote, "and you can't do that until Monday morning. God, it's a good thing we already had a baby-sitter for the night…"

"It's just going to be another expensive pain in the ass," Jonathon said, "but I'll be out by Monday morning."

The cell door opened. "Wrap it up," an officer said.

"I swear, this station has a funny way of telling time," Jonathon mused. "Monday morning, I see the Justice of the Peace. Right after that, I'll be at home."

She stood up, and so did he.

"I love you, Jennifer," he said. They gave each other a quick peck on the lips, and she forced a smile. "Give my love to the kids."

"I will."

Dan Jenkins left with Jonathon, talking about coffee and breakfast. Jonathon couldn't think that far ahead. After spending another weekend with the most gaseous, unwashed and perverted dregs of society, the only thing Jonathon craved was a scalding shower and an incinerator for his clothes.

Before they went their separate ways, they stopped on the sidewalk to regard each other and offer their goodbyes. "Thanks again for all your help, Dan," Jonathon said. "I really appreciate it."

"You're welcome," Jenkins answered. He cocked his head and shrugged his shoulders comically. "If anything, this is certainly a novel case. How goes the collection of evidence?"

"I think I've got what we need. I was hoping for more, but…"

Jenkins had pursed his lips, and he was shaking his head empathetically.

"But I can't let this go on any longer," Jonathon said. "I can drop it off at your office later."

"You'd best do that," Jenkins said as he stuck out his hand for a handshake. They shook on it. "We'll see each other again real soon."

"There's no doubt of that," Jonathon replied.

"I should have a name for you, by the time you get there," Jenkins said.

"A name for what?"

"A name of a friend of mine," Jenkins said. "RCMP." Jonathon frowned, but Jenkins reassured him. "You can trust this one. I'd trust him with my own life. You can trust him to get to the bottom of this for you."

"You'll forgive me if I'm a little suspicious."

"Jonathon," Jenkins warned, "if what you say is true, if these guys are cops, then you're going to need someone on the inside. You're going to have to trust someone."

Jonathon sighed.

"Do you trust me?" Jenkins asked. "Then take my word for this guy. I'll give you his name and contact information as soon as you get back to my office. He'll get you sorted out. I'm confident of that. It may take some time…but we'll get you fixed up."

CHAPTER SEVENTEEN

Jonathon applied the screwdriver to the name plate posted outside his hallway door. One sign at a time, his office was losing its identity as a member of Antonino Enterprises.

He'd called the RCMP officer that Jenkins had recommended, and he'd left a message. Jonathon knew that this would come to an eventual close, with himself as the eventual victor, but time and money were running out. His partnership had dissolved, and while he was still getting passive income, his new business prospects were at an all-time low. To prove his disassociation with a supposed criminal mastermind, Jonathon had had no choice but to remove all evidence of his one-time partnership with Fred Anton.

Jonathon heard timid footsteps on the stairs further down the hall. He turned, nameplate in one hand, screwdriver in the other. *Another hood?* he wondered. *More bad press?*

To his surprise, it was Ivan Petrovski, the nervous little man who had bought two apartment complexes from him in the past. Hope swelled in Jonathon's heart; then he thought, *He's here to complain about a sale, or to demand his money back.*

Petrovski reached the top of the stairs, and as he walked down the hall, he wiped his brow. "Good afternoon," he called.

"Hi," Jonathon replied. "Long time no see!"

"Yes, I know," Petrovski said. "You…you need an elevator."

They shared a laugh, and Jonathon invited him into the office. Petrovski looked around, seeming surprised at the Spartan décor.

"How are things going?"

Petrovski flipped his hand. "I'm tired," he said. "I'm very tired, all the time tired."

"Have a seat."

Petrovski removed his hat and took the nearest chair.

"What's on your mind?" Jonathon asked, once Petrovski had settled into the seat.

Petrovski frowned deeply, and Jonathon sensed bad news. "You know, the real estate market…it's not so good for me. I lost a lot of money. I may even lose my dental practice."

"I'm sorry to hear that," Jonathon said.

Petrovski wagged his pointing finger at Jonathon, making him all the more uncomfortable. "That first deal I did with you? That was the only profit I've made in over a year."

Jonathon released the breath he hadn't realized he'd been holding.

"So, I need to do something, or I lose a lot," Petrovski said. He leaned to the side and pulled a clear plastic bag from his outer coat pocket. "I need to sell things." He set the bag on the table. It was filled with ingots of metal.

"What is that?"

"It's gold!" Petrovski said, as if Jonathon was the village idiot. It didn't look like gold. It looked like someone had spilled melted solder or lead, and the metal had broken up into small, irregularly shaped bubbles. "It's dental gold. This is only some of what I have. I have more, about eighty thousand dollars' worth." He shrugged broadly. "I-I don't need it in my practice so much anymore. So, I need to sell it." Petrovski scratched the back of his head. Jonathon couldn't help but notice Petrovski was avoiding eye contact.

Jonathon smiled and said, "I'm not really in a position to buy this from you."

"No no. I know. I can't just sell this anywhere." He winced and shrugged. "I brought it into the country without declaring it. And you know, Customs, sometimes they appear out of nowhere, like magicians. Here – I have the original receipt." He pressed flat a crumpled, faded piece of typewritten paper. "But I don't have proof I declared it when I came to this country. And if I don't have the right papers, I'll have to pay fines, and duty, to Revenue Canada – fines that are more even than the gold is worth!" He shook his head. "And I can't afford that. Not now. I'm already losing money. And I have a little to owe back to the government already in taxes." He wiped his chin on the back of his hand.

Jonathon asked, "And so you came here, because…"

"I want you to sell it for me. All of it. I don't care for how much. Give me fifteen thousand dollars to pay back my taxes. You keep the rest."

Jonathon hoisted the plastic bag off the table, and he was surprised at the weight of it, even as small a sample as it was. "Where's the rest of it?"

"I keep it hidden," Petrovski whispered, "in the boiler room of my apartment building on College Avenue." While Jonathon considered his options, Petrovski added, "You keep that sample. You check it out, see that it's the real thing. Gold is gold, yes?" He smiled, but he seemed suddenly distracted by Jonathon's second storey windows. "If you want, then we can go get the rest, anytime, and sell it."

Jonathon ran the math in his head. Even if he sold it at half its original value, if Petrovski only wanted fifteen thousand out of the sale, Jonathon would have enough to continue paying some of the bills, and to pay off the legal fees he'd been accruing with Dan Jenkins' office. "There's a jeweller friend of mine I could see. I'll take this over to him and see what he thinks."

Petrovski wiped his brow. "That's wonderful. You are so helpful to me."

"I'll get back to you as soon as I have news."

"Thank you. This is good. You're a good friend." He shook Jonathon's hand. Petrovski's hand trembled, and it was clammy. He stood up, half-bowing and uttering more thanks, and as he left, he clapped his hat to his head. He seemed well-recovered from his trip up the stairs. Spry, even.

I wouldn't be so comfortable walking around with this much gold in my coat pocket either. And if anyone empathize with someone embroiled in business with Customs, it was Jonathon. He had no love for that agency, and if it meant helping a friend, there was no question: Jonathon would help however he could.

Later that afternoon, he walked across to the small jewelry shop where Jonathon's friend worked. They greeted each other, and set down to business. Gerald, the jeweler, was more than happy to conduct business with him; Richard was their mutual friend and drinking buddy.

Gerald inspected the colour and shine of the gold, then weighed it on a precise scale.

"Is it actually gold?" Jonathon asked.

"No doubt of it," the jeweler answered. "It's an unusual colour, but we can refine that out. Is this all of it?"

"No, he says he has more at home."

The jeweler nodded. "How much do you want for it?"

"Here," Jonathon said, "I've got the original invoice to go with it. He says the full amount was worth about eighty thousand. I need at least sixty percent of the original value."

"If you don't need a receipt, I can get the cash ready for when you bring in the full amount. It's good for me that way, too."

"I'll let you know as soon as I have it," Jonathon said. "Ivan said he can give it to me any time I'm ready, and neither of us needs a receipt."

"Well, if you're ready, I am. Gold is gold."

Jonathon smiled. "I'll give you a call as soon as I have it – does that work?"

"Yeah, that'll be just fine." The jeweller put the gold back into the plastic bag and handed it over to Jonathon, saying that he would rather buy all or nothing. Jonathon took the gold and wished his friend a good day, and promised again that he'd call as soon as he had his hands on the rest of the gold. "Hey," Gerald said. "It's Friday. You going tonight?"

Jonathon shrugged and smiled. "I'll have to check with the wife, but I don't see why not."

"Great," Gerald said. He winked. "We'll meet up at Richard's shop."

"Sounds good."

Jonathon had been back at the office only for a few minutes when the phone rang. "Hello?"

"Buddy! It's Friday and I'm thirsty."

"Richard! Your ears must have been burning," Jonathon replied. "Gerald and I were just talking about you."

"So are you up for it? A couple of drinks after six?"

"I'm thinking about it, but I'd promised Jennifer I'd take her out for dinner. We've been trying to take a nice, quiet night away for a while now, and…" Jonathon cleared his throat. "Something always seems to come up."

"Ah, come on. Bring her along."

"I'll ask her," Jonathon said brightly. The very thought of the company of good and happy friends was enough to cheer him up. "Tell you what, even if she doesn't want to come, I'll swing by and say hi, and then I'll go out to dinner with her afterwards."

"Great. We'll see you later then."

"At your shop?"

"Yep."

"Then I'll see you in a little while."

Jonathon went downstairs to help with the clean-up of the store. "So Richard invited us both over for drinks tonight. You interested? I thought we could go there first, then work our way back to the restaurant."

"I'd love to," Jennifer said, "but I promised Kent I'd drive him over to his friend's house for a sleepover tonight. I told him I'd drive him over there right after work." She smiled playfully and said, "Why don't you go over there for a while, and meet me at home later?"

"You don't want to go out tonight?"

She purred and said, "I'll have something nice waiting for you when you get there. I'll put the kids to bed, and we can have a late dinner…" She traced circles on his shirt. "No intruding waiters, no prying eyes… just you…and me…"

"That," Jonathon said, brushing his hands together, "sounds delicious."

Jonathon had a spring in his heels for the first time in weeks. Even the early winter wind couldn't dampen his spirits. He crossed the road and skipped up onto the curb, not caring who was watching. He passed by grated windows displaying televisions, radios and electronic devices. The lights were off, and the sign was turned to "Closed." On Fridays, if business was slow, Richard always closed up shop a little early, but he'd leave the door open so he, Gerald and their mutual friends could slip inside and head for the back room, where Richard kept his private party bar stocked.

Jonathon paused outside the door. There didn't seem to be anyone moving around inside, or anyone watching for his arrival. He didn't see a light on in the back room, either.

He opened the door. "Hello?" He opened it a little wider, and he stepped inside. "Richard?" There was no answer. He gently closed the door behind him. "Hey, anyone here?" If no one heard him, he expected that it would have been because of rowdy conversation in the back room; but as he came close to the rear door, he heard no other voices. "Hey, guys?"

The staff room was closed, but he heard the wind whistling through the rear exit. He went to ensure that the door was closed; what he saw was that the door had been jimmied open and the frame was damaged. He swore under his breath and ran to the cash to pick up the phone. He dialed the police station, and while waiting for someone to pick up, he looked around the store, wondering what – if anything – had been taken.

"Regina City Police," answered the voice on the other end of the line. "How may I help you?"

Jonathon said quickly, "Yes, I'd like to report a break and en…"

The front door was open, and a figure, backlit by the sun, was entering. He could tell by the set of the shoulders and the shape of the cap that the police had already arrived. Outside, a large dog barked. Jonathon could see the dark animal straining against his leash, snapping and plunging toward the door.

"Hello?" asked the voice on the phone.

"Never mind," Jonathon said. He gently set the phone on the hooks.

The first police officer jumped into a braced stance, aiming his gun at Jonathon. "Up against the wall with your hands on the top of your head!" Canine officers and other patrolmen rushed in, guns and batons raised. "Against the wall!" they shouted. "Hands on your head! On your head! Do it now!"

Jonathon did as he was told, though he moved in slow motion. If he moved too quickly, he'd provoke them; but by moving slowly, he

180

angered them. Radios squawked, dogs barked, and a pair of handcuffs rattled around his wrists as someone wrestled first the right hand, then the left, behind the small of Jonathon's back. *Friday night,* Jonathon thought.

Suddenly, he felt very old, and he regretted getting his hopes up.

CHAPTER EIGHTEEN

"So, this is three weekends now," Jennifer said. "Should I just clear my calendar?"

"Jennifer, I said I was sorry."

"What the hell is really going on?"

"I told you, it's all harassment."

"You were harassed at Richard's store? And they arrested you because of it?"

"No, I..." Jonathon exhaled and clapped his hand to his eyes. "The front door was open. Richard would leave it open on Friday nights to let the rest of us in. So I went in!"

"And then they harassed you."

"I went in, no one else was there. So I went to the back of the store, saying, 'Hello, hello!' and no one answered. And then I saw that the back door had been jimmied open, so I called for police."

Jennifer sat back, crossing her arms.

"And as soon as I had the police dispatcher on the phone, telling them that the store had been broken into, the cops came in, saw me there, and jumped to a conclusion."

Jennifer tilted her head, as if to ask Jonathon if she was expected to believe him.

"They have my voice on the police dispatcher's tape recordings. Jennifer, no one in their right minds calls police to say, 'Oh hey, just to let you know, I'm breaking into an electronics store now, so come and arrest me.'"

"No cop in his right mind would arrest somebody calling the police, either."

"I don't know what else to tell you, Jennifer. I'm too tired and too upset to make up a convincing lie."

"Well," Jennifer began, "didn't you tell the guys who were arresting you that you were innocent? They said you just surrendered to police, like you were admitting your guilt!"

"I don't know, I just figured it wasn't worth my while to put up a fight. Hell, putting up a fight would have only made matters worse!"

Jennifer inclined her head. Her voice was soft when she asked, "And what does your lawyer say about *this* one?"

"He says it's just another bullshit charge. There's no evidence that I broke the back door, and like I said, if I wanted to break in some place – even if that place was owned by a close friend of mine – I sure as hell wouldn't have called the police to tell them I was doing it. I'm being set up," he said, "otherwise, how could the cops have gotten there so fast?"

Jennifer slouched. "I'm just getting tired of this routine, Jonathon."

"You and me both. But you know I'll be home Monday morning. Jenkins says the phone logs are all we're going to need for this one. It's just another lost weekend. They're not going to be able to make this one stick. They haven't got a leg to stand on."

Jonathon made it through the following week and weekend without incident, likely because trial was already pending for the next Monday. But it wasn't a pleasant weekend at all. Instead of risking a Friday night on the town, he, Jennifer and the kids stayed indoors for 72-hours, playing board games and reading books. It was a tense weekend, because as soon as Jenkins had entered a not guilty plea, the provincial courthouse judge had glanced over the rims of his glasses and pursed his lips, looking for all the world like he'd already passed judgment. He'd been looking at Jonathon, not at Jenkins. The judge had scribbled something on a note pad to his right, sighed as if disgusted and bored, then asked the clerk for the next available trial date. Jonathon knew the evidence was in his favour, so he had no good reason to fear the judge; but then again, since the evidence was in Jonathon's favour, there was no good reason for the judge to stare at Jonathon in such a manner.

Monday morning, the day of his trial – seven days after he'd last been released from jail – Jonathon and his lawyer stood at the defence table, awaiting the decision. Jenkins looked cool and composed. Even the Crown Attorney seemed mildly disappointed in such a clean-cut defence argument.

Behind them, a crowd of press, strangers and family members had filled almost every seat. Jonathon heard pencils skittering across paper notepads.

"Mr. Parker," said the judge. "I find you guilty of break and enter with intent to commit an indictable offence therein."

Jonathon was the only one in the courtroom who *didn't* make a sound of surprise, and that was because he'd been dumbstruck by the verdict.

"Since this is your first offence," the judge continued, "I'll sentence you to a fine of one thousand dollars." He pointed to the uniformed man at the side of the judge's bench. "The Bailiff will make arrangements to hold you in custody until the fine has been paid. Do you understand?"

Jonathon's mouth was open. The judge leaned over crossed arms and blinked at him. "Yes sir," Jonathon said. He'd responded like an automaton.

The judge sat back and asked the clerk if now would be a convenient time to recess for lunch. The clerk agreed it would be a good idea. The judge formalized the decision by closing the case, announcing recess and cracking his gavel on the block. All rose, and when he left, everyone went their separate ways.

Jenkins was pale. Jonathon was not. Ryder and Callaghan were leaning against their car, where they'd parked at the curb. The constant press of foot traffic obscured them, but Jonathon could see and hear them easily enough. They were laughing and slapping each other on the back.

"I can't believe the old bastard found you guilty," Jenkins whispered. "I still don't understand what went wrong!"

"I know you did your best," Jonathon said.

Callaghan, pouting, had balled up his fist and was twisting it in the corner of his eye. Ryder laughed at his charades.

"The fine's no big deal," Jonathon said out of the corner of his mouth, because he'd rather be damned than let the Dynamic Duo know that they'd gotten to him. But they had accomplished something: he'd been an innocent man, until a crooked judge declared him a criminal.

"I think we'd better file an appeal on this right away," Jenkins said. Some colour returned to his cheeks, and his hands moved with enraged energy. "I'm not going to let them hold a criminal record over you for this, not with so much evidence at hand. That would be unthinkable! This is an absolute miscarriage of justice."

"Do what you need to do," Jonathon said, "because you know I'm good for the fees. I'd rather be cooperative now than give them another reason to call me crooked." He turned his back to Ryder and Callaghan so they couldn't read his lips through their binoculars. "Listen, when do you have time to get together and discuss those other two assholes?"

He regarded Jonathon with a thoughtful expression. "Yes. Come by the office during lunch tomorrow. We'll talk then."

"Sounds good," Jonathon said. They shook on it, said their good-byes, and while Jenkins walked to the parking lot, Jonathon lifted his hand and signalled for a cab. The taxi drove up. Jonathon glanced around, and his heart skipped a beat. He couldn't see Ryder or Callaghan anymore.

Jonathon opened the rear door of the taxi, and the driver asked, "Where to?" The driver's expression changed, and he put the car back in drive. The door slipped free of Jonathon's grasp, and it closed but didn't latch. Jonathon straightened his back. Out of the corners of his eyes, he saw the two mocking shadows at his sides.

"Gotta admit," Ryder said in Jonathon's ear as the taxi drove away, "that old judge surprised even us!" He picked at the elbow patches of Jonathon's tan coat, as if judging the quality of the material.

Jonathon raised his hand to hire another cab, but Callaghan pulled his arm down. "Aw, going so soon?" Callaghan cooed.

"You know," Jonathon said, "if I thought you two were smart enough to figure out the mechanics of it, I would tell you to go fuck yourselves."

Callaghan was quiet for a moment. A cold wind blew along the street, lifting Callaghan's hair. "Now is that any way to talk to the only two men in the world who could save your sorry ass?" Callaghan asked quietly. Another silence. There was no humour left in his freckled face. "No, you know what? Screw it."

Ryder raised his hands and said, "Yeah, I'm with you. I'm done here."

Callaghan fixed Jonathon's tie. "We gave you lots of warning, Parker, and you're too damned stupid to save yourself." He nodded. "So the next time you're in front of a judge, expect five years. And when that happens, we're all going to sit down and have a serious conversation." He smoothed Jonathon's tie and adjusted his coat lapels. "We'll be seeing you around, Parker."

Jonathon gave them hardly a second glance. He threw up his hand and shouted, "Taxi!"

"Your friend," said Petrovski a couple of days later at his dental office, "he's still willing to buy the gold from you?" He asked Jonathon to close the consultation room door.

"Yes, he's still willing to buy it," Jonathon answered. "Why wouldn't he be?"

"Even though you were caught breaking in..."

"I was *charged* with breaking in," Jonathon amended. "I'm no thief. I don't need to be. Besides, if you really thought I was a thief, we wouldn't be doing business right now."

Petrovski toggled his head in half-hearted agreement. "Yes, it's better to do this now. I don't like having this hanging around." His hair was dark with sweat. "Whether you did it or not, the electronic store, it was broken into, yes?"

"Yes."

"And not very far from here! And me, I would rather sell at a loss than lose everything."

Jonathon couldn't argue with that. Petrovski took the plastic bag of gold ingots from his locked desk drawer, and he placed it gently in

Jonathon's palm. "When can you get the rest of it?" Jonathon asked. "My friend's ready at any time, and he'd rather buy it all at once."

Petrovski sat behind his desk and wiped his forehead. "You know the building." He invited Jonathon to sit while he sketched the layout of the ground floor of the apartment building Jonathon had once sold him. "Here, this is the backdoor," he said, pointing to the completed sketch with the sharp end of his pencil. "You go in here, and down the hallway. There's a door marked 'boiler room.'"

Jonathon said, "The boiler room?"

Petrovski sat back, spreading his hands apart. "It's safer than any room! Nobody thinks to look for gold in a strongbox in the back of a boiler room. Besides, you go in the backdoor, nobody knows you have gold when you come back out, nobody chases you and mugs you."

"Good point. Where in the boiler room?"

"You will find it hidden on top of the pipes in the south-west corner of the room, up high by the ceiling." Uncomfortable, Petrovski rubbed his belly. "The maintenance man is nosy, but he always leaves every night about one o'clock."

"In the afternoon?"

"In the morning!" He gave Jonathon a key ring with two keys on it.

Jonathon frowned, but he took the keys.

"You go in after that. Nobody sees you go in. Nobody sees you go out. Then, you only need to wait until morning, and sell it."

Jonathon sat forward. "Ivan, why don't you just come with me? In daylight hours."

Petrovski wiped his forehead again. When he spoke, he kept his eyes closed. "I am in trouble. So much trouble, you would not believe. I have to take a flight to Calgary."

"When?"

"In less than an hour. My mother is very sick, and the doctor said it was urgent I be there."

Jonathon shrugged. "So why don't we do this when you get back?"

Petrovski shook his head vigorously. "You remember, I said Revenue Canada was on to me for some tax problems. I had a problem flipping a property you sold me! So much trouble, and now I have this big problem with my taxes. I need to pay my back taxes by the end of the month – that is only next week! If I don't, they say they will audit me, and that would be a disaster! I could lose everything." Petrovski wagged his hand, shushing any further argument. "You can give me the money on Tuesday, when I get back from Calgary."

Jonathon pocketed the keys and the gold. "I guess we'll have to do it your way."

There wasn't one thing Jonathon liked about this plan. What he needed was someone to watch his back.

He walked into the Neighbour's Pub, which was doing late business for a weeknight. Cory, predictable to a fault, sat at his usual table near the back door. He looked up at Jonathon. He wasn't happy. "As I recall," Cory began, "you were supposed to fly overseas and come back with ten thousand dollars for me. How many months ago was that, now?"

"How does Monday sound?"

"Sounds like a lousy weekend to me." But he was intrigued. "You come here to tell me that?"

"I came to ask you to help me get that money," he said. Cory lifted an eyebrow at that. "What are you doing for the next thirty minutes?"

"It's quarter to one," Cory intoned. "In the next thirty minutes, I'm going to drink, piss, go home and sleep. Why?"

"I could use some company while I pick up a package."

"Why, you scared?"

"I could use an extra pair of eyes."

Cory snorted. "I don't do B & E."

"It's not B & E when you have the key from the owner of the building."

"You lifted the key?"

Jonathon showed him the gold ingots, and he explained everything. "He wants it to be done carefully and quietly, because he doesn't want close to a hundred grand worth of dental gold to go missing – and *I* don't want to get jumped while I'm carrying it. Seriously, it's no big deal. But I figure, if you watch me pick up the rest, you'll see I'm telling you the truth – that you'll get your money on Monday, as soon as I sell it. We get a part of the cut."

Cory watched Jonathon over the lip of his beer glass. "I'm charging you interest."

"Can we discuss it on the way? I don't want to be out any later than we need to be. Jennifer's already got reason enough to worry."

A little past one in the morning, Jonathon held the back door open for Cory, who had been keeping one eye over his shoulder since they left the Pontiac. Jonathon marched down the hall, fishing for the borrowed keys. He walked like he belonged there, so as not to arouse suspicion. Cory rubbed condensation from his nose and kept his head low between upraised shoulders. Jonathon teased him for looking like the world's worst spy, and Cory fixed his posture. Cory pointed over Jonathon's shoulder at the door marked "boiler room." Jonathon stopped in front of it and tested first the one key, then the other, in the lock. The door opened without a sound. "Stay here," Jonathon said, and Cory was happy to linger in the doorway, letting in the hallway light and giving himself the fastest way out.

Jonathon flicked on his flashlight. The boiler room looked like a horror movie set, complete with a maze of blackened water pipes, hulking machines and battered boxes. A pilot light shone in the small space under the boiler.

"You know where it is?" Cory asked.

"Yep," Jonathon said. He directed his feet to the southwest corner. In a few seconds, he reassured himself, this leg of his mission would be done. Once he was out of the boiler room, he was in the clear. He shone his flashlight over the pipes, and not for the first time, he was glad for tall legs and a long reach. He ran his fingers through dust, cobwebs and rust. There were a lot of pipes, but no sign of the strongbox. *Maybe he meant the south-east corner, not south-west,* Jonathon thought.

"Hey," Cory whispered from the door. "Get out here."

"Gimme a sec."

"I think there's some weird shit going on out here."

"What?"

"Get over here!"

Jonathon abandoned his hunt, and he joined Cory by the boiler room door.

"You hear that?" Cory asked.

Jonathon listened, and he heard a splash, followed by a glugging noise and another splash. "What the hell?" He moved Cory out of the way, and he rushed down the hall to see what was going on. Cory followed him.

"God – what…what is that smell?" Cory asked. "Is that gasoline?"

The base of the interior backstairs obscured the figure of the two men near the rear exit. Then one of them moved into Jonathon's line of sight. It was a man, wearing a tan jacket with dark elbow patches – a jacket that matched the one Jonathon was wearing. The stranger swung a red gas canister, emptying the last contents on the hall floor. A second man pushed him out of the way and left by the rear exit, splashing more gasoline as he went. The man wearing the tan jacket tossed his canister outside the open back door, then he left, slamming the door behind him.

"Holy *shit*," Cory said. "I'm out of here."

"Go upstairs," Jonathon said, "and get ready to leave with everyone else by the front lobby doors. Go!"

Cory ran past him and took the backstairs two at a time. Jonathon counted to three, then ran to follow him. He heard a whoosh, like something out of a movie. He smelled the smoke first. As he ran up the stairs, flames raced along the pool of gasoline from under the door, erupting and leaping as they came into contact with the wallpaper and drywall. Jonathon ran up the stairs and down the hall pulling a fire alarm as he ran. He banged on doors as went, waking tenants where he found them, and shuttling them toward the lobby as they emerged in their pyjamas, boots and winter coats, yelling and weeping. A hundred people were talking and pleading at once, and the shriek of the fire alarm was deafening. Smoke billowed down the hallway, and Jonathon had to leave. He emerged outside coughing into his elbow, eyes stinging.

Someone grabbed his left arm and jerked it around behind him. Through bleary, runny eyes, Jonathon saw service lights rolling, red, blue and white.

"And they say there's never a cop around when you need one," Jonathon wheezed as a cop wrestled his right arm down. Cuffs clapped around his wrists. Jonathon doubled over and coughed. The police officer pushed him against the tide of incoming firemen and hoses. Other officers worked crowd control, and Jonathon did what he could to hide his face from their accusing stare.

How in God's name am I going to explain this one to Jennifer? he thought as an officer put him in the back seat of a waiting cruiser.

He rubbed his face on his shoulder to clear some of the dirty tears from his eyes. When he looked out through the passenger's door, he barely caught a glimpse of Cory walking nonchalantly away from a crowd of the confused tenants, making his way safely toward the neighbouring park.

He smiled to himself; at least they hadn't arrested Cory.

CHAPTER NINETEEN

Jonathon had drowsed, but he hadn't realized it until someone banged shut the cell door. He wasn't sure how he'd managed to fall asleep at all. The cot was nothing but a mesh of flat metal strips, there was no heat, and Jonathon had a wracking cough from smoke inhalation.

An officer stood in the cell, too far from the end of the cot to be at risk of getting kicked in the shins. "You're lucky as hell that we got that anonymous tip when we did," the officer said, crossing his arms. Jonathon didn't know who he despised more, RCMP, Customs, or big-shot municipal cops with spreading waistlines and a lot to prove. "If we hadn't gotten there so quick, you'd be facing multiple charges of man-slaughter. As it is, you're looking at no less than 40 counts of attempted murder."

"Can I call my lawyer now?"

"Hell of a good thing we had a guy on the roof across the lane. Saw everything."

Jonathon rubbed his eyes. "Can I call my lawyer *now*?"

"Who was the guy that went in with you?"

"All I saw was people coming out," Jonathon answered.

"You heard me, right?" the officer asked. "We had an officer of the law posted across the road on surveillance. He saw everything. There were two of you. It was the other guy who set the fire, we know that. We just want to know: who was in on it with you? Who's the man actu-ally responsible for the fire? Who lit the match?"

"How about now? Can I call my lawyer now?"

The officer laughed. "God, why do I even bother with you people?" He shrugged and shook his head. "Not like it matters. We've already found Cory Carter." He turned to his partner, who opened the cell door. "We'll wait until you're ready to talk."

"I'm ready to talk to my lawyer now. When do I get to call him?"

The cell door rattled shut. "At four in the morning?" The officer snorted. "We'll drop everything right now for you, Mr. Parker. We'll get right on that. I'm sure your lawyer would be excited to get a call at this time of the morning to find out you're back in jail. What is this, stay number four?" Boots trampled away from the cell.

Jonathon sat on the edge of the cot, his head in his hands.

The following morning around 11:00 o'clock, Jonathon overheard some conversation between guards in the hallway and pieced together that they had somehow just earlier located and arrested Cory.

The next day, they led Jonathon and Cory into a holding area to the side of the judge's bench. They were both wearing the orange coloured overalls of the city jail. Cory wouldn't make eye contact with him.

Jennifer was watching from the gallery, and Michael was fidgeting in her arms. Beside and around her were reporters, plain-clothed policemen, Edward and Norma Parker, Jonathon's in-laws, Bob Myers, Jonathon's one-time secretary Laura, and Pat Burton (who'd just finished telling a joke to Bob Myers, who wasn't listening). Jonathon wasn't sure if he was happy or embarrassed at the turnout; he wasn't sure if they were trying to be supportive, or if they just wanted front row seats to all the action. He was disappointed, however, that his last Christmas party couldn't draw such a crowd.

Dan Jenkins and the lawyers from both sides of the case had wrapped up the time-worn rituals of the hearing. The judge cleared his throat and Jonathon straightened his shoulders. The judge said, "Jonathon Edward Parker."

"Yes, your Honour," Jonathon replied.

"William Cory Carter."

"Yes, your Honour," Cory said softly.

"You're both held to answer to the charges of one count each for arson, one count each for insurance fraud, and forty-one counts each for attempted murder."

Jonathon's knees weakened, and the gallery lifted an collective noise of surprise. Someone sounded happy at the judge's charges.

"Trial is set for the eleventh of December, 1981 in Courtroom 26, Saskatchewan Superior Court, City of Regina. Bail hearing will be at ten a.m., Thursday of this week. Court's dismissed." He banged the gavel, and court sheriffs ushered Jonathon and Cory toward the rear door. Jonathon looked over his shoulder and between two sheriffs at the gallery. Jennifer was already on her feet with her back turned. Norma Parker was trying to console her.

They sat knee to knee in a private cell. Jennifer had left Michael with her parents, but she kept her arms across her chest as if she was still hugging her little boy. "Are you okay?" she asked.

"How are the kids?" he asked instead.

"Fine." She half-laughed. "Well, Michael's becoming a handful."

"And business?"

"It's good," she allowed. "We're busier than ever, which is great."

"Enough to hire more help yet?"

"No, not that great," she answered. "So between that and the kids, I'm pretty much exhausted." She saw his look of helpless grief and took his hands. "I'm sorry Jonathon, I don't mean to complain about it. It's not like you can help it."

He smiled. "I didn't hear any complaint. Besides, I'll be out before you know it."

"I know. My dad agreed to put up whatever bail money you and Cory need. He doesn't believe you had any part in that fire."

"He doesn't need to worry about it," he insisted. "I made arrangements for my bail already with Dan. There's not much I can do for Cory though. Besides, unless they drop a lot of the charges..." He was feeling very tired. "Bail could be set at an unreasonably high amount. Your dad might believe I'm innocent, but one look at that judge, and I know I'm in for a fight. I can't ask your dad to cover something that high."

"Jonathon, it doesn't matter. Whatever it is, my dad will put it up for both of you. Listen, Cory's been a friend of my brother for years. And Dad wants to help *both* of you. Let him help. I need you home, and I don't need any more debts, even if it's to Dan Jenkins. All right? Let him help."

He kissed her hand. She kissed him on the lips.

Once bail had been posted, Jonathon was released to do what work he could before the trial. He spent most of that time working with Jennifer at the flower shop; but he spent a good portion of it dealing with a change in the legal line-up.

Robert Downes seemed young for a criminal lawyer, but he had a surgical way of looking at people, like a man accustomed to seeking a weak spot in armour and exploiting it. He shook Jonathon's hand. "Mr. Parker. How are you?"

"Just fine, thanks. This is Cory Carter, my co-accused."

They shook hands too. Cory said, "Nice to meet you."

"Have a seat," Downes said. He did just that, himself. "I've known Dan Jenkins for many years, and he tells me nothing but good things about you, Jonathon. As you can imagine, he's extremely upset over this current situation."

"I know," Jonathon said. "He referred us to you because he felt he wasn't up to handling a criminal case of this size, or one with its ramifications."

Downes nodded. "He told me about your allegations against these two RCMP officers."

"Yeah, he's more of a real estate lawyer than a criminal lawyer," Jonathon said.

"He's shared his files with me, and he says you had some mini-cassette tapes to bring as well?"

"I meant to give them to Dan Jenkins a few weeks ago, but..." Jonathon cracked his neck. "A couple of things came up. I'll get them to you later today."

Downes crossed his arms. "So why don't you start by telling me what really happened that night, when you two went down to the College Court Apartments."

Jonathon rubbed his face. Ryder and Callaghan aside, arson aside, it wasn't an easy story to tell without someone getting into hot water.

Jonathon gave her a quick peck on the cheek, though she was still with a customer. Jennifer raised her hand and said, "Hurry back. I've got a major order to fill this afternoon, and I could use the help."

"Sure, hun. As soon as I get back from dropping these off at the lawyer's office." He raised the plastic bag of mini-cassette tapes. "Back before you know it."

"Don't go down any dark alleys, all right?"

They shared a smile at that, and Jonathon left, jangling the bell over the door as he went out. He checked in all directions, then walked a bee-line to his Pontiac. His hand was on the door latch when four tires screeched up beside him, an engine revved, and two arms came out of nowhere to hug Jonathon from behind. Suddenly, he was on the cold ground looking up at Callaghan, whose face was full of murderous intent. Callaghan slapped his hands on Jonathon's collar and hauled him up and wrestled him into the backseat of the unmarked car. Jonathon opened his mouth to shout for help, and Callaghan punched upwards, cracking Jonathon's teeth together. Callaghan pulled the rear passenger's door shut after him, drew his gun and pressed the muzzle against Jonathon's lips. Ryder pulled down the gear selector into drive.

No one said a word, and the trip to the snow-covered dump was shorter than ever. Ryder threw it into park, making the car skid to a stop. He jumped out and opened the door behind Jonathon's back, making him fall out; Callaghan came out by the same door, kicking Jonathon in the belly. Then Callaghan threw down the bag of mini-cassette tapes and ground them under the heel of his boot. While Callaghan stamped all of the evidence, Ryder pulled Jonathon to his feet, slammed him against the side of the car and frisked him for any sign of the mini-cassette recorder itself.

"You're suicidal, you know that?" Ryder asked. Jonathon didn't reply. "Is this what you want? Huh? Five years in prison – for you *and* for your little friend Cory? Huh?" Ryder flicked out his hands, shoving Jonathon against the side of the car.

"Cory didn't have anything to do with Anton," Jonathon said. "And he didn't have anything to do with that fire you set. Damn it, you could have killed forty people – and for what?"

Ryder leaned his forearm against Jonathon's throat, bending him backward over the roof of the car. "You listen here, jackass. You either work with us to get Anton, or we'll screw you all. Your father-in-law posted bail for you two, huh? So now, not only are you screwing yourself, but you're screwing Cory..." He leaned extra weight with every name. "And Jennifer, and your father-in-law, your parents, your kids... Now who are you going to help, huh? Anton, or all of *them*?"

It was hard to breathe, but Jonathon smiled. "You two assholes are the ones who torched that building, not us. We didn't do *anything*. Don't count your chickens before they hatch, dumbass – they haven't found us guilty yet."

Ryder bared his teeth in a sick imitation of a smile.

"The trial hasn't even started yet," Jonathon said, "and we haven't started to fight yet. So come on. Let's do it."

Ryder laughed. He pulled Jonathon away, trying to spin him off balance and make him fall, but Jonathon kept his feet under him. Ryder signalled to Callaghan, whose hair was sweaty from his mad jig on the bag of evidence. They got in their usual seats in the front of the car, and as Ryder put it in gear, he drove over the cassette tapes. He backed over them, too, as he executed a three-point turn and fish-tailed out of the dump site.

Jonathon tightened his thin fall jacket around himself. He regretted having only worn shoes. There wasn't so much snow in the city, and he knew from experience that it was a long, slow, snowy walk back to town. He picked up the torn bag and all the broken parts within. Loops had burst from each of the cassettes, and white lines criss-crossed the black magnetic tape, permanently damaging the quality. But the idiots hadn't thought to take the tapes with them. The tapes were salvageable. He knew it. He believed it with all his heart. He had to believe it.

Jennifer was in the living room clutching a crumpled Kleenex against her cheek. When the front door opened, she turned her head, then jumped up, saying, "Oh God, Jonathon, where have you been?" She ran at him and hugged him. "Are you all right? Look at you! You're freezing!"

He shuddered and shivered. "I had an unexpected meeting that took longer than expected."

"Are you okay?"

"I'm all right," he said. He was mildly surprised. Usually meetings with Ryder and Callaghan went far, far worse than that. "Just need a few minutes to warm up." She quickly led him to the kitchen and filled the electric kettle. He set the bag of broken tapes on the table.

She was chewing the side of her thumb nail. She blinked, and new tears fell.

"What's the matter?" Jonathon asked. "Hey," he cooed. He wrapped his cold arms around her. "It'll be okay."

She sobbed against him. "We lost the flower shop today."

Jonathon recoiled and held her at arm's length. "What are you talking about?"

Jennifer wiped her eyes with the well-used tissue. "The sheriff served me with notice, and someone came to change the locks."

"What?"

"The new owner of the building found a way to revoke our lease because your so-called links to organized crime, and something about a clause that allows him to take reasonable action to protect his reputation, and he wouldn't listen to me when I said it was the only thing we had left..."

Jonathon hugged her close while she sobbed uncontrollably against him. He rocked her and tried everything he could to calm her down.

"When is this ever going to end?" she asked. Her whole body shook.

He ran his hand over her head again and again. He needed a plan. He needed help. This had gone way too far. "I'll go see the lawyer first thing tomorrow morning," he said. "I think I've got a couple of ideas. We'll get through this, I swear we will."

CHAPTER TWENTY

Jonathon sat at the kitchen table with a mug of coffee and a plate of toast. He left another message with Joe McElvoy, the RCMP investigator whose name Dan Jenkins had given Jonathon several weeks earlier. He'd begun to believe that McElvoy was nothing more than an answering machine, but he was at a point where he would try anything.

He checked the time. Now that the lawyer's office was open, he dialed out and asked for Robert Downes. "Robert Downes speaking," was the response.

"Hi, Mr. Downes? It's Jonathon Parker."

"Yes Jonathon, how can I help you? I thought you were supposed to come by yesterday with those tapes. Is everything all right?"

"I had a little problem getting to your office yesterday, but I'll explain that in a second. Listen, I called you because I could use some advice."

"I'm listening."

"Yesterday, the landlord of the building where our flower shop is – well, yesterday he revoked the lease and changed all the locks. All of our stock and equipment is inside that shop, and my wife has five big orders to get out today."

"Revoked the lease?" the lawyer asked, surprised. "On what grounds?"

"He used a clause in the lease, something about saying that he had a right to protect his reputation, and, since he claims that I have links to organized crime…"

The lawyer made a noise that was somewhere between a sigh and a groan.

"But listen, our rent is paid up, and we've asked to get access to the store so that we can at least get our stock out. And nothing. No answer.

What I want to know is, can I get a locksmith to let me back in, long enough to get our things out?"

There was a long pause on the line. "Are you asking a hypothetical question? Because anything I say to you can't be taken as legal advice. It has to be taken as completely hypothetical."

"Sure, I understand. The question was completely hypothetical."

Another long pause. "All right. Technically, you would be breaking and entering, but only if you were caught actually inside the premises."

"I know all about that," Jonathon commented.

"If you did, hypothetically, get a locksmith out there, you'd have to make sure he didn't provide you any keys, and that he locked the doors as they were prior to your entry."

"And if we get everything out?"

"You can't be charged with theft of your own possessions," the lawyer answered. "At least, not criminally. But you're at risk of a civil suit. On the other hand, if your rent is paid up, as you said, and as long as you don't damage the premises, he really can't expect to gain much from such an action. Hypothetically speaking, of course."

"Of course." Jonathon exhaled. "Great. That's about what I was hoping."

"Are you coming by with the tapes?"

"Yes, absolutely. I'll be seeing you later today, as soon as I can get there."

As soon as Jonathon hung up and had his mouth full of toast, the phone rang. He swallowed a glug of coffee to wash down the crumbs, and he picked up the receiver. "Hello?" He listened carefully. His eyes lit up and his hair stood on end. "Yes, sure I can be there in about an hour." He was about to hang up, when he stopped and added a sincere, "Thank you." He rushed through the rest of his breakfast, and as he stood up to get ready to leave, he shouted, "Jennifer? Can you come in here for a sec?"

It was cold and the sand was hard, but Michael was happy to be out playing and making a mess. Jonathon watched him from a nearby park bench, breathing white air. A broad-shouldered, good-looking man sat down beside him. He had very short hair, a carved face, and he seemed tired but bright-eyed. They sat in silence for a moment. Then the man asked, "Are you Jonathon Parker?"

"I am."

The rugged man took out his wallet and offered a business card. It had a royal seal for an insignia, and written on it were the words "Sergeant Joseph McElvoy, Senior Officer, Regina Special Branch, National Crime Intelligence Section (NCIS)." Jonathon blew out pent up breath.

"Nice to meet you," Jonathon said.

McElvoy pointed at Michael, who was chucking a shovel full of dirt over his shoulder and catching it instead in the hood of his coat. "Just starting to get mobile, eh?"

"Yeah. He's into just about everything as soon as your back is turned."

McElvoy smiled and stood up, and Jonathon took his lead. McElvoy began to pace around the cobbled path around the playground area, with Michael in plain view and oblivious to their motions.

"Dan Jenkins spoke very highly of you," Jonathon said. "I'm hoping you can help me out of a jam two of your colleagues have got me into."

"I've read our file on you," McElvoy said. It sounded almost like a warning. "It sounds like you've got yourself into a couple of jams all by yourself."

"I had a lot of help," Jonathon said bitterly.

"How?"

"You name it. They defrauded me out of nearly half a million dollars. They arranged a phony arrest on trumped up charges of stealing my own car. Framed me for break and enter with intent. And most recently, framed me and my co-accused for forty-one counts of attempted murder in an arson they themselves set, if you can believe it."

McElvoy raised his chin and watched the sky as he walked. "Those are some serious allegations. And no, without convincing evidence, I wouldn't believe any of it."

"But I do have evidence."

McElvoy regarded him.

Jonathon untucked the bag of broken mini-cassette tapes from inside his coat, and he handed them across to McElvoy. "Add 'tampering with evidence' to the list of my accusations. I'm hoping some of your guys can piece these back together again." Inside the bag was an envelope as well. Jonathon pointed to it. "It's a long story, but I've tried to write it out for you, date by date. In that envelope you'll find a statement from me, plus copies of the bank transfers with my forged signatures, plus photocopies of my airplane tickets for the same period of time. I've put together as much as I could for you."

"And these tapes..."

"Recorded conversations between myself and the two officers that started all this."

McElvoy said, "I'll give you fifteen minutes. If you convince me that any of this is true in that time, I'll give you the rest of my afternoon."

"There are two men," Jonathon began. "Ryder and Callaghan."

McElvoy raised an eyebrow.

"From what I understand, they've had history with a good friend of mine, a guy by the name of Fred Anton."

McElvoy raised the other eyebrow.

Jonathon forged on and told him the rest of the story, assured now that he had McElvoy's undivided attention.

They spoke for three quarters of an hour, then, when Michael became fussy, they took him to a fast food restaurant and talked over lunch.

"I can't comment officially on Ryder and Callaghan," McElvoy said around a mouthful of burger. "But I will say you've gone further than piquing my interest."

"I sure hope so," Jonathon said. "I don't know who else to turn to."

McElvoy drank from his take-out cup. "Give me until next Thursday to get some serious investigating underway."

Jonathon didn't know if wanted to laugh or cry. But his relief was mingled with doubt. "What about Ryder and Callaghan?"

"Until I know for certain what's really going on, there's nothing I can do about them. These things take time, and they require caution."

Jonathon was underwhelmed.

"But you can believe this," McElvoy said. He rarely blinked whenever he spoke. He stared as if he could see through to the back of Jonathon's brain. "If even *half* of what you tell me is true, you won't be bothered by either of them for a very long time. That I can assure you."

Jonathon shrugged. "Next Thursday it is, then."

McElvoy quickly finished his lunch, wiped his hands and face, then shook Jonathon's hand. Without another word, McElvoy got up and left.

Jennifer was vacuuming the floor, and when she heard the front door open, she came to take Michael from Jonathon's hands. "And did you boys have fun today?"

"We were at the park," Jonathon said as he closed the door and kicked off his boots. "And we met a very nice man, didn't we?" Michael giggled at the tickle under his chin. To Jennifer, Jonathon said, "His name's McElvoy, that RCMP officer I talked to this morning on the phone."

"And?"

"And I think he's actually going to help us out."

"Help?" Jennifer asked. "From the RCMP? That would be a nice change. Oh – by the way, your lawyer called, that Robert Downes guy?"

"Yeah?"

"He wants you to call him back right away, but first – you should take a look at what's in the garage."

Jonathon hung up his coat. "Why?"

"Let's just say I had a great day too." As soon as she had Michael out of his winter clothes and laid down for a nap, she came back and led Jonathon by the hand through the mud room into the cold garage. It was filled with boxes of fresh flowers, potted plants, furniture and a cash register.

"Wow," Jonathon said. "That was quick!"

"My brother sent two of his service station attendants over with the truck. We met the locksmith over there at eleven, and we had everything loaded and moved out in forty-five minutes. Can you believe it?"

"Jeez – did anyone see you do it?"

Jennifer shrugged. "No one seemed to notice or pay any attention at all. But, at least now we can fill those orders for this weekend, and we can probably sell off everything else right here from the garage. I can call a couple of people and see if they're interested." She put her hands on her hips. "Just such a stupid, crying shame…"

They talked about the details as they went back into the warmer rooms of the house. "I should call up your brother and give him my thanks," Jonathon said.

"You should call that lawyer first."

"You're right – it's getting late. I'd better call him before the office closes." They kissed quickly on the lips, and Jennifer went back to quieter cleaning while Jonathon went into the kitchen to place his call. "Robert Downes, please," he said, once the receptionist had picked up his call.

After a moment, Downes answered. "Thanks for getting back to me, Jonathon. I, uh…" He cleared his throat. "I've got a bit of a problem here."

"How's that?"

"You remember that 'hypothetical' conversation we had this morning?"

Jonathon closed his eyes. "Yes…" He spoke with more optimism than he felt. "Everything's okay now. Jennifer got all our stuff out of the store, no problem."

"Great…great, I'm glad. At least that part is okay. But uh…listen, did you or your wife discuss that hypothetical conversation with anyone?"

I wonder if my phone has been tapped, Jonathon thought, belatedly. "Well, she called her brother, and they had two guys help move some of the stuff, but they wouldn't have talked to anyone."

"Good. Listen carefully, and please don't respond until I'm finished."

Jonathon sat down.

"I'm not saying that your conversations are being monitored, but somehow, two RCMP officers knew what we talked about. They paid me a visit today. They're threatening to have me brought before the bar on charges of counselling an offence. Frankly, I don't think the charges could stick, but, let's just say that the potential problems for me could be enormous. They've suggested that I withdraw as your lawyer in this arson case, and they've suggested that they agree not to bring me before the bar, if you catch my meaning. I do have a proposed solution, which I'm happy to discuss. But if we go ahead, we won't bring up anything to do with our 'hypothetical' conversation from this morning. You with me?"

"I understand," Jonathon said. "But tell me, do the names Ryder and Callaghan sound familiar to you?"

"Let's leave it at that for now," Downes said, "and maybe we'll talk about this again sometime, in private."

"All right. So what's your proposed solution?"

"First of all, the Crown has asked to postpone the trial date. Of course, we agreed, but we don't know when the new date is. It hasn't been set yet. We've scheduled a pre-trial conference for mid-January to establish a firm date. It may be put off as far as next winter. We'll just have to wait for the new year to find out for sure."

"Okay…"

"Now, because of this other issue, from this morning, I'd like to refer you to another lawyer, a guy by the name of Rus Bentley. Now, he's got lots of experience, and he's a respected trial lawyer. If it's okay with you, I'll call him up first thing tomorrow and find out if he has time on his schedule to handle your trial. Considering the current delay, I don't think that's going to be a problem."

Jonathon wrote down the name.

"If he is available, and if he is inclined, I'll send your entire retainer and all the copies of my files to his office. I'll have to do up a bill for my time to date, but you can pay that later. I know your particular financial situation right now, and I'm empathetic to that."

"Thank you."

"Cory will have to find someone else too. I know Rus won't be able to take on the both of you, for a number of reasons. Your thoughts?"

"Well, I'm disappointed to lose you…"

"I know."

"But yeah, okay. I appreciate the referral. Find out if he'll do it and let me know."

Downes sighed. "I'll talk to him first thing in the morning. And if he says yes, I'll have his office contact you directly. Deal?"

"Sure," Jonathon said. It wasn't like he had a lot of choice.

"Good. You have a good night, Jonathon, and don't you give up."

REGINA, CHRISTMAS SEASON, 1981.

Kent and Lisa had gone off to play with their new toys, while Jennifer and Jonathon remained in the living room enjoying a hot adult beverage. Michael was playing with a new truck, alternately running it across the shag carpeting and sticking it in his mouth. The phone rang.

"Don't answer it," Jennifer said, pressing her hand to her husband's chest and pinning him to the couch. The phone rang again. "No, even crooked cops have to take a holiday some time."

"If I don't answer it, I'll only make things worse," he said as he worked his way off the plush couch. He answered the phone in the kitchen. "Hello?"

"You up for a little drive tonight?"

Jonathon closed his eyes. "Damn it, come on. It's practically Christmas. Just for one night."

"It's McElvoy."

"M...Oh God, I'm sorry Sergeant. I thought you were someone else."

"I can pick you up at the Eaton's Centre Parkade in twenty minutes. Can you be there?"

Jonathon frowned. "I've grown to hate that place."

"Will you be there? I'm sorry about the timing, but it's the only time I have."

"Yeah...Yeah, sure, whatever. I'll be there in twenty minutes."

McElvoy disconnected with a quick goodbye, so Jonathon hung up. Jennifer was standing in the kitchen doorway.

"It's McElvoy," he said. "It won't be long – and trust me, with McElvoy, I won't be walking back for a change."

"Oh Jonathon..."

"I mean he'll give me a lift back to my own car."

She rolled her eyes, but she let him go.

McElvoy put it in park. "You all right?" he asked. "You look a little peaky."

Jonathon was staring out the windows. "Don't you guys have an office or something?" He pointed at the snow covered piles of rubbish that Jonathon had come to know so well. "Some place with walls, and heating?"

McElvoy laughed. "Relax. It's a force of habit."

"So to speak," Jonathon said.

"Out here," McElvoy said, "there's no way for someone to eavesdrop. Besides that, this is the last place they'd think to look for you, now isn't it?"

Jonathon couldn't argue with that. "So what have you found out?"

"It's interesting, I'll give you that. We were able to salvage some of the recordings, but some we'll never be able to recover. Parts of the tapes were too badly damaged."

"Is it enough?"

"Honestly?" McElvoy said. "No. It's not quite enough."

Jonathon sagged and pressed his hands to his face.

"Ryder and Callaghan aren't stupid. They've been very efficient at covering any trace of their involvement with you *or* with Anton. But they're not perfect. We'll get them."

Jonathon aged three years in that car.

"I've got four detectives from three different divisions working on this," McElvoy said. "We'll get them."

"Any hope of getting them before the trial date? You know it's been postponed, right?"

"No, I wasn't aware. How far out has it been postponed?"

"They won't be setting a new trial date until January."

"Well, at least that buys us some time. As for getting them quickly? I'd love to say we can wrap this all up tomorrow, but that's not the case. Nothing's ever that simple. We need to talk to Ivan Petrovski. He's the missing link in this arson case. In order to set you up for arson, someone had to get you out there, someone you trusted and believed, and that someone was your dentist friend. And unfortunately, he's mysteriously relocated, and we've been unable to find him so far."

"Try Calgary," Jonathon said. "The last I heard, he was out there looking after his sick mother, so maybe he's got more family out there."

McElvoy nodded. "And as for your friend Anton..."

"Yeah?"

"All his files have gone missing too. Strange, that, considering how presumably well-connected he is to organized crime."

"And they both went missing at the same time? Petrovski, and all your files on Fred? What a coincidence."

"It's enough to make a lot of important people ask important questions," McElvoy assured him.

"And what do you suggest I do in the meantime? I can't work, we've lost the flower shop, I can't access my overseas accounts – if it wasn't for the fact that I had some passive income from some rental units I own, we'd be eating peanut butter sandwiches every day."

"Just be patient. We'll get them. We always get our man in the end."

Jonathon laughed. He couldn't help himself.

Everyone was well-behaved at Christmas dinner, even if it did sound a little formal. Edward Parker made very few comments, except to his wife, and that was usually "Can you pass me the mashed potatoes" or some variation. Norma and Jonathon's grandfather Jake made up for it by joking around with Kent and Lisa. Jennifer's parents told stories about how, as children, they spent Christmases with their own grandparents in homes that were little more than sod houses. Jennifer's brother and her sister-in-law were there as well. Jonathon said very little, but he was content and relaxed. McElvoy was on his side. Someone finally believed him – and McElvoy was someone in a position to do something about it. He carved the turkey and ate voraciously, laughing with a big mouthful at a wisecrack from his brother-in-law. Even Edward smirked and asked for some green beans.

The phone rang. Jennifer's grin fell off, leaving a pale mask of worry in its place. "I'll get it," Jonathon said. "I'll take it in the bedroom," he added to Jennifer. He took a good, bracing gulp of the sparkling wine before he left the table. He leaned over and kissed Jennifer on the cheek, and while he was there he whispered, "It's probably McElvoy. Maybe he's found Petrovski."

"Hurry back," she answered.

"I will."

In the bedroom, the noise from the Christmas table filtered in under the door. Jonathon waited for the phone to ring, and he picked it up. "Hello?"

"Merry Christmas, Jonny-boy." It was Callaghan.

"What do you want?"

"We've got a Christmas present for you!"

"I'm not interested."

"Don't be hasty now. 'Tis the season of brotherly love and forgiveness, and this could be your 'get out of jail free card' for the next five Christmases. Now what do you say about *that*?"

Jennifer opened the bedroom door and listened in to Jonathon's side of the conversation.

"Let me guess," Jonathon said. "Shopping Centre Parkade, twenty minutes."

"You're getting good at this!" Callaghan hung up. Jonathon did likewise.

Jonathon put on a sweater while Jennifer watched him. "You know I have to do this."

"On Christmas," Jennifer said in a very accusatory tone.

"If I had a choice, don't you think I'd rather be here? Do you think I want to walk out now, while my Dad already thinks I'm the scum of the earth, who always runs out on people at the last minute?" He seriously considered dropping his pants and putting on a pair of long johns, but he decided that would only make Jennifer worry more. "I'll be just a little while, I swear."

Jonathon parked the Pontiac not far from the unmarked, occupied car. He didn't even bother to wait for Callaghan to open the door for him. He opened it for himself and sat in the middle of the backseat, and he kept his foot in the door. Like a comedy duo in a b-movie parody, Ryder and Callaghan turned in their front seats, hooked their elbows over and smiled.

"What, no trip to the dump?" Jonathon asked.

"Got a couple of Christmas presents for you," Ryder said.

Callaghan handed him an envelope. Jonathon eyed it suspiciously, and when Callaghan coaxed and cajoled him, Jonathon took it from him. Inside, there were five plane tickets for Qantas Airways. Callaghan handed him a second, fatter manila envelope. Inside this were several bundles of hundred dollar bills. "And there'll be another half million transferred to an account in your name, as soon as you land in Sydney."

"And," Ryder said, lifting a finger, "all of your pending charges will be dismissed publicly before you leave." He looked and sounded slightly drunk.

"You're bribing me to leave the country, and you're offering to drop the charges for things I didn't do," Jonathon said. "You're offering to drop the charges on crimes that *you* guys committed."

Ryder sighed, reached down into the front floor well and pulled up a plastic bag. "By the way. Christmas present #3. Sergeant McElvoy sends his regards." He dumped the bag. Mini-cassette tapes fell out, most of them Scotch-taped and repaired. Ryder didn't look so drunk anymore. "Really? Did you think you could get us with one of our own?"

"Jonny," Callaghan said. "Don't you get it? We all work together! We're all members of the same big team!"

Ryder plucked a pen from his inside coat pocket, and Callaghan handed Jonathon a multi-paged witness statement. This one was far bigger than the last one they'd written for him.

"This is the way out," Callaghan said, putting the pen in Jonathon's hand. "No other way out. Only this one. You sign this, and we'll be out of your life forever – no more fighting!"

Ryder said, "It's the *best* Christmas your family will ever see!"

Jonathon flipped through page after page, statements against Fred Anton, accusing him of graft, fraud and outright murder. "This isn't half bad," Jonathon said to them. "Have you found a reputable fiction publisher for it yet?"

Smiles fled all three faces, and for a moment, they were suspended in time. Jonathon made the first move. He kicked open the door and had made it as far as his own car door when Callaghan and Ryder caught up to him, both hands loaded with pointed guns. "You're gonna get back in the fucking car," Ryder said, grabbing hold of Jonathon's shirt collar.

Jonathon twisted, swinging his fists. He hit something, and a gun went off. The bullet punched a hole through the shoulder of Jonathon's coat. The shot ricocheted. Callaghan swore and froze in position. Jonathon tried to swing again, but he shouted instead, surprised by the burning pain and non-responsiveness of his arm. He looked at his shoulder. The bullet had punched a hole through more than his overcoat. He was bleeding. Callaghan swore louder, as if it was Jonathon's fault and as if Callaghan was the wounded party. Ryder rushed Jonathon, spun him around and pinned him against the Pontiac with one arm behind his back. Jonathon shouted as Callaghan grabbed him by the wounded arm and wrestled him into handcuffs; in the tussle, all three fell face first to the ground, with Jonathon at the bottom of the pile.

"You want another Christmas present, Jonny? Huh?" Callaghan said in his ear. "Then Merry fucking Christmas." Ryder got two good kicks in before Callaghan pistol whipped Jonathon across the back of the head. Jonathon flattened, all the fight knocked out of him. Someone unlocked the cuffs and wrenched them off. A moment later, and tires squealed out of the lot, their shriek echoing a second time when they turned a corner and sped away.

Jonathon lay in a twisted, dazed heap. He didn't know for how long.

In the distance, he could hear tinny Christmas music played over the exterior speakers of the shopping centre nearby. It was Christmas night. No one was coming by, not until after Boxing Day. Jonathon grunted and rolled onto his side. His head spun. His shoulder burned. No matter how much he coaxed or urged himself, standing up seemed too far away and too pointless. He was grateful at least that the night wasn't that cold.

Warm, yellow headlights ran over Jonathon's head and shoulders. Then the lights changed colours: red, blue and white. The cruiser parked inches away from Jonathon's head and outstretched arm. A man got out, scratching the salt and pebbles under his boot; he walked over. Subdued voices and squelch came over the officer's radio handset, as updates, instructions and questions were relayed in a language unique to the police.

The officer gently kicked Jonathon in the back. He didn't move. "Hey," the officer said. He kicked him again.

Jonathon caught the officer by the ankle and pulled. The cop's other foot shot up, and he fell down, hard. In a blind rage, Jonathon tumbled upon the fallen officer and punched him across the face with his left and right fists, and using the cruiser as support, Jonathon got up and kicked the officer in the side. Jonathon clutched his shoulder and stopped when he couldn't catch his breath. It was neither Ryder nor Callaghan. The uniformed city cop had stopped moving, and his bloody eyes were closed. Jonathon swore. He ran for his car, got in and drove away before the fallen officer could see who had hit him.

Jonathon snuck in by the back door and went straight to the washroom. All the lights were off in the house, except for those on the tree; the TV was also on in the living room. The volume was turned down. Jonathon closed the bathroom door behind him. His coat had been torn through, as had his sweater and his shirt underneath, and all of them were caked in blood. The shirt peeled away like a bandage stuck to arm hair. He winced, and he showed the mirror his wound. For something that bled so badly and hurt so much, it didn't look like anything more than a scratch. He cleaned up the edges with water and rubbing alcohol, then bandaged it with whatever he could find in the first aid kit. His face wasn't badly bruised, but his chest was dappled with red and purple bruises, each the size of a softball. His lower back looked as bad.

He came out of the bathroom without his shirt on, and he went straight to the wet bar for back to back tumblers of Scotch. Jennifer roused, where she'd fallen asleep on the couch in front of the TV. "Well

I had a great time tonight," she muttered, "trying to keep your parents entertained while you were out."

He finished his second tumbler. "I'm sorry," he said. "It wasn't McElvoy."

She sat up and roused a little more. She noticed his bandage. "Damn it! Won't they ever give up? There's nothing left they can do!"

"I wish you hadn't said that," Jonathon said. He refilled his glass.

Rus Bentley's office was in a prestigious, three-storey, turn-of-the-century mansion on a half-acre, well-treed lot. The finely crafted sign on the lawn read "Bentley & Company, Barristers and Solicitors".

Rus Bentley himself was a prestigious looking man with jowls, a man who looked like he belonged with the Conservatives in the House of Commons, and not in a lawyer's office. "Mr. Parker," he said. "Nice to meet you. How are you?"

"I'm fine, thanks."

They shook hands and sat down to business. "I've reviewed the files that Robert Downes sent over, and I can confirm that your retainer has been put into our trust account." He opened the file folder on his desk and handed Jonathon a receipt for the retainer. "He also mentions in his notes that you may have some mini-cassette tapes to bring to me as well."

"Unfortunately," Jonathon said, rubbing his bruised abdomen, "those have been since lost."

The man frowned, making his jowls look even bigger. "Well then, that is unfortunate. Never mind then. Now, where shall we start?"

REGINA. SPRING, 1982.

They'd been sharing a couple of beers to celebrate the launch of a new flower shop under Jennifer's name, and until then, it had been a quiet night in front of *The Alan Thicke Show*. Outside, the

January windstorms blew through. It made for poor reception on TV.

"It's been a while since you heard from that new lawyer," Jennifer commented. "Have you heard anything new from him? Is he ready for the fall?"

"I don't see why not," Jonathon said. "But why worry now? We don't even know when the new trial date is."

"Yeah, but will he be ready?"

"Probably. He's supposed to be one of the best in the city, and he's got all of our files. And Cory says his lawyer has talked to him a couple of times too. If there was a problem, he'd call us."

A couple of days later, Rus Bentley called with a problem. "Mr. Parker," he said, "I'm sorry to have to inform you of this, especially after this much time having passed, but a serious conflict of interest has come to our attention, and I must withdraw as your counsel on this matter of the arson."

Jonathon said, "What? I can't believe this!"

"I am truly sorry, but the matter is out of my hands! The rules are very clear with respect to the potential conflicts."

Jonathon's lips flapped, but no sound came out.

"Mr. Parker, are you still there?"

"Yeah. Yeah, I'm still here. Well...jeez...then send back what's left of the retainer to Dan Jenkins and I'll figure out what to do from there, I guess."

This time it was Bentley who was slow to respond. "You must realize your retainer has already been spent on research by our firm. There's nothing left to send anywhere."

"Well that's just fantastic! All right then, I'll come by later today, myself, and pick up the research you've done. Would two o'clock be okay?"

Gently, the lawyer said, "I am sorry, but that research clearly belongs to our firm." Bored, haughty, inconvenienced, he added, "I can release a copy of our case file and that of Mr. Downes, of course, but that's all."

"Seriously. You'd do that to me?"

"Mr. Parker, I'm sorry, but this conversation is now at an end."

The line went dead. Jonathon crushed the receiver in his hand, and when his anger boiled over, he screamed a curse and slammed the handset onto its base.

A few days later, after dinner while the kids were playing or watching TV, Jennifer said, "Lawyer number four...Is this one any good?" They were washing dishes together.

"McGuire?" Jonathon asked. He dried the plate that was handed to him. "I doubt it. All the good lawyers have been warned off the case."

"By Ryder and Callaghan?"

"Probably. Oh, but I did get this *fascinating* letter back from the law society. You remember, the complaint I sent about Rus Bentley?"

"Yeah. Why fascinating? Are they going to do anything about him?"

Jonathon laughed at that. "Well, essentially, they say they've completed their investigation into my allegations of his misconduct. And they came back and said that 'he has not acted with any improprieties', and that my 'allegations are without substance.'"

"That's not fascinating. That sucks!"

"No – the fascinating part is this: the letter exonerating Russell L. Bentley of any improprieties was signed by the president of the law society of Saskatchewan – who just *happens* to be Russell L. Bentley! Talk about a conflict of interest, eh?"

"That's disgusting," Jennifer said. "So now what do we do?"

Jonathon shrugged. "We trust in the evidence and hope for the best."

CHAPTER TWENTY-ONE

REGINA. FALL, 1982.

It was several days into the trial. The judge, a shrunken relic of an old man, would balance his chin on his hands and periodically close his eyes as if asleep. He jolted when the Crown Prosecutor asked a loud question, and he turned to listen more intently to the Regina City Police Constable David Salisbury, who was in the witness box. Jonathon and Cory sat at the defence table with their two lawyers. Of the two, Malone was a sharp, cynical but reliable looking young lawyer, with dark curling hair cropped close to his head. McGuire on the other hand was the dictionary picture of a dunderhead. He was a doughy man in his early sixties, ill-dressed, wearing a gaudy orange tie, and he had a habit of picking his nose, rolling the specimen between his finger and thumb, and examining it before "subtly" flicking it away under the defence table.

Once again, the gallery was filled with reporters, Jonathon's family and in-laws, Bob Myers, and Pat Burton, who was again trying to tell a joke to Bob Myers. But this time the composition of the audience was a little different. Ivan Petrovski was trying unsuccessfully to disguise himself as a very small, very empty wooden chair. Jonathon wondered if he'd settled his affairs with Revenue Canada.

The prosecutor coughed, waking the judge. "Are you absolutely certain that the two men you saw entering the building with the gasoline containers were the Accused?" He flung his arm backwards and pointed blindly at Jonathon and Cory.

Salisbury adjusted his tie. Like most beat cops, he seemed completely uncomfortable in a suit and tie, but his voice and mannerisms were confident. "Yes I am. From my position on the adjacent roof-top, I was able to make a positive identification."

Cory sat forward, grinding his teeth. Malone touched him on the shoulder, pushing him back into his chair. But Jonathon had caught the discrepancy too. He wrote it on a note and passed it to McGuire, who quickly flicked his latest booger under the table and took the notepad from Jonathon. He read the note, hooked his thumbnail into his nostril, picked out another bit of white gunk and promised he'd act on what Jonathon had written. Malone leaned over and read the same note. He didn't give any reaction.

The prosecutor asked, "What did you see next?"

"A couple of minutes passed, then the door opened and they backed out of it, splashing liquid from the gas cans onto the building and the ground around the back door area. They tossed the cans down near the back door, and Carter made a striking motion near his foot, and the fire immediately ignited. The flames shot up about fifty to sixty feet."

Cory had jumped to his feet, but Malone caught him by the elbow and sat him down again. The judge, in a rare moment of alertness, shot a scolding glare at the defence table. Jonathon wrote another note and passed it to McGuire, who didn't react.

Later, the prosecution asked its final questions and turned the floor over to the defence for cross-examination of the witness. What Malone lacked in volume, he more than made up for in class. He had a tendency to pace before the bench and the witness stand like a bullfighter, pelvis first.

Jonathon heard a cough behind him, and the hairs on the back of his neck rose. Thinking he recognized the voice, he slowly turned. Joe McElvoy crossed his legs. How long he'd been there, Jonathon had no idea. And whether the NCIS investigator was there to help or hinder, Jonathon couldn't guess. He was the last one to have the mini-cassette tapes. There was no way to know whose side McElvoy was on. He had lost his ability to judge who was an ally of Jonathon Parker or an accomplice of Ryder and Callaghan. Everyone seemed to turn against him, sooner or later. It was like living in a slow, dull remake of *The Bodysnatchers*.

"Constable Salisbury," Malone said, "is it true that your stake-out position was just over three hundred feet from the rear door of the building?"

"Yes," Salisbury answered, "but it was a very well lit area."

"Even so," Malone mused aloud, "I find it difficult to believe that you could positively identify anyone from such a distance. You previously testified that they appeared from the darkness in the area of the westerly side of the parking lot. Then they entered into your well lit field of vision, but were then heading toward the rear door, which, when considering your vantage point, would indicate that they were facing *away* from you at all times. Is that correct, Constable?"

"Yes it is, but…"

"Just the answer to the question, Constable. And you also testified that when they came out with the gas cans, they were…" Malone checked his notes. "'The door opened and they backed out, splashing liquid from the gas cans onto the building and the ground around the back door area.' Is that correct?"

"Uh, yes it is."

"So, until this point, you only saw the two men from behind, so you could not yet have identified those two men, correct?"

Salisbury answered, "Yes, I guess that's correct."

"Yes or no, Constable. We don't guess in court."

"Yes, it's correct."

"Thank you." Malone flipped the pages of his notes. "Yet you testified earlier, that at this point in the sequence of events, 'Carter made a striking motion near his foot, and the fire immediately ignited.' Would it not be more accurate, Constable, to say that 'one' of the two men, neither of whom you could identify at that point, made that striking motion that ignited the fire?"

Salisbury hesitated, and he seemed to chew his words before letting them fall out of his mouth. "Yes, at that point, that would be more accurate."

"What did the two men do after the fire ignited, Constable?"

Salisbury shifted his position, leaning forward slightly, as if he'd regained his confidence. "They immediately turned and ran behind a row of evergreen hedges at the east side of the parking lot, and then they were out of my sight. But I assume they ran toward the front of the building where Parker was arrested."

Malone's eyebrows had risen from the word *assume*. "That's an odd assumption, Constable. The arresting officer has testified that he apprehended Mr. Parker coming *out* of the *front door* of the building, not from beside it."

The audience mumbled and muttered, sounding like something out of an episode of Perry Mason. The judge didn't react.

Malone said, "From your stake-out position, what direction were you facing, Constable, when looking toward that rear door?"

"Almost due south."

"So someone running east from that door to the row of hedges would essentially be looking away from you again. Correct?"

"Well, yes, but – "

"Well my question is, Constable Salisbury, how and when did you identify these two men, having now admitted to never seeing either of their faces during this entire sequence of events?"

Salisbury answered smugly, "I could tell who they were by the *clothing* they were wearing."

Members of the audience laughed. The judge didn't. His eyes were closed.

"I see," said Malone. "So if I'm understanding you correctly, what you are saying is that the two men you saw going in the building carrying gas containers are presumably the same two men you saw coming out of that building splashing gasoline all over the place, because they all wore the same clothing. But in any event, any of those men could have been anyone wearing similar clothing as the accused were?"

Salisbury had been turning red in the face during Malone's summary. He looked at the Crown Prosecutor, who was studiously avoiding eye contact with him. "I assumed they were the same men."

"The same as which men, Constable?"

"As the two I saw go in."

"Yes, the two you saw from behind," Malone said. "Constable, what colour were the jackets the two men you saw wearing?"

Salisbury checked his own notes. "One was light coloured, and one was darker coloured."

Malone blinked. "Sorry, could you tell what *colour* their jackets were, or for that matter, do you recollect whether or not they were wearing jackets, or some other form of clothing?"

Salisbury referred back to his notes. "I could tell one of them was wearing light coloured clothing and the other was wearing darker clothing. As to the exact color, or type of clothing, I couldn't tell for sure. It was too far away."

Malone nodded. "Yet you would have us believe that you somehow were close enough to make a 'positive identification' of the two accused?" Salisbury said nothing. Malone turned away from the witness stand, saying over his shoulder, "I have no further cross-examination for this witness at this time, your Honour."

Jonathon and Cory both relaxed. The prosecutor was visibly unimpressed. The judge, drowsy as ever, dismissed Salisbury from the stand and said, "Call your next witness."

On the evidence table, there was a large plastic bag full of clothing, presumably the clothes that Jonathon had worn. Beside it was a second plastic bag labelled as Cory's clothes. Two red plastic five-gallon gasoline containers had also been entered into evidence.

A different police officer was on the witness stand this time, and Malone was asking all the questions in his subdued but clear voice. The witness was Corporal Willard Scott, a veteran RCMP officer and an expert witness called to testify about chemicals found on the evidentiary clothing. While the rest of the courtroom seemed alert and stapled to the edges of their seats, the judge had once again propped up his chin on a fist and was fading fast.

"Corporal Scott," Malone said. "You testified to the prosecution that the clothing you received, presumably the clothing belonging to the two accused, was all *equally soaked* in gasoline. Is that correct?"

The corporal answered, "That is correct."

"And you performed the chemical analysis yourself."

"Yes I did, in the presence of my lab assistant."

"In your expert opinion, if a person wearing any of this clothing was to strike a match or be within arm's length of flames that were leaping fifty to sixty feet into the air, would you expect this clothing to have ignited?"

Scott replied, "The amount of gasoline that was on this clothing at the time I conducted my analysis would produce sufficient fumes to risk ignition if it were that close to even a very small flame."

Malone nodded. "Is there any way that you are aware of that this clothing would not have ignited if it were within the proximity of the flames as described by Constable Salisbury?"

Scott thought it over. "In my opinion, it would be impossible for anyone to be that close to open flames wearing any of this clothing and not burst into flames themselves."

A chair screeched across the hard wood floor. The Crown Prosecutor had leapt to his feet, and he was signalling to the judge. "Your honour, may I have a moment to confer with the witness?"

Cory glanced at Jonathon, who was helpless to explain. It seemed fishy to Jonathon as well. But the judge waved his hand, bored with the whole ordeal, and the prosecutor approached the witness stand. The witness answered a few questions that were too quiet to be held on the record, and after a few moments, the Prosecutor returned to his table and sat down, looking angry. McGuire picked his nose, rolled the nostril turd into a flickable wad and got rid of it under the table.

Malone glanced at the Crown Prosecutor with visible sarcasm, as if to ask if he could now continue. He didn't wait for a response. "Is it true that gasoline evaporates quickly, particularly gasoline residues such as what might be found as a result of splashing onto clothing?"

Scott raised a shoulder. "I wouldn't say 'quickly'. The rate of evaporation varies greatly depending upon a number of variables."

"You are the expert, Corporal Scott. Please elaborate regarding these 'variables' and how we lay persons should consider them."

"Well, there is first the manufacturing brand of the gasoline, the grade, the amount, the type of clothing or material the gasoline has contaminated…And perhaps the most significant of these are the timing between the contamination of the materials and the collection of those materials as evidence, and particularly, the method of preserving those materials from the time they were collected and processed as evidence to the time they were analyzed in the lab. All of these variables, or rather each of them, has significant effect upon the rate at which the gasoline would evaporate from the clothing in question."

Malone inclined his head. "Thank you, Corporal Scott. That was very helpful. Are you familiar with the testimony of the two Regina City Police constables who were the arresting officers in this case, regarding their handling of the clothing as evidence in this matter?"

"No, I was not present in court when they testified."

"Let me briefly recap portions of their testimony as I believe it applies here. First, Mister Parker was arrested at approximately one thirty in the morning, coming out of the building almost immediately after the fire ignited. He was taken to the City Police Station, stripped, and his clothing was placed in this evidence bag within forty-five minutes of his arrest, according to the city police evidence technician. My client, Mr. Carter, on the other hand, was not arrested until approximately ten thirty the following morning. His clothing, the clothing in this bag, was removed by one of the arresting officers from a washing machine, after it had apparently gone through the wash, rinse and spin dry cycles, but before being put into the dryer. That clothing was then placed unbagged into the trunk of the arresting officer's car, and left there until approximately three o'clock in the afternoon, when it was retrieved, taken to the evidence room, and finally placed into this plastic evidence bag, at approximately three thirty. What do you conclude from this sequence of events, Corporal Scott?"

The corporal looked from the judge to the prosecutor, then back to the judge. Then he looked toward McElvoy; Jonathon followed his line of sight. McElvoy nodded ever so slightly. No one else seemed to notice. No one spoke. No one moved.

"There is only one plausible conclusion," Corporal Scott said.

"I agree, Corporal Scott, but please elaborate for everyone's benefit."

"The clothing in those two bags was contaminated with the same amount of gasoline at precisely the same time, and preserved identically thereafter, until it was delivered to my laboratory."

When the noise level of the gallery grew too loud, the judge banged his gavel and demanded order. Several of the Regina City Police officers sitting in attendance got up to leave.

Malone said, "Thank you, Corporal Scott. I just have one more question for you. I noticed you *were* present during my cross-examination of Constable Salisbury. I'm going to refresh your memory to some small part of that. Constable Salisbury testified that, just prior to the fire being ignited, the two men both 'tossed the gas cans down near the door.' My question to you, Corporal Scott, as the chemical expert in this case, do you believe it to be in any way possible for someone to toss one or two of those presumably emptied gas cans onto the area that those same cans had just been emptied upon, ignite that spilled gasoline, and then expect to have the fire department arrive sometime later and retrieve those same plastic gasoline containers, with absolutely no evidence of them being scorched or otherwise damaged in anyway, by a fire that supposedly caused flames to leap sixty feet into the air?"

With the audience muttering its own testimony, Corporal Scott answered, "No, I do not believe such a result would be possible."

Malone smiled and said, "Corporal Scott, if I may, just one more quick question. If Constable Salisbury did in fact see two men toss two plastic gas containers onto the ground near that back door, could these containers be the ones he saw?"

"No sir, they could not be."

Reactions from the audience made Jonathon turn in his seat. Constable Salisbury was getting up and leaving.

"Thank you, Corporal Scott. That's all I have for you at this time."

Cory turned to Jonathon and grinned. McGuire picked his nose, sat back and crossed his arms. This time, he flicked the dried snot across the top of the table.

CHAPTER TWENTY-TWO

Given enough time, Ivan Petrovski could drown in his own sweat. All eyes were on him – except for the eyes of the judge. Petrovski answered questions as flatly as he could manage, as simply as he could manage, and only occasionally did he sweep a handkerchief across his brow. The Prosecutor had gone back to his table for a glass of water, and Petrovski took a moment to drink as well. He no sooner had the glass to his lips when Petrovski froze, eyes locked on the back door. Jonathon looked over his shoulder. McElvoy had also turned to see who was coming in. It was Ryder. Petrovski made sweating an Olympic sport, and his voice quavered.

The Crown Prosecutor returned, oblivious to the comings and goings of the audience behind him. "Dr. Petrovski, were you the owner of the College Street Apartments at the time of this fire?"

"Yes sir, I was."

"Did you make any insurance claims, or receive any compensation as a result of this fire?"

"N-no. Nothing." He made a subtle motion with his chin and shoulders; the look seemed aimed at Ryder, and it seemed like a question.

The prosecutor continued. "Have you ever had any business dealings with either of the accused?"

"Yes, I bought two buildings from Mr. Parker a while ago."

"Did you have any dealings with him regarding the College Street Apartments or any dealings with him on the day before, or the day of the fire?"

"No, I was out of town on the day of the fire."

Jonathon seethed. Cory looked like a deer caught in headlights; he turned to Jonathon, but Jonathon could say nothing.

Initial testimony for the prosecution continued for the better part of an hour. The clerk cast a quick glance around the courtroom to see if anyone was watching; then he nudged the judge out of his doze. Members of the gallery thought it amusing, but neither Cory, nor Jonathon, nor Malone – nor even the prosecutor – were impressed. Jonathon gazed over his shoulder to see what McElvoy made of it; he was busy watching Ryder, and Ryder was busy locking eyes with Petrovski, as if feeding him testimony by some force of psychic power. Callaghan sat with him now; he seemed to be enjoying himself. The prosecution concluded its questions, McGuire picked his nose and Malone rose to cross-examine. Malone began by asking, "Have any members of the RCMP ever approached you to partake in any schemes to entrap either of the accused?"

Petrovski's mouth opened and closed several times before he managed to say, "No, of course not!" He glanced at Ryder. So did Jonathon and McElvoy. McElvoy turned his attention to Jonathon, who nodded slightly.

Malone asked, "Is it true that you suffered a substantial financial loss on the building you purchased from Mr. Parker last year?"

"Yes, but that was just the way the market went. I did not blame him or anyone for that."

"Dr. Petrovski, do you owe a substantial debt to Revenue Canada for unpaid income taxes and for duty on undeclared items?"

Petrovski made an upset noise, and, trembling, he looked again at Ryder. Callaghan looked alarmed; he showed his expression to Ryder. Ryder raised his arm and shook it, presumably to shake his cuff loose from his watchband. The judge sat up, suddenly alert, and he looked at his pocket watch.

"Excuse me, Mister Malone," said the judge. Louder, he announced, "The court will take its morning recess now." He banged his gavel to make it official. Without another word, the judge stood abruptly and went to the door toward his chambers.

Jennifer got up and waded her way toward the defence table. Ryder put his hands on her shoulders and moved her aside as he rushed across the courtroom to the judge's chamber. Callaghan followed, hot on his

228

heels. McElvoy waited, then bolted from his chair like a man on a mission. Jonathon spurred the defence lawyers to action as well.

"Those two guys that followed the judge into his chambers," Jonathon said, "they're the two RCMP I've been trying to tell you about. They set us up. *They* set the fire, not us. And it's obvious now – they also made Petrovski's tax debts disappear, or why else...?"

Boogers McGuire had turned to Jonathon. He mumbled, "Now, let's not aggravate the situation."

"Wha – What do you mean? The first and only time the judge could stay awake was because those two assholes motioned for his attention."

McGuire was lifting and raising his hands, palm down, as if to tamp down the volume of Jonathon's voice. Malone was frowning, though. Jonathon had gotten his attention, and Malone was now watching the door of the judge's chambers. Cory was aghast, until he said, "That was them? And now they're with the judge?" He turned to Malone and said, "Well, aren't you going to do something about it?"

Malone didn't answer.

"And what's with the judge falling asleep all the time in the first place?" Jonathon asked.

Malone did answer that question. "To be honest, I was surprised when I first heard he was sitting on this case. He's been retired for nearly a year now."

"What?"

Malone nodded. "Those two RCMP must have something on him. Nothing else makes any sense at all. The problem now is: the trial is virtually over. We can't try now to introduce any of this as new evidence, because we really only have speculation, nothing concrete!"

"Wha..." Jonathon raised and dropped his arms, slapping his hands against his legs. "You've gotta be kidding me!"

Jonathon had no more fingernails left to chew. Cory had lost all of his on the first day of the trial. McGuire scratched his nose while Malone read his summation from his papers. "...that due to the absence of any firm identification of the accused having committed this offence, and in light of the obvious tampering with the evidence – that is, *all* of the alleged evidence – taken together with the remaining inconsistencies in both Salisbury's and Petrovski's testimonies, I beseech the court to allow the accused the benefit of the doubt, and to find them both 'Not Guilty.'"

The judge sighed. "Thank you, Mr. Malone. The court will waive the Prosecution's summation and proceed with its verdict."

Even the court reporters looked up and murmured *what?* and other exclamations. The prosecutor raised his eyebrows.

"Jonathon Edward Parker," the judge declared. Jonathon rose. The gallery was dead silent. "William Cory Carter." Cory also stood. "I sentence each of you to five years in the Federal Penitentiary."

Jonathon alone was silent; everyone had something to cry out. The lawyers from both sides of the case stood and spoke at once, and Malone said under his breath, "You're not supposed to pronounce sentence before you read the verdict – what's he doing?"

The judge seemed amazed by all the hubbub. Then he made a face of sheepish annoyance and said, "Oh yes! The court finds you both guilty of arson pursuant to the Criminal Code of Canada. At the Crown's request, all counts of attempted murder have been dismissed. The sentence of five years to each of you stands."

The prosecutor's mouth was open. "Your Honour! Due to the callous disregard for human life which was exhibited by these men during the perpetration of this *extremely* serious offense, the Crown wishes to be on the record as intending to appeal this sentence, and will seek to *increase it* to maximum of fourteen years as provided in the Code."

The judge shook his head and muttered too softly to be heard over the hue and cry in the courtroom. Cory jumped up and added his voice to the angry replies, and a sheriff rushed over to restrain him. Jonathon sat and closed his eyes.

"Appeal?" the judge asked, as if he'd been offered cold soup and some uncooked escargot. "Fine. It's your call. Court is adjourned."

Cory was beside himself. Two constables assisted the sheriff in removing Cory from the courtroom. Jonathon stared at McGuire, who shrugged and looked away, seemingly embarrassed but helpless – and unwilling – to offer any additional support.

"You son of a bitch," Jonathon said to McGuire. "You sold out too, didn't you?"

McGuire cleaned out his ear. A sheriff came to escort Jonathon from the room, and as Jonathon stood up, he gave one last look at his wife, who was sobbing, bereft and inconsolable.

CHAPTER TWENTY-THREE

DRUMHELLER INSTITUTION, DRUMHELLER ALBERTA. FALL, 1983

Jonathon and Cory had been brought to the same prison at the same time, and though they were housed in the same isolation annex – the fish tank – they rarely saw each other. The prison block was smaller and quieter than he had ever imagined a provincial prison to be. There seemed to be as many guards as prisoners here – maybe thirty of each at most. He later learned that all newcomers spent their first three weeks or so in this fish tank, under observation, until prison authorities could classify them into various groups before assigning them to cells in general population.

During this time, Jonathon was eager to get his appeals preparation underway. But the prison system had some hoops for him to jump through, first. During their first week, both Jonathon and Cory were brought to the prison psychologist for an interview. They sat quietly in an anteroom until a clerk called Jonathon and pointed him in the direction of a small, locked room. Inside, there was nothing but a desk and chair. He sat and waited in silence and in curiosity for something to happen. A few minutes later, the clerk returned with a test.

"This is a three part IQ test. The first part is a vocabulary test," the clerk said as he set down a dull pencil beside the stapled bundle of papers. "Second part is for abstract thinking. Third part is a logical IQ test. You can answer the questions in any book in any order. Do as many of them as you can in the next ninety minutes. I'll be back then to collect your test. You can start as soon as I close the door. When you're finished, slide the booklets through the slot over here, for marking."

Jonathon thanked him out of habit, and waited for the door to close before he opened the packages. He skimmed the questions. They seemed to get harder the farther through the booklets he went. So, as he used to do in high school, he attacked the questions from hardest to easiest; that way he would rush through the easiest questions when time was running out. The very last logic test question was over his head, but after that, as he'd expected, the questions got progressively easier, and he was able to gain speed as he worked backwards through the booklet. He took his time, filling out the multiple choice and long form answers, not because he had to, but because it was the first good, healthy, relaxed mental stimulation he'd had in days. When he was done, he closed the booklets and slid them through the slot.

Nothing happened.

He went back and sat patiently. A few minutes later, he got up and looked through the slot to see if the test had maybe gotten stuck. He only saw an office beyond, and no one was moving. A few minutes later, he got up to stretch and pace.

About half an hour after he'd finished his test, the door opened behind him, and he was called out. Two prison guards put him in manacles, walked him out of the room, down the hall, past his assigned cell, into an elevator and down to a lower hall. "Where are we going?" he asked.

"The hole," one of the guards said.

"The hole?" Jonathon asked. "What's the hole?"

They'd entered a bleak hallway lined with what looked like storage lockers, or restaurant refrigerators. One guard kept his hand on Jonathon's shoulder and one on his manacled wrists. The other opened the solid, metal door. The window in the door was about as long as Jonathon's forearm, and crisscrossed with what looked like chicken wire, embedded in the glass. Behind this door was another one, a barred barrier like the cell Jonathon had been in the past few days. Once free of his manacles, Jonathon was pushed through the double-secure doors.

"Solitary?" Jonathon asked. "What for? What have I done?"

They didn't answer. One of the guards closed the interior door.

"How long am I in here for?" Jonathon asked. "Can you tell me that much at least?"

"Two weeks," one of the guards said. Then they closed the exterior door.

It was as quiet as a tomb, and if not for the buzzing overhead light, it would have been as dark as a crypt, too.

If he'd known what crime he'd committed to deserve two weeks in solitary, Jonathon would have used the time to consider his actions and make amends. Instead, he spent those two weeks pacing in the six-by-ten cell, wondering what the hell he'd done to deserve such punishment, and cursing the names of Ryder and Callaghan.

He couldn't count the hours. He wasn't allowed a watch, and there was no clock. Mealtimes were arbitrary – sometimes twice a day, sometimes only once. He was allowed no literature with which to pass the time. For twenty-three hours of every day, he stayed in his cell; during one quick hour, he was rushed through exercise in a separate part of the courtyard under heavy guard.

At the end of those two weeks, different guards came to claim him and put him in manacles and escort him up to the prison psychologist. The shrink was drinking coffee out of a Styrofoam cup. "So, prisoner 4373," he began. "Do you understand why you were put in solitary confinement?"

"No, doctor," Jonathon answered flatly.

The psychologist regarded him, dumbfounded. "For cheating on your tests, of course."

Jonathon blinked at him.

"I've been marking these tests now for almost fifteen years, and no one has scored anything like this. No one is that good. Even I can't get that many answers correct. How do you explain that?"

Jonathon swallowed his initial response and said instead, "I don't know, doctor."

The psychologist pointed out the various answers and the weighted scores. "I can't submit these test results. No one can score this high without cheating, and we don't tolerate this behaviour in our institution. Now, unless you want to spend more time in solitary, I suggest you cooperate this time. I'll let you take a similar test, and this time, I expect honesty. There won't be any preparation or collusion this time, will there be?"

235

"No doctor," Jonathon answered. "Doctor?"

"Yes?"

"If I get a lower score this time, will you take that as my coopera-tion?"

The psychologist sipped his coffee. "Well yes, that's the general idea. It would prove you're not cheating."

Jonathon's eye twitched. "Do you want me to take the tests right away? Right now? I'd be happy to cooperate."

The psychologist sat back, seemingly appeased. "I'll call for a clerk to take you to the test-taking area." He picked up the interphone and called for someone to escort Jonathon to the next room.

About ninety minutes later, he was brought back into the psycholo-gist's office. This time, the psychologist was eating an apple, and he had no more coffee. He was reviewing Jonathon's scores again. "Bet-ter," was all he said. He flicked his finger at a guard, and Jonathon was brought back up to his original cell in the fish tank.

Over the intervening months since his sentencing, Jonathon had spent his time reading, researching and trying to prepare himself for the appeals process. His cell was hardly as cozy as Fred Anton's old office, or even his own office, back when he had one: he worked alone in his cell, sitting on a hard chair under a book shelf bolted to the wall beside the mirror. There was hardly enough floor space for both the chair and the cot, but it was enough. Most days, he had papers and books scattered over the remaining floor space and along his cot; somewhere between the pages, he would find his way out, he was sure of it. Jail was a pain in the ass, but anger drove him on, and every day he made a little inroad into his appeals case. Every day brought the appeal hearing that much closer.

The red tape was getting to him, though. In order to finalize his notes for the appeal, he asked one of the guards if he could use one of the typewriters assigned to the prisoners' pool. The guard said he could. Nothing ever came of it. So, a few days later, Jonathon asked someone else for it. He was eventually brought a form to request use of the typewriter. A week passed. Another week went by. He asked a guard what had become of the typewriter, and he explained that he'd already filled out the form. The guard shrugged and said that the form must have been lost; so he brought a new copy of the form for Jonathon to fill out. Another month went by, and still no typewriter. When he complained about it to a third guard, and when he explained it was for his appeals process – he needed to submit something more than hand-written notes drafted in charcoal pencil – the guard told him he'd filled out the wrong form, and that they were all out of the correct forms; in order for him to fill out the correct form, he had to fill out a form to request that form. At some point, Jonathon stopped trying to make sense of it; he filled out all the forms he needed to, and as the appeals date came closer, he asked daily for the typewriter. A few weeks before the appeals process, a guard explained to him that no typewriter had been found. Jonathon told him to forget it: his notes had been final-ized by hand, and there was no point in typing it out. Fifteen minutes later, a guard brought a typewriter over to his cell. He refused it, saying again that there was no point to retyping all his notes. He spent two more weeks in solitary confinement for 'willfully provoking a security officer.'

And every action was timed by the system, from the moment he woke up to the moment he dressed and shaved, to the moment he was sent back to his cell for sleep. Every hour was long, and every day had forty-eight of them – seventy-two, if he was in The Hole. It was a long year. And though he had a kind of corner office, he had come to hate the view; from the dizzyingly wide horizons of the open prairies he'd come to this place, as seen through a barred window: consecutive bar-riers of cinderblocks and barbed wire, and beyond that, the sculpted but dead, dusty Badlands of Alberta.

Whenever he was in general population, Jonathon spent a lot of his time working out in the courtyard with several other of the prisoners in the medium security facility. As a result, he'd lost some fat, but he'd gained muscle. It showed especially in his shoulders and neck, and it helped to deter most of the younger punks from making trouble. He hadn't noticed it, himself; there were no reliable mirrors in the facility, except for the cheap plastic things that were bolted to his cell wall. It was Jennifer who first pointed it out. She said that, if it weren't for the prison greens, the irritating fluorescent lights and the paleness of his skin, she would have said he looked sexier than ever.

She looked understandably tired. It was a long drive between Regina and Drumheller. And for her sake, he remained optimistic. They pressed hands against the glass. Jonathon made a kissing sound into the foul-smelling mouthpiece of the phone.

"I feel good about the appeal," Jonathon said. "Those two bozos can't get to all three of the appeal judges."

"I sure hope you're right." She massaged her brow. "It seems those two can do a lot of things we never expected."

"Well, my new appeal lawyer is optimistic about getting us off completely."

She forced a smile, but she was too tired to make it look convincing.

"Or at worst," Jonathon said, "getting the sentence reduced to time served. He thinks the evidence we have against the dynamic duo is finally enough to do us some good."

"How's Cory holding up with all this? Have you heard?"

"Pretty good, all things considered. He's riding on my lawyer's coattails for the appeal, but that's okay. It's the least I can do to help him out."

Jennifer shook her head. "I don't understand what's taking so long with this appeal!"

"The Crown is actually the one that filed the appeal to increase the sentence."

"Oh, that inspires confidence."

"We're just filing a defense, arguing to reduce the sentence, but we're also hoping to find a way to introduce new evidence to get the conviction overturned – or at least to get the sentence reduced. So, to some extent, the timing has been mostly in the Crown's hands." He leaned toward the glass and said, "I have a feeling it would have taken even longer to get an appeals court date if my own lawyer had tried to file one."

"Not that McGuire guy again."

"No, hell no. But Malone…We talked about it after the trial, and he says we have no grounds for an appeal."

"What?"

"Malone was so confident that we would win the initial trial – since there was no actual, valid evidence against us – that he chose not to object to anything that might have otherwise given us grounds to appeal. And of course that idiot McGuire went out of his way to make sure *he* didn't create any grounds for appeal. The only thing *that* guy excelled at was picking his nose."

Jennifer smiled. "I think we're both looking forward to your appeals date. At least then you'll be closer to home, and I don't have to drive all the way out *here*, just to see you."

"Yeah," he sighed. "God, I just hope these judges will actually stay awake long enough to take our case seriously. I think – "

They heard a click in the receiver. When Jennifer asked a question, Jonathon didn't hear it. The line had gone dead. Their time was up. Jennifer looked up over Jonathon's head. He felt the presence behind him before he heard the voice.

"Come on, Parker. You've got other visitors waiting."

Jonathon kissed his fingertips and pressed them against the glass. She did likewise, but Jonathon was being escorted away by the prison guard.

"Who's waiting for me?" Jonathon asked. The prison guard marched him down bland walls to a room marked "Case Visitors."

"Couple of Mounties to see you," the guard said. He unlocked and opened the door.

"Can't you tell them I'm unavailable?" Jonathon asked. The guard didn't answer. He drew his black baton, and another guard came from further down the hall to assist. Jonathon turned and went in without another word. He was thoroughly unsurprised to see Ryder and Callaghan. He was glad they'd come shortly after his visit with Jennifer. Whether she knew it or not, she'd bolstered his spirits. The guard closed the door with a bang.

Ryder threaded his fingers together behind his head. "So. You missed us?"

"I was all broken up," Jonathon answered, "but I'll get over it."

Callaghan was looking him over. "Saw your wife today," he said. "Bet you miss her." Jonathon didn't rise to the bait. "What's say we arrange for you to go home for Christmas this year? And what if we arranged for you to stay with her indefinitely?"

There was a packet of papers on the table in front of Ryder.

"Three meals a day, no dishes to wash?" Jonathon said. "No ringing phone calls, no rat race, all the legal documents I can read…and you want me to leave a place like this?"

They didn't smile. Ryder put his hands on the table. "Listen, we're eventually going to get Anton anyway. You help us out a little, we help you out at a little. That's how things operate. Everyone wins in the end."

"The relocation offers still stands," Callaghan said. "And we're feeling generous today, so we thought we'd up the cash to say…uh…an even million dollars, plus whatever it takes to buy you a place in Sydney, just like the one you have now. I mean, uh – heh – just like the house you have in Regina."

Jonathon sat down. Ryder and Callaghan watched him intently. Jonathon peered over the multi-page document, reading the accusations and the false evidence against Fred Anton. They hadn't spoken in a couple of years, Fred and Jonathon. They'd thought it safer that way, in case one phone or the other was bugged. It was safer for both of them that way. They'd been fighting Ryder and Callaghan too long to give them any ammunition now.

"I want out first," Jonathon said. "And I want the judgment completely overturned and my record wiped clean."

Ryder slid a pen across the table. "Sign the document," Ryder said. "We'll hang around, make some calls, and we'll get the warden to remand you into our custody before the day's over."

"Wouldn't Jenny be surprised to see you," Callaghan said.

Jonathon took up the pen and hovered it over the final page of the document. "I bet she will be," Jonathon said, sharing a smile with them.

He snapped the pen in two and dropped it on the table.

"But not today." Jonathon picked up the document and walked it over to the waste paper basket beside the door. "Guard!" He sensed Ryder and Callaghan moving behind him. "Guard!"

A key grated into the lock and the door opened. The guard looked mildly confused. He chucked his chin at Ryder and Callaghan, asking, "Is everything all right in here?"

"Absolutely!" Ryder said. "But could you give us a couple more minutes alone with Mr. Parker?"

"No problem." The guard lifted his hand in salutation, and closed the door again. Jonathon heard the lock turn.

Ryder collided against Jonathon, crushing him against the wall. He had his forearm braced against Jonathon's neck, bruising his chin against the cinderblocks. "Here's the deal. You don't like our olive branch? Fine. We don't like your attitude. Your sentence appeal is *just* around the corner." He emphasized his words with an extra thrust of weight against Jonathon's neck. "You like it so much in here? We're going to get your sentence *increased* to six years. That should give you ample time to adjust your attitude."

"You think you can sway three appeals court judges?" Jonathon asked. "I don't think so." It was hard to breathe, and the forced bend in his neck made it hard to speak. "They'll be the real deal this time, and not some old fart you can bribe out of retirement."

Ryder took hold of Jonathon's head and bashed it against the wall. Jonathon stumbled, arms pin-wheeling backward, and Ryder wasn't there to catch him. He fell against the table and caught himself from falling to the floor. "Guard!" Ryder called.

The guard returned, and at an affirmative glance from Ryder, he plucked Jonathon away from the table and launched him into the hall, where a second guard caught him and yelled at him for trying to run. They all but frog-marched him back to his cell.

SASKATCHEWAN SUPREME COURT, APPELLATE DIVISION. REGINA. FALL, 1983.

The three judges sat at their crescent shaped bench, each watching Jonathon, Cory, and Jonathon's lawyer. The man sitting behind the name plate marked "Chief Justice J. R. Compton" was speaking. Ryder and Callaghan were sitting behind the accused, poorly disguised as reporters. Jennifer and Norma were there too – Jonathon had seen them come in – but now he didn't dare look away from the presiding judges.

"…I have great difficulty appreciating how two intelligent men, in full command of their faculties, could plan and execute such a callous and terrifying act. Whatever your motives, you were criminally corrupt and neither of you showed any remorse, each contending your own innocence."

Jonathon kept his mouth shut, because judgment hadn't been handed down yet. Cory, on the other hand, stepped forward and was restrained by the sheriff.

"We're innocent, dammit!" Cory shouted. "Why would we show remorse?"

The Chief Justice glared at Cory, then at Jonathon, who hung his head. "In the interests of general deterrence, and in maintaining the public's respect for the administration of justice, I feel more than justified to increase Mr. Carter's sentence from five years to *eight* years."

Cory screamed and ranted. They dragged and carried him out of the court.

When it was quiet enough, Chief Justice Compton resumed. His voice was level and firm. "And since Mr. Parker gives indication of learning the hard lesson which Mr. Carter seems incapable of learning, I will only increase his sentence from five years, to six years."

The blood drained from Jonathon's face. He heard both Jennifer and Norma gasp and sob.

CHAPTER TWENTY-FOUR

STONY MOUNTAIN INSTITUTION, STONY MOUNTAIN, MANITOBA. JULY, 1984.

Jonathon spent some of his free time either spotting or lifting with several of the weightlifting buffs in the gym and in the courtyard; over the months that passed, he added more than thirty pounds of muscle to his tall frame, and, more importantly, he'd made a few friends. Some days, he spent time playing chess and card games with some of the quieter prisoners in the recreation rooms. He spent a great deal of his time reading quietly in his cell with the door open. He'd gone months being the Grey Man, neither the model prisoner nor the troublemaker. He made a point of being so uninteresting that guards routinely forgot his name and prisoner number.

It was nearing the end of free time, so Jonathon was rushing to read to the end of the article before they were filed away to their cells. He was sitting in the TV room reading the well-used news magazine when he heard the first shot. All noise stopped. Every prisoner froze. There was another shot, a loud crack as from a pistol. Most of the guards fled in the direction of the disturbance, leaving only a skeleton crew of very raw, very nervous guards to watch over the prisoners. Some of the prisoners set down their reading material and stood up facing the remaining guards. Jonathon kept his mouth shut and watched for the slightest instructions. Voices and guns were raised, and the prisoners were ordered to their cells. A handful lingered, posturing and challenging the guards. There was another shot, as flat and loud as a blast from a shotgun. Jonathon locked himself in his cell, waiting to know what had happened. He listened anxiously for news as other prisoners were ushered to their cells or returned by their own volition. He heard the shouts of prisoners and guards, doors jangling open, and full-out war. Prisoners were rioting.

Then things went quiet.

Jonathon sat on his bunk, waiting for the worst.

Hours later, men came running down the corridors wearing bala-clavas, Plexiglas face guards and bearing automatic assault rifles. Jona-thon got up to see what was happening – it looked as though Cuba had invaded and taken over the prison.

They announced a lockdown.

One cell at a time, prisoners were called out of their cells, and all possessions were pulled out, inspected and dumped into large plastic containers on a wheeled trolley. "Against the wall!" someone shouted. "Against the wall, feet apart, *move!*"

Jonathon stepped back from the bars.

"You! I said against the wall!"

Jonathon turned and complied. He wasn't sure who was talking, or to whom, but he complied anyhow. His cell door opened, and some-one pulled him out. His books were pulled down from the shelves and pulled apart. The guard confiscated a picture of his son Michael, who was looking like a five-year old little man beside his mother. His tooth-brush was thrown out into the corridor.

"Strip down," the guard said, poking Jonathon in the neck.

"What?"

"Get the fucking clothes off. Take 'em off now! Do it now!" There were two or three guards shouting at once, all saying the same things, even though Jonathon was already doing what they were ask-ing for. Out of the corner of his eye, he saw several other prisoners from his block stripping out of their clothes and out of their under-wear. One of the guards handed his weapon to someone standing beside him; he pulled blue latex gloves out of one of the pockets of his paramilitary uniform. "Assume the position," someone shouted in Jonathon's ear.

"I don't understand what this is about."

Hands grabbed Jonathon by the shoulder, forcing his head toward the cinderblocks between cells. "Strip *down*," the guard screamed in his ear. Jonathon raised his hands in surrender, and with trembling fingers, he complied.

At the far end of the row of naked prisoners, someone drew a sharp intake of breath. Jonathon could see the prisoner fidget and grimace.

Jonathon pressed his head against the cinderblocks. He wished himself a million miles away. Anywhere but there.

The second prisoner in the line-up cried out.

Jonathon closed his eyes and tried to withdraw deeper into his mind, but subtle noises and shouted commands drew him back to the here-and-now. *But I'm not a criminal*, he thought. *I'm not supposed to be here.*

"Assume the position!" someone howled in his ear. "Do you hear me? Assume the position!"

Jonathon put his hands against the wall and copied the posture of the prisoner to his left.

All that remained of Jonathon's possessions, if they could be called his, were the lidless toilet, a sink bolted into the wall, and the lattice-framework of his cot. There was no mattress, no blankets, no books, not so much as a means of keeping count of the days by writing a tick on the wall. He'd been naked since the riot and lockdown. TVs bolted along the common wall played the CBC during wakeful hours, but Jonathon's cell was between two of the sets, so he could only hear the news, not see it. Aside from the rare times guards came by with the meal trolley, he saw no other human face for days.

It was small comfort to think that Cory Carter was missing all this. He'd been sent to a penitentiary in British Columbia, far away from this lower level of hell.

"How much longer, do you think?" Jonathon asked. "Until we get let out, I mean?" His voice was raw. The tap gave nothing more than a drizzle, even with the faucet cranked open, and he had nothing but his hands to drink from.

The man in the cell beside him said, "I know what you mean. By my count, we've been in here at least forty-three days."

"You count funny," Jonathon said. "But that does explain why we smell so bad. God, what I wouldn't do for a shower." *What I wouldn't do for some clothes*, he thought.

"Careful," someone warned.

"How can you stink?" Jonathon's neighbour asked. "I'm too cold to work up a sweat. Damn near froze to death last night. Least they could do was give us a blanket, or turn on some heat or something. Damn."

Conversation dwindled away. It wasn't winter, not yet. And suffering a winter without blankets, clothing or hot food was too plausible to contemplate.

"What I want to know," Jonathon's neighbour whispered, "is how much longer until we *eat* something!"

"I'm guessing another eight or nine hours before the next feed cart," Jonathon said.

His neighbour chuckled. "Feed cart. Some kinda damned zoo, and we're all a bunch of shit-flinging chimpanzees." He was at the height of sarcasm when he added, "Jeez, I wonder what it'll be today. Should I eat the half slice of rancid bologna first, or should I eat the whole slice of yummy old bread? Did you know penicillin comes from mold? Just think of all the infections we're fighting. Oh, I know! I'll plug up the sink, run some water in it, and I'll make bologna soup! Decisions decisions."

Jonathon laughed at the tirade – until he heard the words *Stony Mountain Institution* on the TV. Someone else shouted for quiet.

"Officials report that conditions at Stony Mountain Institution have returned to normal. The scene of July's tragic stabbing deaths of two prison employees led to a lengthy lockdown, following threats of a prisoner-led riot..." The report went on about how some prisoners had been drinking contraband homebrew and had become belligerent, but since the lockdown, conditions had vastly improved. Jonathon couldn't see the video, but the reporter narrated a scene set, presumably, in the cafeteria. She dispelled any rumours that the prisoners were being deprived of food – as made obvious, she said, by the video. Jonathon wondered if they'd been actually filming the inside of Stony Mountain Institution, because sure as hell he hadn't seen the inside of the dining hall in well over four or five weeks. Someone down the corridor catcalled the reporter, and three others booed and shouted and mocked the report. The TVs went off, to everyone's disappointment.

A few minutes later, he heard the rattle of a gate. "Everyone against the back wall," a guard called. "Lunch wagon coming through!"

"That was a fast eight hours," Jonathon's neighbour declared.

Jonathon waited until he heard the paper plate slide under the bars before he dared move.

Dinner was unsurprisingly lean: one thin slice of white bread, half a slice of bologna, and half of a small apple. Jonathon caught the briefest glimpse of a prisoner in a green jumpsuit on food detail. Jonathon daydreamed of hand-knit sweaters, jeans and clean underwear. He remembered long winter nights curled up on the couch with Jennifer, a bowl of popcorn in her lap and a drink in his hands, watching the TV while listening to the fire crackle.

The lockdown dragged on. They were into their ninth week, and the news had long ago stopped feeding them updates on their situation.

Jonathon's hair was matted and his skin had begun to scab with dirt and caked on sweat. He hadn't said a word in thirty-six hours. He sat on the very edge of his cot near the bars. "Hey," he whispered. He heard his neighbour shift positions.

"Hey. You finally finish that apple core?"

"Yeah," Jonathon said. "And the orange peel."

"How the hell'd you finish the orange peel?"

"Put it in the sink with some water. I made some tea."

His neighbour dared a quiet laugh.

"There wasn't enough for two, sorry," Jonathon said.

"Was it any good?"

"Tasted like shit," Jonathon said. "Watery, citrusy shit."

"God, I'm so hungry I could eat dog food. I don't know what I want more, food or a blanket."

"You'd probably eat the blanket," Jonathon answered. His friend snickered.

At the sound of locks opening, they shut their mouths.

Jonathon ran his hand over his face. The mirror was little more than a square of plastic with a reflective coating on the back, but it was better than nothing. For the first time in months, he was clean-shaven, and he was scheduled for a hair cut in a few minutes. Just because he could, he ran the water and thoroughly brushed his teeth a second time, then washed up and pressed a towel to his face. He'd lost weight and muscle mass, and no matter how many times he'd brushed his teeth, his breath smelled. But he'd slept. For the first time since the start of the lock-down, he'd curled up in a blanket on a thin mattress and slept for hours at a time.

He didn't look quite like himself. His face was too skinny, his hair too big and too wild. He looked like the Count of Monte Christo, the day he was rescued from the sea.

STONY MOUNTAIN INSTITUTION, MANITOBA. SPRING, 1985.

Jonathon, along with some of the other prisoners, had replaced some of the weight lost during the lockdown and the winter that followed. He wasn't as bulky as he had been before the lockdown, but he was cut. Many of his friends and fellow inmates wore the haunted, skeletal mask of men that had been starved. On the upside, the Institution had replaced some of the free weights – which could easily have been used as blunt force weapons during the riot – and in their place there were now multi-station work-out machines. He had clapped a hand with the man sitting on the chest-press bench, and was about to switch places with him when one of the prison workers called him away. One of a pair of guards gave him enough time to wipe down his face and chest with a towel, and the guard told Jonathon to come along. They led him upstairs. There, he spoke with another clerk, who told him he had a visitor.

Jonathon's heart fell into his bowels. Things had been stable for six weeks running. The last thing he needed was another visit from Ryder and Callaghan.

They gave Jonathon five minutes to get cleaned up and present-able, which was odd. If it was Jennifer come to visit, they didn't care if he had shat his underwear. If it was Ryder and Callaghan, they would have cared even less how he presented himself. So he cleaned up and emerged from his cell looking presentable and feeling like he was being led to the slaughter.

They took him to a room marked "Parole Review Room."

The last three times he was up for a parole review, he'd been denied, owing to his supposed links to organized crime. He hadn't been sched-uled for a fourth review.

One of the guards opened the door, and Jonathon was mildly relieved to see it was McElvoy. McElvoy didn't seem overjoyed to see Jonathon; he was all business, as usual. McElvoy nodded at the guards and told them to close the door.

"Take a seat," McElvoy said. He'd aged. "I finally have some good news for you."

"Don't tell me it's a late Christmas present."

McElvoy didn't get the joke. "I'm serious. I know it hasn't looked good from your point of view. And I know you haven't been getting a lot of updates from me."

"Try 'no updates.'"

"I've been working hard on the Ryder and Callaghan investigation. I couldn't risk a leak."

Jonathon relaxed his shoulders. "Really. Rumour has it you're all on the same team."

"Supposed to be," McElvoy admitted. "Until someone gets out of line. Turns out you were right about those two." Before Jonathon could launch a sarcastic reply, McElvoy said, "They've been running their own team."

Jonathon nodded. "So you believe me."

"We have evidence against them."

"Well...great," Jonathon said. "So...what do we do now?"

McElvoy canted his head. "It's complicated. For now, I've made arrangements for a parole review board to hold an emergency sitting. It's scheduled about..." He checked his watched. "About half an hour from now."

"Holy shit," Jonathon breathed.

"They don't know why, but they will release you into a half-way house in Toronto, ostensibly in my custody."

"That's funny," Jonathon said. "They turned me down three times already. Someone still believes I have links to organized crime."

"Oh, they will let you out," McElvoy said. "Now, you'll have to follow the rules of the half-way house, but it won't be for long. We'll have to settle on a place for full parole later, but for now, it's Toronto, in the half-way house."

Jonathon could hardly believe his ears. "I have a parole hearing in thirty minutes?"

"And they'll release you to the half-way house."

Jonathon shook his head. "Bu…but what about Ryder and Callaghan? They'll only follow me there and this is going to start up all over again."

"Oh, there's no question they'll be dealt with. But for right now, my main concern is getting you the hell out of here."

"But…"

"I've still got them under surveillance." McElvoy leaned close and said, "We're investigating several other matters at the same time, unrelated to your case."

"You mean…I'm not the only one?"

McElvoy blinked, but he neither acknowledged nor denied that there were more victims. "I'm hoping to have Ryder and Callaghan completely boxed in by the end of next month. Then you and I will have to have another serious discussion about testifying against them."

Jonathon smirked. "I think I might just enjoy that."

"Can't say as I blame you. Anyway, I've got a few quick calls to make before your parole reviewers get here. Then I'll see you in a few weeks."

"Wait – what happens to Cory Carter?"

"Right. Glad you asked. I was in B.C. last Friday. He was granted parole to a half-way house in Vancouver just yesterday."

"Really," Jonathon said. He stifled a relieved laugh. "Really!"

"He knows virtually nothing about our investigation of Ryder or Callaghan, but we'll deal with that later, too. For now, he thinks he negotiated his own early release by giving a statement to the Regina Police about his involvement in another matter."

"…You're not shitting me?"

"Parker, I haven't got time enough to fly all the way out here just to shit you." McElvoy stood.

Jonathon didn't trust his own legs. "Well…thank you!"

McElvoy extended his hand, and Jonathon shook it. "You're certainly welcome. One question though." McElvoy sat down again. "Why on earth didn't you take their offer? That was one hell of a lot of money. You must have figured out by then that they were serious about giving it to you."

Jonathon shrugged. "Yeah, it was a lot of money. And yeah, I knew they were serious. They may have been idiots and assholes, but they were always serious. But everything they wanted from me was a lie. I couldn't lie about Fred like that. Send him to a hell-hole like this, make him suffer for crimes he never committed? Just to satisfy those two assholes? Not bloody likely!"

"Well, Parker." McElvoy rose, this time with the intention of making up for lost time before the parole review. "You're one in a million, I've gotta say that." He patted Jonathon on the shoulder as he passed by. "Stay here until I come for you, for the parole review."

Jonathon entered the room. There was one folding table, three chairs, three parole reviewers and no place for either McElvoy or Jonathon to sit. McElvoy excused himself. The members of the parole review board sat down, and one of them opened the file folder labeled with Jonathon's name. The reviewer in the middle looked at the member on his right, then the one on his left, and with a nod, they got started.

"Good afternoon, Mr. Parker."

"Good afternoon."

"On carefully considering your appli…" The reviewer coughed. "On further consideration of the information provided to us, we've decided to reserve our decision to grant parole for another…" He referred to the open file. "Another six month period."

Jonathon closed his eyes and breathed.

"For this interim period..." The reviewer stalled again as he read through a note in the file. "During this interim period, you will be transferred to a day parole facility in Toronto, where your case will be re-assessed in due course."

Jonathon's knees buckled. He mashed his lips together to keep from crying out from joy and relief. He was getting out.

"Conditions of this day parole will be: that you report to the facility immediately upon your release. A transportation allowance from this institution to the destination facility will be provided as part of your release documentation. You will present these documents to the facility immediately upon your arrival. You will abide by the rules of the facility. You will seek and secure gainful employment. You will have no further associations with known criminals or criminal organizations. Do you understand?"

"I understand fully," Jonathon said.

"Congratulations, Mr. Parker. The security level classification of your incarceration has just gone from level 6 to level 2 – federal day parole."

CHAPTER TWENTY-FIVE

KEELE COMMUNITY CORRECTIONAL CENTRE. TORONTO, ONTARIO. SPRING, 1985

The taxi dropped Jonathon off at the corner after a pleasantly dull day at his job downtown. He paid the fare and thanked the driver. Coffee in hand, Jonathon walked up the steps of the half-way house, through the common room, and he stopped in front of the Commissionaire's desk. The security guard there opened the sliding Plexiglas panel and passed Jonathon the log book for the time and his signature. They exchanged pleasantries. Once Jonathon was logged in, he went to the pigeon holes to check his mail. There was an envelope waiting for him.

He carried the envelope down the hall to the recreation room. Other men were there playing pool and reading the newspaper. Jonathon said hello to someone he'd come to know and sat down beside his friend with his coffee and the envelope.

Inside the envelope was a snapshot. Michael was six years old, already off to school, and he had his father's eyes. Jonathon hadn't seen the boy since Drumheller. He could only guess how tall the kid was now. He wondered if Michael would recognize his own father.

He unfolded the lined paper, and he quickly raised his hand to his face to hide the surprising upwell of emotions. It was his son's blocky handwriting, using a fat pencil and a useless eraser. "I miss you Daddy. Love Michael." Jonathon draped the letter over his knee and took a quick slug of coffee. *I'm coming home, Michael. Real soon, I'm coming home.* He waited until he could trust himself to read. Jennifer had closed the letter. She'd written, "I'm sorry. Jennifer."

Jonathon ground the ball of his hand against his eye. When his friend asked him if he was okay, Jonathon replied that he had never been better. He took his coffee and went to his assigned bedroom.

Jonathon walked into the government-owned skyscraper with long strides. He was the first one to arrive, so the receptionist of the Attorney General's Office asked him to sit in one of the well-padded chairs in the waiting area. About ten minutes later, McElvoy entered. He went straight to the receptionist, and she asked him to sit as well. McElvoy nodded at Jonathon.

"Good morning," McElvoy said. He didn't smile, but his voice seemed happier and more enthusiastic than it had ever been before. "We'll wait a few minutes, and then we can use one of their private conference rooms so I can get you up to speed. Then we'll meet with the Attorney General to get things underway, okay?"

"Whatever you say. You're the boss."

"Damn straight," McElvoy said.

Jonathon shook his head. "No, I can't agree to that. The conviction's got to be overturned too."

McElvoy's jaw muscles were flexing. "Listen to me. That'll just cause everyone a lot of embarrassment."

"Embarrassment!" Jonathon echoed.

McElvoy waved his hands, pushing back Jonathon's argument. "We can probably make it happen. But it's no doubt going to take a lot of trade-offs on your other demands."

"Negotiation used to be a hell of a lot more fun," Jonathon commented. "Okay, forget it." He had a new idea anyhow. "Let's volunteer to shorten the list."

"What are you thinking?"

"A compromise." With a bitter smile, Jonathon added, "Everyone wins."

Had everyone left, the Attorney General's office still would have been crowded. Matching books lined walls, and plants grew out of pots balanced on the frame of picture windows. The AG had a spectacular view of the Toronto skyline. At the round meeting table, there were seated

Jonathon, McElvoy, a lawyer, a stenographer and the Attorney General himself. Jonathon was the only one not taking notes or scribbling addendums. There were two documents in the middle of the table, both titled RCMP Confidential Memorandum; one had Ryder's name on it, and the other, Callaghan's.

The lawyer smacked his notepad. "But that kind of negative publicity is not tolerable. We can't have the nation thinking that the RCMP are all a bunch of hoodlums. We'd lose all credibility!"

McElvoy interceded. "I think you've missed Mr. Parker's main point. He doesn't have any interest in embarrassing the RCMP in general. He simply wants to rid the country of these two bad apples – to rid the country *and* the RCMP of a blight against its reputation."

"Exactly," Jonathon said. "Obviously, I want Cory and myself absolved of all this crap – that goes without saying. But most importantly, I just want – no, not just want. I *demand* that Ryder and Callaghan be permanently banned from Canada after having their citizenship revoked, their pension plans terminated, and their domestic assets seized and donated to charity. It doesn't have to be a big public spectacle. Just get *rid* of them."

The lawyer scoffed. "That's a tall order, Mr. Parker. You can't expect us to..."

The Attorney General uncrossed his legs and sat forward. "Now hang on, Bob. I think Mr. Parker is being more than reasonable. For Christ's sake, he's just served almost four years of a six year sentence for something we all know he didn't do. He's had his licenses revoked, his property damaged and stolen, he's been blackmailed, beaten unconscious several times, his assets frozen – and stolen – What do you think? We should just say 'oops' and apologize?"

The lawyer seemed cowed.

The AG turned to Jonathon. "Mr. Parker, I admire your fortitude. If indeed, you will sign the twenty-five year non-disclosure as discussed, I see no reason not to proceed as you suggest. Bob, go with Helen and get this into a simple letter agreement right away. And do up the non-disclosure at the same time." He smiled. "We don't want Mr. Parker here to change his mind."

Jonathon's limbs trembled with giddy energy. He was hungry but too excited to eat. It was already past sunset. And he could eat whatever he wanted. He could hardly wrap his head around the concept. From rancid cold cuts twice a day to whatever the hell he felt like having for dinner. He puffed and laughed. It was good to be out of there.

It was good to be done with Ryder and Callaghan.

He couldn't believe it. It was over. Jonathon was free. He had won in the end. He'd *won*.

"Well," McElvoy said. They stood inside the government building exit, facing the steps down to street level. "Certainly a longer day than I had anticipated. But we did manage to get a lot accomplished, didn't we?"

"Yeah," Jonathon said. He smiled briefly. "Yeah, we did. I wish I could have gotten the criminal records cleared, though. But I can deal with that, especially since I'll never have to deal with the dynamic duo ever again."

McElvoy turned to him, regarded him, then offered his hand. Jonathon grabbed the man's hand and squeezed it in a handshake. "Good luck, Parker," McElvoy said.

"Thank you," Jonathon said. He'd never said anything with greater sincerity.

He watched as McElvoy did up his coat and left. They waved once, and McElvoy disappeared into the thick of evening commuter foot traffic.

It was over.

It was time to pick up the pieces.

REGINA. APRIL, 1986.

Jonathon had finished his work contract and returned to Regina as quickly as he could afford it. He called Jennifer from the airport, but there was no answer. He went to visit his parents first.

Norma had fed Jonathon cookies and snacks, but she'd been cool and quiet since he'd arrived. Jonathon sat across from his father, and she sat between them, looking at nothing but the kitchen wall. Edward's face was red despite his farmer's tan. A vein in his neck was standing out.

Jonathon pulled out an envelope from his inner suit jacket pocket. He set it down in the middle of the table.

"What's this?" Norma asked.

"Open it," Jonathon said.

Edward clutched a napkin in his hand. He squeezed it like he meant to wring the crumbs out of it. He flicked his chin at Norma, indicating that she should be the one to open it. She used a butter knife to cut the seal. "Oh Lord," she breathed. Her eyes sparkled. "What's this all about?"

It was a bank draft payable to Edward and Norma Parker: $350,000 to cover what they lost during the Corpus Christi deal.

"It's part of my settlement," Jonathon said. "I asked them to pay you back for what was taken. It should cover what you lost, plus a little interest."

Norma dropped her hands to the table. "But Jonathon, what about you? You need this to get back on your own two feet." She put the cheque back in his hands. "You need this more than we do."

Jonathon said, "It's okay. I have enough of my own. Don't worry about me."

"But Jonathon..."

Edward banged his fist on the table. "You throw money at us, and you think that'll make everything okay?"

"Edward!" Norma said.

"You think we can ever trust you again? You think this makes up for everything you've done to your mother and me?"

Jonathon averted his gaze and clenched his teeth.

"Hell of a lot of nerve you've got. I don't know where the hell you got that arrogance from, but it wasn't from me, because you're sure as hell no son of mine."

Edward got up from the table and stormed out of the kitchen.

Norma sat stunned. She was on the verge of tears. She still had the cheque in her hands.

Jonathon got up, kissed his mother on the top of her head, and he left for the front door. Jake stopped him, and they hugged. They didn't say anything to each other. They didn't have to.

Jonathon paid the taxi driver, and the driver wished him a good night. He knocked on the door.

Michael answered it. It took him a second. Then his eyes widened and sparkled. His mouth opened in an enormous grin. "Daddy!" he screamed. Jonathon bent at the hips and Michael took a flying leap into Jonathon's arms.

"I missed you so much!" Jonathon said in his ears. "You've gotten so big! Look at you!"

"I missed you Daddy," Michael said. "I missed you a lot!"

Jennifer emerged from further down the hall. She'd darkened her hair, and it was pulled back into a scrunchie. Her face was a blank.

Michael leaned back in Jonathon's arms and toyed with Jonathon's facial features as if they were made of putty.

A car drove up into the driveway. Thinking it was the taxi again, Jonathon turned.

It was a late model Dodge. The driver parked and got out, taking a briefcase with him. He cast a glance at Jonathon, but then passed through the open front door and kissed Jennifer on the lips as he walked inside.

Then the stranger stopped in the middle of the front hall, his back turned. He returned to the door way and asked Jennifer, "Is…is that…"

"Yes it is," Jennifer said. She couldn't make eye contact with any of them.

"Are you coming home for keeps now, Daddy?" Michael asked.

Jonathon stood on the front stoop with Michael in his arms. "I think your Mom and I have to talk over some things first, kiddo." The stranger was wearing Jonathon's favourite tan jacket, the one with the patched elbows. "And it looks like we have a lot to talk about."

Jonathon had aged, and so much had happened over the last four years that no one recognized him, no one but Jennifer. For the first time in a long time, they could sit at a table in a café and be left undisturbed.

"It's no problem," Jonathon said.

Jennifer toyed with her coffee mug. Her eyes misted, so she quickly finished her coffee.

"I'll call Dan Jenkins tomorrow and have him arrange to transfer the house into your name."

"We'd appreciate that," she murmured.

"The only stipulation: don't sell it so long as Michael is living at home. You can have custody, if you want, so he can stay at home. But please…I don't want to have any hassles over visitation rights."

She shook her head vigorously. "You won't have any problems there." She set her mug on the table. "He adores you, and I'd never take that away from him." Her eyes dewed again, and she turned her gaze to the rainy Regina streets. "You really are amazing about all this, you know that?" She looked at him. When she blinked, a tear fell down her cheek. "I am so sorry about all this."

Jonathon cleared his throat. *First Rita, then this. Why is it so damned hard…? First Rita, and now you. I trusted you.* "It is what it is." *Never make a pretty woman your wife…*

The waitress came by to clear the table. She asked if they wanted anything else. Neither did. The waitress left them to the sounds of cheesy pop music on the radio and the sound of the rain against the windows. "I really should get going," Jennifer said. "It's almost the kids' suppertime."

"Yeah," Jonathon said. He was free, and he had nowhere to go. He had absolutely nowhere to go. "Yeah, I understand."

CHAPTER TWENTY-SIX

VANCOUVER. FALL, 1986.

Jonathon stood in front of the table facing three national parole board review officers. Sitting with the reviewers was Joe McElvoy, who was trying very hard not to smile.

One of the reviewers made little referral to his notes. He'd either memorized what he had to say, or he was speaking from the heart. "… And the last two years of your parole will be unsupervised."

Jonathon smiled and thanked each of the reviewers in turn, shaking their hands as he walked from one end of the table to the next. He stopped in front of McElvoy, who'd stood up. Jonathon gripped his hand and gave it a firm shake; McElvoy clapped him on the elbow and winked. "Now get out of here," McElvoy said.

Jonathon didn't wait for a second invitation, but it was hard to say goodbye to the RCMP officer who had turned the tragedy around, and had defended him.

Jonathon was preparing an appraisal report on his computer when he heard a loud shout in the neighbouring office. There were only three private offices at Mitchell Stewart Industries, and as far as Jonathon knew, there were only four people at work. Jonathon leapt out of his chair and went to see what was the matter. Andrew Garnet fell out through his own office door looking like an excited fan boy. The sound had come from Rowan Howell's office.

"*Yes!*" Rowan shouted. He dropped his hands on his dreadlocks and hooted again. "*Andy, you've gotta…*" The middle-aged Jamaican turned and saw that both Andy and the company's president Jonathon were already peering through his open office door. "You've gotta hear this."

"What?" Andrew laughed.

"I did it," Rowan said. "My client in Amsterdam just signed the deal for three hundred metric tonnes of sugar from my supplier in Brazil. Our commission..." He paused for dramatic effect. "Is almost half a million."

"Wow!" Jonathon said. "Congratulations!"

"Yeah," Andrew said, "I guess you could say that's a real *sweet* deal." They laughed.

Jonathon raised his finger and said, "There's just one thing missing."

Rowan was crestfallen, but Jonathon crooked his finger and invited his two colleagues to join him in Jonathon's private office. "What?" Rowan asked as Jonathon opened a cupboard beside his desk. "What am I missing?"

Jonathon took out three snifters and said, "Cognac!" He showed them the bottle, and they eagerly agreed to a share.

VANCOUVER. SPRING, 1987.

Chris Burnette sat back and scratched his head, whistling low and in amazement. Jonathon nodded at the skinny documentary writer, saying, "It's a hell of a story, I know."

They had met in Jonathon's private office back at Mitchell Stewart Industries.

The private investigator, James Arnold, was cut from the same mould as McElvoy: husky, distinguished-looking, and despite his casual attire, he was all business. His was a master-class poker face. While he waited for Burnette to finish writing a reminder to himself, Arnold thumbed through his own notes. Arnold looked like a man with a question.

"So, other than getting our hands on those few items, I think we've fairly well covered it all, from beginning to end," Jonathon said.

"Okay then," Arnold said. "I seem to have my work cut out for me. Let me see if I've captured everything." He licked his thumb and flipped to an earlier page. "I need to get copies of all the court transcripts, plus all four trials, *plus* the appeal. I'm gonna need the Regina Leader-Post newspaper articles for the dates in question, a copy of the article in January '78 issue of the Edmonton Journal Week-Ender magazine, and transcripts from the local television newscasts and radio broadcasts for the relative dates. I'm going to need statements from the Regina City Police, from the RCMP, the Attorney General's Office, from the Parole Board and from all the lawyers involved. I'm going to need copies of the Mansard Reports for the Saskatchewan Legislative Assembly for that period, and a statement from the Attorney General's Office. I'm also going to need copies of the Customs Search report in Regina back in '79. Oh – and I'm going to have to get statements from Fred Anton and his lawyer. I think that's it. Did I miss anything?"

"I think that fairly well sums it up," Jonathon said. "I can go through some of my old files and see if I have any of it left, but it's probably best for you to plan on having to find everything from scratch. You can imagine, but it's been hard keeping all my files intact, after the last couple of years."

"No doubt," Burnette said. He rubbed his lean hands together and said, "Well, at least I have enough of an outline to get started on for the documentary, and a rough draft for the narration. But I've got to tell you, I'm not sure I want to take it to the screenplay stage or not. Either way, this type of exposé is definitely going to ruffle some feathers, big-time."

"All right," Jonathon said, reaching across the table. "Let's go back to the non-disclosure agreements, the ones I signed in the A.G.'s office. When you cut through all the legal jargon, what you get is an agreement not to make any of this information public for a period of twenty-five years. Obviously, that's meant to cover whatever's not already on public record. So what I can do is have you both sign a similar non-disclosure agreement, at least until I get the okay from my lawyer to release any of it further than for our own private discussions."

"We'll have to change the names in the story," Burnette said.

Arnold grunted. "Gee! You think so?"

Jonathon was feeling better and worse at the same time. His story had to be told, if only for the sake of making others aware that they, too, could become a victim. Jonathon was just an average guy, intelligent and caring; if it could happen to Jonathon, it could happen to anyone.

VANCOUVER. SUMMER, 1987

Jonathon's office had become a jungle of files and banker's boxes. The amount of research that James Arnold had compiled was simply staggering: there were loose documents captured in file folders, and there were videotapes, audio tapes, newspapers, magazines, everything. Jonathon's colleagues Andrew and Rowan had helped bring all the material up from James' car.

Chris Burnette's burden looked skimpy by comparison. He dropped five, ring-bound documents on the table, each about an inch thick. "So there you have it," he said. He'd provided enough copies of the documentary script for everyone. "It's still very rough, but now that we have all of the research material..." He seemed intimidated by the stacks of materials the private investigator had collected. "Now that we have all this, I can quickly and easily fill in all the blanks." He shook his head. "And it still makes for a hell of a story."

Andrew was studying the details as he handed Jonathon a copy of the two-part invoice. Neither the services of Arnold Investigations nor the writing skills of Chris Burnette came cheap. Andrew commented, "For that price, it had better be a hell of a story."

"That 'story' cost me a hell of a lot more than that over the last few years," Jonathon reminded them. "A hell of a lot more." He pointed at the boxes. "Do you need this?"

"Oh, God, no – thanks," Burnette replied. "I already have it. Your P.I. friend here gave me a copy of everything and delivered it to my place this morning. The last thing I need at my place is another box of research."

VANCOUVER. SPRING, 1988

Jonathon was sharing a quiet laugh with Fred Anton over dinner at Anton's house. Anton's wife guffawed at Anton's awful puns, and the lawyer Harvey looked like the joke had gone over his head – which only made Jonathon and Anton laugh that much harder.

Anton had suffered a heart attack in recent months, and though he showed signs of slowing down, he showed no signs of stopping. But he had become demure, somehow, and he'd lost some weight, making him look unkempt and deflated.

But there was a shine in Anton's eyes like never before. When he looked at Jonathon, it was with a fire in his eyes; Jonathon didn't know if it was because Anton was proud of Jonathon, or because he was furious at what had happened between Jonathon and his two persistent attackers, or because he looked at Jonathon and was reminded of wilder days of champagne and high-stakes gambles. Anton had a way of expressing many conflicting emotions with a single look.

They'd kept up a meagre correspondence while Jonathon was in jail, and to keep Anton from worrying too much, Jonathon spoke rarely and vaguely of his experiences there. Once Jonathon moved to Vancouver, they resumed their friendship, though their social lives were hardly so adventurous or chaotic as before.

Anton had explained why Ryder and Callaghan had hated him so fiercely over the years. All three had been in high school together. All three had been on the football team, and when it came time to choose a new quarterback for the varsity team, it came down to Ryder, Callaghan and Anton. Anton was chosen. Ryder and Callaghan had despised him – an immigrant and a success – from that day on. As they had done with Jonathon, they had looked for every opportunity to threaten and prosecute their old high school friend, Fred Anton.

Jonathon didn't bring up the topic again. It was impossible to believe that all this – these years and decades of torment – had been because of a personal animosity, that it had been all because of high school politics.

Anton never asked why Jonathon hadn't betrayed him. He never had to. He was a good judge of character, and Jonathon never had to explain himself.

When conversation petered out, Anton turned to his wife and asked, "Honey, would you excuse us for a second?"

Harvey looked up and grinned. "No problem, sweet-cheeks."

Anton threw his napkin at Harvey's face. Then he wiggled his fingers at Jonathon, indicating that he should get up and follow Anton for a brief walk outside. They walked through mist and under street lamps, saying nothing for a while. Anton's shoes scuffed the sidewalk. He turned to Jonathon, so Jonathon stopped to face him. Anton offered his hand.

"Thank you," Anton said. His voice broke.

Jonathon ignored Anton's hand and embraced him like a brother. "You're welcome."

Anton thumped him on the back, then turned away, nodding once. He coughed and they kept walking. Anton quickly changed the subject with a joke he'd forgotten to tell over dinner, and in no time, he had Jonathon in stitches.

A couple of weeks later, Jonathon was reading over some of the recent revisions in the transcript when he heard a couple of raised voices. Jonathon set down the document and stood up, wondering what all the fuss was about. He opened his office door. The voices were coming from the waiting area. Andrew and Rowan also poked their heads out.

"What the hell was that?" Jonathon asked.

Rowan shrugged. Andrew started down the hall to see what was happening. The other two followed. They rounded the corner just in time to see one of two uniformed Vancouver City Police officers push the receptionist out of his way. They'd both drawn their guns and were holding them down at a low guard. Behind them came two plain-clothed RCMP officers with badges on their lapels, and several other men in suits, all with laminated ID cards identifying them as British Columbia Securities Commission investigators.

"Against the wall," said one of the uniformed officers. He was pointing at the wall beside Rowan's door. "Face the wall, all of you, with your hands on your head. Move."

Andrew looked confused. Rowan didn't show any emotion at all; he'd been shocked into obedience, it seemed, by the timbre of the officer's voice.

"Move now," the officer shouted at Andrew. Andrew nodded and turned to the wall beside Rowan. He watched as Jonathon slowly complied.

Jonathon turned his head slightly. There was a grey-haired man standing beside him, and according to his ID, he was a senior securities investigator. "Can I ask what this is all about?"

"We're here pursuant to this warrant to conduct a search of these premises in relation to an allegation of securities fraud." He showed Jonathon the warrant. "The municipal police officers and the RCMP have accompanied us to ensure your full cooperation."

"You already have it," Jonathon said. "So can we put our hands down now?"

"What 'securities fraud' are you talking about?" Andrew asked.

Instead of answering directly, the senior investigator said, "You'll not be placed under arrest today, so long as you don't interfere with the men conducting this search. If I could have your acknowledgement of this, then I'll leave you here in the care of these two RCMP officers, while we conduct the search. Otherwise, you'll be removed and detained until we are finished. Is that understood?"

Rowan and Andrew were looking at Jonathon, who gave his acknowledgement. Looking and sounding confused, Rowan and Andrew also said that they understood. While Jonathon took his hands down from his head, the two RCMP officers drew their weapons from their underarm holsters and indicated that all three of them should move into Jonathon's office. "Go," said the fatter of the two.

"Sure," Jonathon said. "That's where the cognac is."

The officers followed Jonathon, Rowan and Andrew into Jonathon's office. "Can I offer you a drink, Officer..." He squinted at the senior officer's name tag. "McNaught?" The man didn't answer. He offered drinks to everyone, including McNaught's partner, but no one else seemed interested. He served himself a drink, since it was better than worrying and complaining.

"Hell of a front," grunted McNaught. With his red, bulbous nose, his weight problem and saggy face, the officer reminded Jonathon a little of Rodney Dangerfield, if he had his sense of humour surgically removed. He even had a way of talking out of one side of his mouth, though on him, it was an affectation of derision and superiority. He was looking around Jonathon's office, and picking paint off the sign on the door that read *Jonathon Parker, President.* He closed the door. "You must think you're some real big shot, living like this when you should be on parole."

"I am on parole," Jonathon said. "And steady work is one of the conditions."

"This is a hell of a lot more than a common criminal deserves," McNaught said. He jabbed his partner in the shoulder and pointed at Jonathon. "Get a load of this guy, will you? Christ." To Jonathon, he added, "Mickey told me you were an asshole."

"Who?"

"Mick Ryder, dumbass," McNaught said.

Jonathon walked over to his desk chair and sat down before his knees gave out. Andrew and Rowan studied his face. Both were speechless.

McNaught sat on the corner of Jonathon's meeting table, making the table legs creak. "Apparently he was right." He snorted a laugh. "By the time we're finished with you, Jonny-boy, you'll wish you'd never heard of Mick Ryder. *That* I guarantee you."

Jonathon sighed and closed his eyes.

CHAPTER TWENTY-SEVEN

VANCOUVER. SPRING, 1988.

Trapped in a tiny office with four other men, being unable to see what people were getting into in the other rooms, that he could tolerate. But being trapped in a tiny office with four men, being unable to see what people were messing around with, and knowing that an ally of Ryder and Callaghan was front and centre, it was more than Jonathon's composure could bear. Knowing the dynamic duo, there was no telling what kind of "evidence" was being found, or whether or not it was being planted in convenient places by cronies of McNaught. So when McNaught and the other RCMP officer were excused from the room by the senior investigator, Jonathon was mildly relieved. The senior investigator's monotone voice was a breath of fresh air compared to McNaught's muttered insults and veiled threats.

The investigator brought Jonathon out into the hall to show him the line-up of boxes and computers. Only a few of the investigators remained, and one of them had a trolley to carry the boxed papers, hardware and floppy disks away.

"Mr. Parker, I'll need you, or someone else in a position of authority, to sign this inventory list of the items seized today. You will note that there are seventeen boxes, numbered zero-zero-one, through zero-seventeen, each with their contents individually catalogued and numbered in separate sub-categories, as well as these pieces of equipment with their serial numbers as shown next to each of them. Please initial all line items, and then sign right here."

Among the boxes were all of the notes and scripts as provided by the documentary maker and the private investigator. $45,000 worth of research and vindication had been inventoried for confiscation.

"Mr. Parker," the senior investigator droned, "sign right here."

Jonathon signed the inventory list and handed it back to him. *Let it go,* he thought. *Burnette has copies of his own at home.*

"Thank you," said the investigator. He tucked the folded list into his coat pocket. "Now I must also inform all three of you gentlemen we have frozen your company bank accounts as well as those personal bank accounts that we are aware of, pending this investigation."

Andrew's face had turned a worrisome shade of purple. Rowan kept his fists at his side, but his whole body shook.

"All monies currently in those accounts, together with any that may arrive to any of those accounts during the course of this investigation, will remain under our authority without exception."

Rowan asked, "How the hell are we supposed to support our families?" Jonathon stopped him before he could say anything more.

"Further," the investigator said, "your real estate assets and any registered vehicles have also been liened as of today. Any attempt to sell, trade, hypothecate or otherwise dispose of any of these assets will be considered fraud pursuant to the British Columbia Securities Act. Do each of you understand?"

"What about our families?" Rowan blurted.

The senior investigator tilted his head and said, "You should have considered them at the very beginning."

McNaught was standing near the front office door, grinning behind his pudgy hand.

"I think we all understand," Jonathon said. "Don't we?"

Rowan and Andrew both opened their mouths as if to shout "No", but Jonathon narrowed his eyes at them. Whether the charges were false or not, impeding the investigation would only be taken as an admission of having something to hide. And worse, any raised voices – or fists – would only give McNaught an excuse to drop additional charges on all three of them.

"Yeah," Rowan said. "Yeah, sure. What the hell. We understand."

"I understand," Andrew said. His voice was soft and boyish, and a little frightened. He looked like he was going to cry. Jonathon empathized.

"Thanks," Jonathon said. "Now please." He pointed at the door. "You've got what you came for. So leave."

"Have a nice day," the senior investigator said.

If he'd been a little closer, the senior investigator would have been pulling shoe leather out of his ass crack for a month.

VANCOUVER. SPRING, 1989.

Mitchell Stewart Industries had long ago patched the holes "accidentally" punched in the drywall when the B.C. Securities Investigators carted out boxes and boxes of records and notes. They'd been able to replace many of the confiscated computer terminals and PCs. They'd even been able to get back to business-as-usual, despite weeks of upheaval and staff trauma. But the memory of that day, when police officers had stormed the place, and, with little clarification of the investigation, had taken so much away. The team spirit had been badly bruised. Their reputation had taken the biggest hit. It was hard to make a profit when all their accounts were frozen.

The phone rang.

"Mitchell Stewart Industries, Jonathon Parker speaking. How can I help you?"

"Mr. Parker?"

Jonathon placed his hand over his eyes. "Yes, it's me."

"I'm calling you from the British Columbia Securities Commission."

Jonathon squeezed the bridge of his nose and winced.

"I'm calling to inform you that the investigation concerning your company has been completed, and all charges have been withdrawn."

He dropped his hand and sat up straight.

"You will receive a formal written acknowledgement of this from our legal counsel shortly. In the interim, we would like to know what you wish us to do with the items that were seized from your office as part of the investigation."

"Well, you could return them," he said.

"Oh, I'm sorry, Mr. Parker. If you want them back, you'll be required to make your own arrangements to pick them up and transport them from our storage facility."

"Oh, I get it. So…you take all our things, you admit we've done nothing wrong, but you won't even bring our stuff back to us." There was no answer from the B.C. Securities caller. "Fine, so when and where can I get them?"

"The same building as our office, on the fourth floor." He gave the full address, and Jonathon wrote it down on a scrap piece of paper. "Just give them your case number and identify yourself to the staff there, and they'll help you out."

Jonathon confirmed the case number and the storage office hours of operations, and as soon as he'd hung up, he cancelled his meetings for the day and headed downtown.

Jonathon had never seen so much black ink before. They'd returned all his notes, including the records from the era of Ryder and Callaghan, but they'd never promised to keep the records in pristine condition. As he, Andrew and Rowan compared the inventory list to the contents of the – somewhat lightened – now eleven boxes short of the original seventeen, they began to notice a trend.

"Inadvertently shredded," Jonathon read. He ran his fingers down the page to the next row that had been blacked out with magic marker. "Inadvertently shredded."

"I can't believe those assholes," Rowan said.

"I know!" Jonathon said. "And the thing that pisses me off is that they wouldn't let me go with what I have here – not without putting my initials beside every case of 'inadvertently shredded.'"

"Hell of a shredder," Andrew said. "I'd be afraid to walk in the door, if I worked around a shredder like that."

"Seriously. How the hell does anybody 'inadvertently shred' eleven boxes full of documents?"

"Apparently quite well," Andrew said.

"Methodically," Rowan said. "And probably on purpose."

CHAPTER TWENTY-SEVEN

Jonathon snorted a laugh.

"Hey, do you guys see a pattern here?" Andrew asked.

Jonathon looked over the list again. "What do you mean?"

"It's all the research we paid that PI for," Andrew said. "And if I'm not mistaken, there's not a single copy of that documentary in anyone of these boxes."

Rowan was on a mission of his own. He checked Jonathon's inventory list, then attacked the boxes. "Bastards!"

"What?" Andrew asked.

"They took more than that. They got all the contact information and every single one of my contracts for the trades I was doing."

Jonathon shook his head. "They didn't keep them. They shredded whatever they thought could cause us the most grief. They couldn't get us on a trumped up charge, so they had to go another route."

Rowan bit his knuckles to keep from screaming out loud.

"Come on," Jonathon said. "Whatever it is, we can recover from it, all right? Let's just unpack whatever's left, and we'll head out for a drink."

"Or two," Andrew said.

"Screw that," Rowan said. "If I'm coming out of the bar on two feet, sit me down and give me another drink."

Jonathon laughed. "Listen, at least we can access our bank accounts again."

"Amen," Rowan said.

"Then let's work up a thirst," Jonathon said. He handed a sheaf of papers to Rowan to sort and file away.

At the very least, Jonathon was glad to have his accounts re-opened. He could do business openly again. He had a few plans in the works for recovering from his losses in a hurry, but for that, he needed a partner, someone with cachet.

He had called up Bill Lang, a real estate developer in his late fifties, to talk over some ideas. They were sitting in Jonathon's private office at Mitchell Stewart Industries.

Bill cracked his knuckles. "A lot of us small developers in Hawaii lost everything. It wasn't just me. When the Japanese came into that market with their wagon loads of money, the rest of us, we just couldn't compete. They drove us out. They drove some of us right into bankruptcy."

Jonathon could empathize. "Well, the market's still strong here, thank God for that. In fact, a realtor friend of mine just called me yesterday about a project. He asked to meet up with me tomorrow morning at a project he's just listed in Richmond."

"Virginia or British Columbia?"

"B.C. You want to come along? Maybe we can work something out together."

"How big is it?" Bill asked. "Because I gotta tell you, I really don't have any money left to work with. The only asset I have left is my brother-in-law." When he realized that Jonathon didn't catch whatever joke Bill was trying to make, Bill explained: "Roger's a well-known local architect. In terms of development, he can work for me on the cuff, as it were."

"He'd work for free?"

"No, but for me he'll work for a percentage of the project instead of for cash remuneration, if I sweet talk him into it. But otherwise, I'm broke."

"The project's big," Jonathon said, "and there's a lot to be gained. A group of six, four-storey apartment buildings, strata-titled, so we can sell off units as condos."

"How many units?"

"278," Jonathon said. "Just over sixteen million for the asking price."

Bill whistled at that. "Is it in that bad of shape? How old is the building?"

"Only about fifteen years, and I don't get the impression that it's in *bad* shape, but my realtor friend says it could fetch thirty million, if we completely renovate it. He knows I work with some great subcontractors so he thinks I'm a good fit for the project. The original owners have gone into receivership. Couldn't keep up with the interest rates."

Bill nodded then, satisfied now with the unusually low price. "Yeah, but the last time I checked my account balance, I didn't have sixteen million lying around."

"I wouldn't worry. We had a bit of a setback too, this last year. It took a big gouge out of our resources. But if there's one thing I've learned, it's that you can recover from just about anything, so long as you don't give up hope. Besides there's always lots of eager investors around."

"You're a hell of an optimist," Bill said.

Jonathon shrugged. "It's in my nature, I guess. I wouldn't be here now, if I'd ever given up hope. So what do you say? Head out with me to Richmond tomorrow?"

Bill said, "Nothing ventured, nothing gained, I guess. It won't hurt to look at the papers and see what we can come up with."

"That's the spirit."

A week later, Jonathon and Bill were back at Jonathon's desk. This time, instead of reclining in their chairs with their hands behind their heads and their legs crossed, now they were bowed forward over their papers and analyses.

"So the project is now split into two halves," Jonathon said. Bill nodded, encouraging Jonathon to carry on. "We've committed fifty grand as a non-refundable deposit on each half in thirty days. The balance we have to pay sixty days after that, no conditions."

"I think I just shit my pants," Bill said.

Jonathon smiled. "Cash on simple terms, instead of complicated and conditional terms from the other buyers? The receiver couldn't turn us down. Our deal's so clean they couldn't help themselves. I told you: simple is the way to go. The other offers were so complex the buyers had to hire a legal team just to interpret all the clauses. We simplify, the buyer knows exactly what he's getting into…"

Bill groaned as if he had indigestion.

Jonathon raised his hand and smiled. "Relax!"

Bill piped an uncomfortable, dubious laugh.

"That mortgage broker I told you about has found us two joint venture partners. They've each agreed to put up one *hundred* thousand dollars non-refundable in thirty days, to cover our deposit. And they've each agreed to put up one hundred percent of all the money to complete the purchases, and to cover the renovations and improvement costs."

"Good God," Bill breathed. "All that? What's in it for them?"

"Each one gets a fifty percent interest in their half of the project. That leaves you and I with a hundred grand in our pockets, *right now*. Plus, we retain half the project, all the development rights, all the marketing rights…and did I mention we keep half the profits?"

Bill's mouth was agape.

"I figure we should each end up with a little over three quarters of a million dollars, or the equivalent in paid-for condos. Our choice. Does that work for you?"

Bill laughed. "Sheeyit! I'll manage somehow." Like a man who'd just discovered he's won the lottery, Bill rubbed his head and laughed again. "You really know how to make something out of nothing, don't you?"

Jonathon smiled.

"You got horseshoes jammed up your ass or something?"

Jonathon twinkled his fingers. "I've got the magic!"

NORTH VANCOUVER, BC. FALL, 1989.

The Richmond project was finished and Jonathon and Bill were on to their second project together, a sixteen storey high rise apartment to condo conversion in the prestigious Lonsdale area of North Vancouver. Life was good – for the moment.

It wasn't that Jonathon didn't appreciate his good fortunes. In fact, he appreciated his good fortune as many ways as he could – paying bonuses to Andrew and Rowan, buying a new house, leasing a new Mercedes convertible…eating three square meals a day…It wasn't that he was unwilling to do whatever it took to sell off the condos, either. If he had any say in the matter, he would sell off all units in record time, and to hell with the ridiculous spike in interest rates.

Regardless, in that moment, Jonathon would rather have been a million miles away. He could have joyfully disguised himself as one of the construction workers and pitched in to help with both hands. Anywhere was better than in front of a television camera.

Still, in that real estate market, they needed all the good publicity and exposure they could get. Having a reporter from CBC news come over for an interview was the best – and worst – that he could have hoped for. An aspiring reporter had noticed the very unusual sign Jonathon and Bill had erected in front of their project, and he insisted on including both partners in the interview.

If this CBC reporter recognized Jonathon from bigger news stories out of Regina, she gave no sign of it. Jonathon wondered who might be watching, and who might recognize him. He hoped that they would let Bill take most of the airtime. Bill was grinning from ear to ear.

"I'm here in North Vancouver at Harbour Castle Condominiums with local real estate developers Bill Lang and Jonathon Parker, who seem to have found an innovative approach to the slow real estate market, caused by the recent climb in interest rates. They call it…'Honda-Miniums.' Buy one of their condos, and they give you a *free* Honda Accord." The reporter turned to Jonathon and asked, "Is it really that simple, Mr. Parker? Or is there a catch?" She tilted her microphone toward his mouth.

The news camera focused on Jonathon. He thought of reporters in his face, boxing him in against the door of the flower shop in Regina. "It is just that simple," he said. "And there is no catch. Simply put, we want to sell out as quickly as possible, and if we sell a condo by giving a car away, it actually costs us less than the interest charge on the sale price, so everyone wins. It's a simple choice for us; give a car to a buyer and sell a condo, or remain stuck with that condo and have to pay back interest to the bank – which in turn only drives up the cost of the remaining condos."

"There you have it," the reporter said into her microphone. "This developer's innovative method of dealing with high interest rates promises to be a real win for home buyers this year."

Jonathon was afraid to go back to his office and answer the phone. He was happy to let Bill Lang handle the sales for a while. He didn't want to pick up the phone and hear a familiar but unfriendly voice. He knew too many of them.

Deep Cove, B.C.. Fall, 1989.

Jonathon had pulled up into his driveway and parked the Mercedes. It was a very nice car.

Jonathon was back in the chips, and to hell with people like McNaught. Still, he was tired, and ever since the reporter had shot that piece, he'd felt utterly exposed. But more than that, he was tired. It had been a great few months, and now, though he didn't have time for a vacation, he decided it was time to take the weekend off and disconnect.

He was just putting up the roof when he heard a car park on the road in front of his lawn. He didn't think anything of it. He was totally focused on getting inside, closing the curtains and taking the phone off the hook. He jogged up the walk and he had his key in the lock when he heard heavy, hard-soled shoes slapping the flagstones behind him. He turned in time to see McNaught extend his arm and put his hand against the door frame beside Jonathon's head. McNaught's jacket was open. Jonathon could see the gun in McNaught's underarm holster.

"Parker," he said. "It's been a while. Thought it was about time we had a visit."

Jonathon took the key out of the lock and faced McNaught with his arms crossed.

"I have an invitation," McNaught said.

Jonathon stared at him.

McNaught pulled his gun and stood close to Jonathon. He let his spacious, open coat shield all sight of the gun from the prying eyes of Jonathon's neighbours. "See? Here's my invitation. Now open the door. We can talk this over in private."

When Jonathon didn't move, McNaught flicked the safety off his service pistol and poked Jonathon in the abdomen with the muzzle. Jonathon unlocked and opened the door, saying, "You people never give up, do you?" McNaught was peering out the door as if looking for witnesses. He closed the door while Jonathon walked further into the house and took off his jacket.

"Sit down," McNaught said. He walked across Jonathon's white carpet, leaving dusty tracks in the pile. He sat down in a chair facing Jonathon's couch. "Sit down!" McNaught looked around. Jonathon was no interior decorator, but McNaught seemed to like what he'd done with the place. He especially seemed to like Jonathon's large television set. "Hell of a place you've got here, con."

"What do you want?" Jonathon was bored and irritated.

McNaught lowered his bushy grey eyebrows. "So you think you can ruin a good man's life, then live high on the hog, huh? Imagine my great surprise when I'm finally takin' a night off, one decent night off, to watch the hockey game. And what do I see in the middle of my game, but this CBC 'breaking news' shit. And whose smiling dumbass face do I see? Knew I shoulda kept my eye on you. I turn my back, and the next thing I know, you're on TV with some harebrained scheme, flaunting all the gains of your criminal activities and making yourself look like some clean-cut, oh-so-innocent *business* man…"

Jonathon sat on the couch and sighed. McNaught, Ryder and Callaghan were all tropes from the same script. They liked to wave their guns around and indulge in preamble and hyperbole.

"You try to ruin a good *cop*, and you think you can get away with it? I don't know what kind of crooked deal you made with the Attorney General, but it totally fucked up Mickey's life. His life and the life of his whole goddamned family, and you think you can get away with it, consequence free? No – not just consequence free – look at this place. You're makin' a goddamned *profit* off it. And I'm not going to stand for it. He's in *exile* because of you. Nobody can see him, not even his family. They have to go all the way to Australia, fer Chrissakes."

"I hear it's beautiful this time of year."

279

McNaught sat forward, pointing his gun at Jonathon from between his knees. "Here's how we're gonna play this." He laughed. "You think you can hide from somebody like me? Hell, I've had my eye on you for a long time. I figure you've got a little over a million dollars in the bank right now, a little equity on this house of yours, and about another million or so potential in that Harbour Castle deal you've got going on with Bill Lang." He smiled. Like a car salesman trying to convince a buyer that he's giving away the farm, McNaught said, "You give me what's in the bank, sign over your interest in Harbour Castle to an off-shore company of mine, and we'll call it a deal. I'll look after Mickey and his family, and everybody wins. Oh – and yeah, you can keep the house. It's nice, but the mortgage payments are too high for me. I *will* enjoy driving that pretty little Mercedes though. Never had a convert-ible before. Call it a…a handling fee."

"You're a sad little man, McNaught."

McNaught's smile crumpled into a grimace.

"You're nothing but a gun, a badge and a big mouth," Jonathon said.

"And you're a son of a bitch who's playing with fire," McNaught said, getting to his feet and standing beside the couch.

Jonathon also rose. "If you have the balls to use that gun, I suggest you do it now." He waited. "No? Then you'd better get the hell out of my house before I take that gun from you and shove it up your fat ass."

Jonathon stood toe to toe with McNaught. Jonathon was taller by four or five inches, and he'd had his fill of big talkers. At least Ryder and Callaghan knew how to fight.

McNaught put the gun between them, trying to push Jonathon back and failing. He thrust the muzzle into Jonathon's abdomen again. "That's far enough," McNaught said. McNaught had taken a step back-ward, toward the door, but he kept his gun locked at the same distance from his body. "You think you're so smart, eh?" McNaught sneered. In a low voice, he said, "I'll have that mortgage company call your loan on Harbour Castle by noon tomorrow." He took another step toward the door, keeping the gun now level with Jonathon's chest. Jonathon took a step forward, closing the distance between them. McNaught took another step toward the door. "And you can kiss your bank balance goodbye too, asshole." Jonathon followed him to the door. With one shaking hand, McNaught fumbled for the door knob and let himself out. "We'll be seeing each other again real soon." He put his gun away and walked down the path. Jonathon closed the door.

Jonathon felt like a hundred year old man. He was bone-tired. He was soul-tired.

Bill Lang was unhappy. "Christ. We've gotta do something, Jonathon."

"I know." It had been four days since McNaught had come to Jonathon's house to issue threats.

"I mean, what the hell?" He regarded Jonathon with a mix of confusion, disappointment and disgust. "Our monthly payments are still over a hundred and sixty grand – I mean, how the hell can we keep that up?"

"We'll figure something out."

"Seriously? Tax evasion, Jonny? Tax fraud?"

Jonathon turned red in the face. "It's all lies, Bill. I told you that."

"Three years, they said – three years of tax evasion. That's a hell of a thing to make up out of thin air."

"They have no proof of any wrong-doing," Jonathon said. "It's just another trumped up charge – this is no different than the hassle I had with the B.C. Securities Commission, you remember? They dropped all those charges because they couldn't find any evidence of fraud. And they won't ever find any evidence of fraud *or* tax evasion, because I don't do that, Bill."

"They've put a lien on the property," Bill said. "They've seized *your* accounts, and every penny is *gone* from our joint account – I mean, I sure as hell can't keep up monthly payments of that size all on my own!" He raked his fingers across his scalp. "I mean, what the hell happened here? One minute we're farting through silk, and the next we're up shit creek!"

Jonathon dumped his elbow on the desk and rubbed his weary eyes. "That, we are."

"I mean, what are we going to do about this?" Bill asked. "What are *you* doing about it?"

Jonathon didn't know how to answer. It had taken long enough to
get Ryder and Callaghan out from under his skin. He didn't want to
spend the next six years fighting McNaught too. And after McNaught,
who next?

This just goes on, and on, and on…

Bill Lang watched him, waiting for a response.

"There's something I need to tell you," Jonathon said. "And you may
not believe any of it, but you can ask Rowan. You could ask Andrew
too, if you want to call him up in Montreal. This is not my first legal
battle, and it probably won't be my last. But believe me when I tell
you, time and time again, when someone tries to wrap me up in a false
charge, *I win*. It's a pain in the ass, and I know I'm sick to death of shell-
ing out for legal fees, but that's all it is: an unnecessary cost and a pain
in the ass. And depending on how bad things get, yeah, we might need
to downsize some of our personal comforts, but all is not lost, you hear
me? I have an ace in the hole."

Bill sat forward. "All right. I'm listening."

"For one thing, I've been dealing with thieves and liars for a long
time now, and if there's one thing I've learned, it's that you should never
keep all your eggs in one basket. See, back when I was having some…
some *problems* with my first wife, I flew over to Zurich and I set up a
Swiss bank account."

Bill listened a little more closely.

CHAPTER TWENTY-EIGHT

VANCOUVER. FALL, 1992.

Jonathon hung up his call feeling but worn out and used. He wasn't defeated – there was always another way to recuperate from a loss, even one of this magnitude – but he was something else. There wasn't a word invented yet that could best describe the worry, grief and outrage he now felt. He needed time, and more than anything, he needed McNaught to go curl up under a rock like the maggot he was.

Over the last year, he'd been working with a few fellow businessmen on a high yield investment plan, a type of foreign exchange trading conducted through a private bank. The initial investments were high, and the trading was conducted by some of the sharpest traders in the world. The plan was simple, and everyone had a role to play. For Jonathon, it was simply a matter of acting on behalf of Worldwide Enterprises to seek out new potential investors and bring them on board; the rest was left up to his associates, including Jonathon's good friend, John Reimer.

And now, one of those associates was enmeshed in a huge legal battle in the U.S., and another – the one who had set up Worldwide Enterprises in the first place – had fled the country to avoid prosecution. Jonathon had also been one of the contributing investors. His losses stung, but he knew, with enough time, he could recover all of the lost investments. Unfortunately, his fellow investors weren't blessed with the same patience and optimism as Jonathon, and they took their ire directly to the US civil courts. Jonathon, having been the public face of the company, was taking the heat for a combined $45M loss – the total combined investment.

And worse: his colleagues were in trouble for reasons that smacked of baseless accusations and falsified evidence. Their assets – including the investment monies held in escrow by Worldwide Enterprises – had been frozen by the US Departments of Justice and Treasury, and after his tangle with the BC Securities Commission, Jonathon was now feeling a bad case of déjà vu. It was bad enough that Jonathon had lost a fortune, but Reimer had lost a huge chunk of change, and Jonathon felt just as responsible for the dozen investors he'd brought into the mess on promises of quick and easy capital gains. It was because of Jonathon that they'd invested, and it was because of Jonathon that someone had prompted the U.S. authorities to conduct such a sudden and unfounded investigation of his partners.

Jonathon's suspicions were confirmed late one afternoon.

Jonathon had been sitting at home going through his mail when someone knocked on his door. He'd been expecting a visit from the Rastafarian Rowan, so he got up to answer the door. He turned the bolt. Someone else turned the knob, and the door slammed back into Jonathon's face. Jonathon shook off the shock and braced his shoulder against the door, but whoever was on the other side had greater speed and the advantage of numbers. Something struck Jonathon on the side of the knee, making his leg buckle. The door was forced open, and two men entered, slamming the door behind them.

One of them was smiling. *McNaught*, Jonathon thought, with no sense of surprise at all. McNaught had brought with him a much leaner, much faster partner; RCMP officer or no, the younger man fought like a Russian martial artist, and all Jonathon could do was protect his head with his arm and hope no bones broke.

"Enough," McNaught shouted.

Jonathon narrowed his eyes. A broad fist had stopped within an inch of his eyebrow.

"You'll never learn, will you, dickhead?" McNaught asked. He pushed off from the wall beside the door and sat heavily on a bar stool near where Jonathon lay half-sprawled on the floor in the shadow of the boxer who'd flattened him. "You could have done it my way."

"I have nothing to say to you." Jonathon wiped his upper lip and found blood. He wasn't sure if it was because of a split gum or because of the shot to his nose. Either way, he was seeing red. "Nothing, except for 'get the hell out of my home.'"

McNaught laughed and toyed with an apple in the fruit basket on Jonathon's kitchen counter. "See, if you'd just paid me, I could have helped Mick out of a bad spot. You'd hurt a little, Mick's situation would improve, we'd all move on with our lives."

Jonathon worked his way to his feet. Glaring had little effect, so Jonathon withdrew to the kitchen in search of a paper towel.

"But no, you had to get all obnoxious on me. You never take me seriously, Jonny. And now look what you've made me do. I had to go and contact the US Departments of Justice and Treasury, tell them about that cute little pyramid scheme of yours…"

It wasn't a pyramid scheme, for one, and for another, it was completely legal. But even false accusations are costly, when $45M is frozen, potential interest is lost night after night, and investors summon you to civil court. Jonathon ran the paper towel under water and cleaned his face.

"And what does that get you, huh? Your buddies are in a world of hurt, aren't they? Assets frozen – you must know what that's like, huh?" McNaught snorted a laugh. "Criminal charges of money laundering. Civil suit against you and all your cronies. Reputation's now all shot to shit. Good luck finding someone who'll ever trust them with so much as a pocket full of lint, let alone any investment capital. And while that's all good fun and everything, what the hell's that done for me? Jon-boy, you've got to start thinking about the future! You're a bright boy. You start figuring out a way to get me the money directly."

Jonathon turned abruptly, and the fighter shifted one foot backward, as if preparing for Round Two. Jonathon dumped his fists on the counter and rolled a bruised shoulder. He was already raring for another go.

"I can't touch any of that. It's confiscated. Property of Uncle Sam," McNaught said. "Now how the hell am I supposed to help Mick if I don't have any cash? I ask you."

Jonathon knocked the bowl of fruit from under McNaught's hand. McNaught jumped to his feet, pouting in fear, and his partner drew his gun. McNaught followed suit, sweating.

"Look at you, you sons of bitches," Jonathon said. "Two armed pansies against one unarmed man? Am I so scary to you cowards that you've got to hold me at bay with a pair of government issued pistols?"

"You back off," McNaught shouted. "Get back!"

Jonathon came around the counter, spreading his arms and exposing his chest to an easy shot. "You break into my home, you try to extort money out of me like a pair of common crooks – what's the fucking use of your guns if you're not going to use them, huh?" He took another step toward McNaught and his anonymous friend. "And so, what, you can't break me all on your own, so you have to attack a dozen other people you've never even met?"

"I'm warning you, Parker – get the fuck back."

"And for what? Huh? To send pocket change back to that son of a bitch who stole everything I'd ever made? Who cost me my marriage and my kids? Sent me to prison after putting forty lives at risk, just so he could get back at a guy he knew in *high school?*" Jonathon jabbed his finger in the direction of the door; both men jumped and adjusted their aim. "Go on, you son of a bitch. Pull the trigger. Use the damned gun or I'll take it from you. I'll fucking take the gun from you, I'll shove it up your ass, and after I'm done, I'll call up your superiors and ask them why the hell one of the RCMP's finest can't find his sidearm without an X-Ray and a proctologist."

McNaught's partner dropped his aim and fired a round into the floor between Jonathon's feet. The man brought up the muzzle again, aiming for a spot between Jonathon's eyes. "You just made it personal, asshole. That's a big mistake."

"We're gonna make your life *miserable*, ball-sack," McNaught said.

"I was just along for the ride," said the other. "I was gonna give you the benefit of the doubt, and now I see you're every bit the strutting bastard Mick told us about. And you just made it personal."

"Good," Jonathon said, stepping over the bullet hole in the floor. "Personal. Fine." He had momentum now, despite the smoke drifting from the muzzle of the fired gun. He'd been grazed before. He knew he'd be shot this time. But until that happened, nothing short of a mortal wound would stop him from laying his hands on McNaught's throat. "Then let me have a personal moment with McNaught first. You'll have your turn after I'm done with him. Hell, you can call the fucking hearse while you wait, because when I'm finished with McNaught..."

McNaught called him a crazy fucker, stashed his weapon and turned about face for the door. "This is not over." His partner walked backward toward the door, gun cocked and rock steady in his grip.

"No shit," Jonathon said, chasing them to the door. McNaught pushed his partner out of the way and jumped outside. Jonathon grabbed hold of the door and slammed it, catching the other gunman's jacket between the door and the jamb. The tongue of jacket withdrew, and Jonathon locked his door.

Jonathon's hands trembled like he was standing on an electrical current, but for once, he felt no nausea from the combat. He'd never been so ready for a fight.

He withdrew from the door, his shaking hand over his bloody mouth.

He'd never been so ready to fight to the death.

CHAPTER TWENTY-NINE

VANCOUVER. SUMMER, 1996.

Jonathon handed a box over to Rowan.

"I really appreciate you doing this, Jonathon," Rowan said. He set his burden down at the end of a line of boxes piled in the front hall behind the door.

"I can't say it's my pleasure, because I hate saying goodbye," Jonathon said. "But I'm happy to help you however I can."

Rowan smiled and took the next box from him.

"When does your moving truck get here?" Jonathon asked.

"Should be here any minute now. I'd like to get it to Victoria tonight, if I can. What about you? You all packed and ready to go?"

"Yeah, my movers should be there in the morning. As soon as I get to Armstrong, I'll give you my contact information." He sighed. "I'm just sorry it's come to this."

Rowan shook his head. "I know. But I'm getting on in years, you know. Getting too close to retirement to take on those high-stakes gambles like we used to."

At forty-four, Jonathon knew what Rowan was talking about. At twenty-five, Jonathon had lost everything, including his wife, and his grandfather had reminded how easily the young could bounce back from the biggest losses. Twenty years later, it wasn't so easy to bounce back. He was tired of the sleepless nights and the nail-biting.

He was tired of always having to look over his shoulder when things started looking up.

"Hey," Rowan said, offering a warm smile. "At least we're both leaving with a handsome chunk of change in our pockets."

"It's been a good year," Jonathon agreed.

"You sure you're going to like being out in the sticks like that? After all that high-rolling and city night life?"

Jonathon grinned. "Are you kidding? I grew up on a farm. I'm looking forward to the peace and quiet, to be honest." And by peace and quiet, he meant anonymity and distance between him and McNaught. He could live in total obscurity and not mind it one bit.

Rowan looked around the studio apartment. With the exception of a few bits of furniture, there wasn't anything else left to line up. "The movers can take over the rest of the work, when they get here. That's what I'm paying them for." He sized Jonathon up. "It's been a hell of a good ten years workin' with you, Jonathon."

"We've certainly been through some ups and downs."

Rowan reached over Jonathon's shoulder, and they hugged, slapping each other the back. "You take care of yourself, Jonathon. And for God's sake, try to stay out of trouble, will you?"

Jonathon smiled a wry smile. "I *always* try to stay out of trouble."

"Yeah, well, don't let it follow you out there this time. You drive safe, and you call me as soon as you get settled in, all right?"

"It's a deal."

VERNON, B.C. SUMMER, 1996.

Jonathon had sold his Mercedes and his condo, and with the proceeds from their sales, together with a wired transfer from a line of credit on his Swiss bank account, Jonathon was able to buy a pick-up truck and hole up in a hotel until he found permanent accommodations. He'd forgotten what fresh country air smelled like, so far away from the Pacific as he was now. He'd forgotten what it was like to wake up to birdsong instead of a screeching alarm or a telephone call.

He was at peace.

And he needed a new bank account.

It was a short drive into Vernon B.C., and the town wasn't so big that it was hard to find the local branch of the Bank of Montreal. He waited his turn in the line-up, amused and somehow relieved to be in the company of people wearing jeans, and flannel button-down shirts over tank tops and t-shirts. There weren't so many false pretenses, here. People weren't trying so hard to make a big impression on one another.

One of the tellers was a charming and down-to-earth redhead. Her hair was loosely tied back behind her slender shoulders. When she smiled, her eyes crinkled. It was a genuine smile, not some ill-used, worn-out grin. She took her time with the older clients, listening intently to some story that had nothing to do with the business at hand.

She noticed Jonathon was staring. He lowered his eyes and smiled, suddenly self-conscious. When he looked up again, she was passing an elderly woman her updated bankbook.

Two tellers became free at the same time, and Jonathon was second in line. The person ahead of him went to the wicket where the red-haired teller was waiting. Jonathon went to the other teller, a frumpy but giggly middle-aged woman wearing a frilly pink blouse and too much perfume.

"Hi. I'd like to open a new account, please." He set down a money-envelope on the counter between them.

"Sure thing," the teller said.

Jonathon leaned back to get another look at the teller he'd missed out on. The red-head saw him do it, and she cracked a wide but shy smile.

"Sir?" the teller asked.

"Oh – sorry." He smiled at the middle-aged teller. He apologized and set his mind again to the transaction.

Jonathon walked back to his truck with his keys in one hand and new bankbook in the other. He slowed, bouncing indecisively on one foot.

He clutched his keys and pocketed them again.

This time, when he went into the bank, he went to the customer service desk, where a skinny young man was sitting behind a name plate. "Can I help you, sir?"

"Yes, I need to speak to that young lady over there, please." Jonathon pointed to the dark-haired woman at the near end of the row of tellers.

"Who, Linda?"

"Is that her name?"

"The one with the red hair? Linda."

Jonathon nodded. "Can you tell her I'd like to talk to her, as soon as she has a free moment?"

"Can I tell her what this is about?"

"Sure, just tell her it's a personal matter."

"All right," the clerk said. "Give me a second, and I'll give her the message. Can I give her your name?"

"Jonathon," he replied.

"Thanks." The clerk wrote down a quick message and went to deliver it. While he was standing with the red-haired teller – Linda – he pointed in Jonathon's direction. Jonathon had taken a seat in the waiting area and picked up a magazine. Linda was smiling again when she turned her head and said something to the clerk. The clerk nodded and returned to his own post. "She'll be with you as soon as she can. As you can see, it's unusually busy today."

"That's fine," Jonathon said. "I can wait."

The afternoon sun had turned brassy by the time she joined him in the customer waiting area. "I'm sorry to have taken so long. How can I help you?"

"I was wondering if you would like to go out with me for a drink. Or dinner. Or a night on the town."

Linda pressed her hand to her chest and laughed, disbelieving.

"Seriously, no joke," Jonathon said.

"Are you always so direct?"

"Actually, no. Not when it comes to something like this. Frankly, I'm new in town, and I hate dining out alone."

Linda considered it. "All right. Tomorrow night?"

"Sure. Could I get your number, so we can plan something?"

She walked away, and for a second, Jonathon thought she'd changed her mind. But she returned with a pen and a block of paper from the clerk's desk. She wrote the number down, tore off the page and gave it to him.

"I'll see you tomorrow night," he said, tucking the piece of paper into his shirt pocket. He winked, and she smiled. *Maybe the old magic hasn't left me yet,* he thought as he left the bank.

After Jonathon had been released from the Toronto halfway house, after he'd visited his parents in Regina, his parents had cashed the $350,000 settlement cheque he'd given them in 1986, and they had moved to Prince Albert, Saskatchewan. His father had said he was too embarrassed to stay in Regina any longer, not since his son had become so notorious there. He'd moved with Norma north to Prince Albert, but the place was barren and cold, and Norma was bored to tears.

In 1995, a year before Jonathon moved to Armstrong, his mother had come to visit him in Vancouver (and dragged Edward Parker along with her). During their vacation, they'd spent some time in Armstrong, and both Norma and Edward had grown to love the Okanagan Valley. It was because of Norma's impressions of the place that Jonathon decided to check it out for himself – and later, to move there. Now that he had the means again to make amends with his parents, Jonathon invited them west, this time to stay.

In the summer of '96, Jonathon met his parents, checked them into the hotel, then took them out to meet a local realtor. He'd hoped to find them a nice little farm to retire on. The realtor introduced to them to a hobby farm with fruit trees, a barn and a custom built log home already built on the property. The view was idyllic with its mountains and orchards, and it was only a few minutes' drive into town. They fell in love with it almost on sight. There was no question in Jonathon's mind: while it wasn't a resort in Corpus Christi, the price, the location and the view couldn't be beat. Once they had possession of the place, Jonathon helped them to move in and get settled; his mother was genuinely happy, and his father was at peace. While their relationship was forever strained, Edward accepted Jonathon's olive branch and offered a measure of forgiveness in return; but Edward made it clear: "forgiven" did not imply "forgotten."

Jonathon had his eye on a few other properties as well. Just a mile down from his parents' new home, there was a 100-acre property with a house and some horse barns. He also put a few offers on another 25 acres next to his parents' place, and an additional 5 acres across from the 100-acre property. This time, he had no aims to flip it or to lease the acreage. He'd had enough of that. He would rent out the house on the 5 acre property, but for the rest of it, he had every intention of making it a profitable hobby farm.

The purchase of his parents' farm went off without a hitch, same with the 25 acres nearby. But because of his recent acquisitions, he had intended on finalizing the sale of the 100-acre property by the end of his fiscal year, so he called up the seller and asked for a three-day extension, though that would make the new closing date a Saturday, and not the Wednesday. The vendor had no problem with it at all, and over the phone he agreed to extension, so long as he increased the initial deposit to $150,000. Jonathon agreed to it and put through the deposit.

On the Thursday before the closing date, Jonathon went back into Vancouver to sign all the necessary papers at his lawyers office and to transfer the balance of the money to his lawyer in advance of the Saturday closing date. And since the Monday was a statutory holiday, his lawyer and the seller's lawyer agreed to exchange the signed documents on the Friday prior to the possession date, and everything would be registered on the Tuesday. Jonathon stayed over in Vancouver for a few days, visiting friends, closing out accounts and collecting late mail. He went back to Armstrong on the Wednesday.

When he returned home, Jonathon checked his answering machine. His lawyer had left him an urgent message. Jonathon called him back right away.

"I don't know what to say, I mean…I've never had anything like this happen before!" the lawyer said. "You know the other lawyer, the one representing the vendor of that 100-acre property?"

"Sure. What about him?" Jonathon asked.

"He returned the payment!"

"What?"

"The payment you transferred to me, I transferred it to him on Friday, like we'd agreed."

"Right…So why did he return it? Was there a problem with the transfer?" Because God knew, Jonathon had had money transfer problems in the past, and a thousand questions and scenarios came to mind.

"That son of a gun said we missed the official closing date."

"What?"

"Yeah – he still says the closing date was Wednesday, not Saturday. He says we missed it by two days."

"But that's…we had an agreement!"

"I know! But that sumbitch says he's prepared to deny any and all verbal telephone agreements. Jonathon, I swear to God, I did everything I could."

Who did it? Jonathon wondered. He hadn't told anyone but his few, closest friends that he was moving out of Vancouver, and even fewer knew that he was moving to Armstrong. "What the hell!"

"Jonathon, you have to believe me. I swear to God, I thought we had this thing locked down! Nothing like this has ever happened to us before."

"Christ," Jonathon snapped. "And the deposit?"

It took a long time for his lawyer to confirm that the deposit had been non-refundable. Jonathon had lost another $150,000, and he had nothing to show for it.

"I know you must be upset about this."

"Upset?" Jonathon asked. "Upset!"

"Angry," the lawyer said, "and with good right. Listen, we can negotiate something between us, I'm sure. If I were in your shoes, I'd sue for damages too – you'd have a good case for it."

"No," Jonathon groaned. "Damn it…"

"Look, our firm is prepared to waive all the legal fees in this case…"

Jonathon stood beside his bed with his hand on his forehead. He mouthed another curse and kicked a shoe clean across the room. "All I wanted to do was just settle in some place quiet and be nobody for a while."

"I know…"

"I've lost too damned much on legal fees already, damn it."

The lawyer waited, but when Jonathon couldn't think of something productive to say, he suggested that Jonathon think over his options, and he offered his assistance, top priority, as soon as Jonathon knew what action he wanted to pursue. Jonathon agreed to think about it for a couple of hours, and he'd call him back.

But Jonathon already knew what he was going to do.

He was going to keep his name out of the papers as long as he could. He could have sued the firm, but in the end, he decided staying out of the courts was the cheapest and best option for his own mental health.

He called up the lawyer again. Before he explained that he wasn't going to pursue legal action against the vendor's legal firm, he asked his lawyer if anyone had stated reasons why the seller would suddenly change their minds and "forget" the verbal agreement.

"You'd have to ask them, I guess."

So Jonathon did. After speaking with his own lawyer, he called up the legal firm representing the vendor, and he asked, point-blank, why the seller would not honour the verbal agreement.

"We've been provided certain information," was the initial, cryptic response, and right away, Jonathon began shaking his head. "The spouse of the vendor brought forward information that we all found rather…uh…disconcerting."

"Really." Jonathon sighed.

"Quite compelling, too. She remembered your name from the news some years ago, and she went and did a little research to confirm her findings. She brought it all into my office after showing it to her husband…Newspaper archives, TV news transcripts, transcripts from radio broadcasts…your criminal record sheet…"

"And she *happened* to remember my name from something that happened in Regina…in 1982."

"Phenomenal memory," the lawyer admitted. "I can't even remember what I had for breakfast yesterday!" He laughed.

"Well, that sure as hell explains why you can't remember any verbal agreements you made with my lawyer," Jonathon said. He didn't know what else to say. So he hung up.

He sat on the edge of the hotel room bed with his head between his hands.

Since it was obvious Jonathon wasn't going to be purchasing the 100-acre property after all, he had no interest in the 5-acre lot across the road from it. He called up the seller of the smaller property and arranged to cancel the purchase and to have refunded the $50,000 deposit he'd put on the place. The seller said he was disappointed, but when Jonathon explained that he was no longer interested in the place because he wasn't buying the neighbouring lot after all, the vendor agreed to cancel the sale and return the deposit.

A few days later, the vendor's realtors launched a lawsuit against Jonathon, claiming the $50,000 deposit as damages for loss of commission and loss of reputation. They claimed that the reversal of the sale they had arranged was without cause, and had cost them time and money, and that Jonathon had caused some other prospective clients to believe the realtors were at fault for the lost sale – meaning the loss of potential business, on top of everything else.

A few months later, Jonathon was bounced through a rustic kangaroo court. The plaintiffs made their case, and the defendants' arguments fell on deaf ears. The realtors and the vendor of the 5-acre property were awarded $240,000 in damages.

Jonathon, however, had declared personal bankruptcy in 1992, after one of McNaught's more successful machinations. The money he had was locked into business accounts, and though he was signatory to the company, legally speaking, it wasn't his money. He was on the hook, however, for even more legal fees.

Even in Armstrong, he was under siege. And because it was a small town, there was no way to keep anything under wraps, or to shelter his parents from knowing what had happened.

And in a small town, rumours spread like wildfire.

"...And I've been working at the bank ever since," Linda explained over dinner. It was a quiet little roadside restaurant with a woodsy feel, but the local Okanagan wines they offered were to die for, and the view of the river valley couldn't be beaten. "It's a boring story," she added with a laugh. "Well, other people don't think so, I guess. 'Ooh

– divorced single-woman raising two kids on her own…let's talk about that for years and years and years because we have nothing better to talk about…'"

Jonathon tried to assure her that it wasn't a boring story at all. Linda called his bluff. He laughed and said, "Okay, well 'boring' is perfectly all right with me, trust me. You live a life like mine, and 'boring' seems like paradise."

Linda's attention was elsewhere.

"What are you looking at?" Jonathon asked.

Linda shook her head and told him it was nothing.

People had been looking in their direction. Three women were sitting at a nearby table, and one of them was asking a question of the waiter who had stooped to hear her question. She was pointing at Jonathon.

"Compared to your life, I mean," Linda said, "mine must seem pretty dull and uneventful." She fell quiet after that, sipping her wine and toying with the last of the vegetables on her plate.

Jonathon picked up only a few words from the table across the way: "…Parker?" being one of them – that from the woman. The waiter had said a few things too low to catch, but another woman at the same table had a voice that carried well and she didn't seem to care who overheard what she had to say. Jonathon missed some of it, but he heard in sing-songy, know-it-all tones: "…buying up the *farm* land so he can make a golf course for all his so-called *friends*." She leaned forward, shielding one side of her mouth with her hand, so Jonathon could neither hear what she said nor read her lips.

Linda touched Jonathon's fingers. "Don't let it bother you."

"What?"

"It's a small town," Linda said. "People talk. And sometimes they talk without thinking first."

"You've already heard some rumours then, have you?"

"I'm a bank teller," Linda said. "In a town like this, it's the same as being a hairdresser, or a bartender."

"What do they say about me?" Jonathon asked.

"That you're some soul-sucking businessman, a modern Snidely Whiplash or something. And I say they're wrong." She kissed his fingers. "You're not some soul-sucking businessman. You're *my* soul-sucking businessman, and they can kiss my butt."

Jonathon grinned.

"Trust me on this," she said. "I know this place better than you do, and I know…this too shall pass. They'll eventually get bored of the rumours – especially when they don't see any stupid golf courses or big land purchases, and they'll go off in search of someone else's bones to pick. Either way…" She lifted her wine glass and clinked it against his. "At least you'll have me by your side to keep you company."

CHAPTER THIRTY

VERNON, B.C. SPRING, 1997.

Edward Keith was a personable but rather disorganized fellow. He had legal files stacked on all corners of his desk, but he seemed to thrive in the chaos of his small legal firm. He was a thin, middle-aged man who avoided ties like they were nooses, and he usually wore loose, button-down shirts under a sports jacket. His eyes flicked from one person to the other, as if he was watching a high-stakes, multi-player game of tennis. If he had the ears of a cat, they would have been perked forward in rapt attention.

There was hardly enough room for all four of them. Ed didn't take up much space, but Joe Davidson was accustomed to elbow room, John Reimer was built like a running back, and Jonathon himself was a corn-fed farm boy almost six and a half feet tall. Their close proximity made the office awfully warm.

Joe Davidson had been leading most of the conversation. "…And Jonathon here will help us to find some additional investors, to ensure that we have that opening balance of $10 million. So basically, Ed, all the heavy lifting is done for you."

"Okay," Ed said. "So what do you need from me?"

"First," Davidson said, "our clients will need to send their money to you in trust. You'll need to assure them that's it's safely and completely under your control – not ours, not anyone else. And secondly, you'll have to be with us in Antwerp, to meet the bankers with us and to review the contracts. If you're satisfied with the contracts, you can assure the other investors that everything is all right. You can explain the details of the contracts directly to the investors, before they commit to any transfers."

Ed shrugged. "Sounds good to me. When do you boys figure on arranging this trip?"

301

Reimer answered, "I'm thinking Monday next week? If we're all available." The others agreed, including Jonathon. "I know that Cook is planning to go to Lisbon next Thursday, so that would give us time to get it all done and signed before he leaves. Otherwise, it'd be another three week delay."

"Yeah," Jonathon said, "and if we wait, we might lose one or two of the bigger investors I've managed to line up."

Ed had raised his hand, as if he was back in school, asking a tricky question. "And Cook is…"

"Bill Cook is one of the two bankers over there," Reimer answered. "He's a good guy."

Davidson said, "Yeah, I had a friend of mine already check him out. Cook is the president of the Pacific Crown Bank. In terms of international banks, it's a pretty small one, but it's got a good reputation. So do you think you can arrange a few days away?"

Ed turned in his seat and fished for his day-by-day calendar. He flipped to the next week, checked a couple of days, then said he could be available and he'd be happy to go. "I've never been to Belgium!" he said. "Let's do it."

VERNON, B.C. SPRING, 1998

It's like history is stuck on instant replay, Jonathon thought as he rubbed his eyes. Linda was in the kitchen washing the dishes, and the kids were upstairs doing their homework. Fortunately, they were all out of earshot when Davidson stood up and swore.

"God, what a mess," Davidson said.

"Stop shouting," Jonathon said. "The kids are upstairs."

John Reimer said, "I feel just awful about the whole thing – I mean, Ed…"

"I know," Jonathon said.

"Poor bastard," Reimer continued. He paused to sip his drink. "Bad enough the Law Society's threatening to suspend his license, but all the investors are going after him! To sue him! The guy can barely retire, let alone…"

"And it's not even his fault!" Davidson said. He swore again and ran his fingers through his thinning hair. "God, I can't apologize enough for this, guys. I had no idea Cook was such a crook."

"We don't know that," Jonathon said.

For all Jonathon knew, Cook was a patsy. Another private bank in Belgium – Leader's Credit Bank – had been administering all of Cook's overnight banking. Jonathon and the others had been told about the Leader's Credit Bank by Cook himself, and although Cook had only been working with that bank's President, Jean-Paul Bastienne, for about eight months, Cook thought very highly of him and trusted him implicitly.

"You kidding?" Davidson asked. "Guy's got warrants out for his arrest on half a dozen charges, in half a dozen countries!"

Jonathon had flown to Belgium personally, and he'd tried desperately to recuperate funds that had been spirited out of the Leader's Credit Bank Accounts. *Life stuck on instant replay*, he thought again. He'd tried through a number of collection agencies large and small, some more aggressive than others, and he'd failed.

By luck or by design, he'd actually met Bastienne himself at a hotel bar in Belgium. At first blush, Jonathon could understand why Cook would take Bastienne at face value; Bastienne had been self-confident, extremely intelligent, master of many languages, and seemingly in command of every situation.

Bastienne had bragged about how the money would never be found again. He knew who was talking to, and that seemed to be the ultimate prize – more than the money, it was the stroking of his enormous ego that turned him on. Bastienne seemed to find an epicurean delight in knowing that he could brag about the details of his Ponzi scheme and still betray no evidence of his crimes.

"And Bastienne." Davidson had said it with the same intonations and sneer he might have used if he'd said *Bastard* instead. "Grade A con man, him and his brother. You should see the list of charges he's wanted on – and no one can find him."

"Oh yeah?" Reimer asked. He was watching Davidson with all the keen watchfulness of a sleuth as his suspect walks into a trap. Jonathon's mental alarm bells were ringing too.

Davidson seemed to know a lot more about Bastienne and Cook after the fact than anyone else in the room did. It made Jonathon wonder where he was getting his information from.

"Bank fraud," Davidson listed off, "theft, international money laundering…" He shook his head and said, "I'm sorry I ever got you guys into this mess. Had I known what Cook was into…"

"You seem to know a lot about it now," Jonathon said.

Davidson nodded. "Yeah, my friend did a little checking on my behalf. He's got friends in Interpol."

"Which friend?" Jonathon asked.

"The one who introduced me to Cook in the first place. How the hell he'd ever met Cook, I'll never know. I mean the guy's a cop, not an investor, so how'd he ever find this guy in the first place? In Belgium?" Davidson snorted at the absurdity of it all.

Jonathon rolled his eyes closed. "This friend of yours," he asked, "what's his name?"

"Huh?" Davidson shrugged and said, "My neighbour. Elwood."

Jonathon sunk in his chair with his face in his hands. "McNaught?"

Davidson laughed and said. "Jeez, you know him? God, what a small world, eh?"

"You have no idea," Jonathon said. He dropped his hand to his lap. "Elwood McNaught's an RCMP officer, isn't he?"

"You do know him," Davidson said with a nod. "Good guy. He cashed in a few favours with Interpol to find out the latest on Cook and Bastienne."

"Yeah, well, fat lot of good it does for Ed!" Reimer said. "It's *him* the investors are going after. He's the one on the hook for breach of trust."

"Screw him," Davidson said. "He's got insurance for that kind of thing. What I want to know is how we're gonna get *our* money back."

Jonathon stood up and poured himself another drink. "You want your money back? Then maybe you should start with your old pal Elwood McNaught. Find out why he didn't tell you about these charges *before* we got involved with Cook and Bastienne. Maybe *he* can get some money out of them."

Jonathon tossed back the Scotch, and he remembered the look in McNaught's greedy, sneering eyes the day he burst into Jonathon's home, laughing about what he'd done to Jonathon's investors and partners in the U.S. *You're doing a great job of helping your buddy Mick Ryder, aren't you, McNaught?*

Jonathon poured himself a refill and said, "I'm not done trying yet. We'll find a way to get that money back."

"And if we don't?" Davidson asked. "I lost two hundred grand, here. It's nothing to sneeze at."

Jonathon smothered a smile, and caught *"What, that's all you lost?"* before it came out of his mouth. "If we can't get it back, then we'll just have to find another way to make more." He turned to Davidson and added, "I mean, unless you want to cut your losses now and give up." He pointed at Davidson. "But I, for one, am not going to give up. For Ed's sake. Because he's got a hell of a lot more on the line than two hundred grand."

Davidson closed his mouth. Less than a quarter of an hour later, Davidson had left, and Jonathon didn't see him again for a few months. Not until the trial.

CHAPTER THIRTY-ONE

ARMSTRONG, B.C. SUMMER, 1998

While out working on a tractor in a field next to his home, Jonathon had been thinking about Linda and his two step-children, hating the small-mindedness of some people, and wondering what the hell he was going to do about the situation at the school. Jonathon and Linda were big enough to take on any rumour or haranguing. After almost a year and a half, Linda had gotten used to answering the phone, engaging in pleasant conversation with a friend or a family member, only to rise to a heated debate and a terse goodbye. Even after a year and a half, they still argued with her, telling her that she was out of her mind, hanging around a no-good criminal like Jonathon Parker. And gossip was the least torment Jonathon had suffered in the last couple of decades; but it was irritating, and it was affecting his step-kids. Not a day went by without one or both of his kids getting off the bus and running directly upstairs to their bedrooms. The school principals chalked it up to ordinary teasing, but explained – as if it was inevitable – that the other kids were only teasing, because their mother had married a crook, and now they had a criminal step-dad.

At the very least, he'd tried to make it up to those kids by securing for them a good home and putting money away for their education. And now, thanks to McNaught and Bastienne, even that had gone south. Fortunately, no one had caught wind that Jonathon had inadvertently lost yet again to *actual* criminal activity, or the gossip mill would have overloaded.

He'd been seriously considering moving the family out of the area, if only to protect his step-kids from the taunts at school. He considered how the kids would take it, if he brought the topic up. After all, they'd gone to the same school since kindergarten; it didn't seem fair that they

307

should have to leave it, especially considering it might come across to the wrong people as an admission of guilt or defeat.

Out of the corner of his eye, he spotted a truck driving up. It was his neighbour, the one from whom he'd originally tried to purchase the five acres. His wife had been the one to supply the lawyers with "research" she had supposedly pulled from the library. Jonathon wondered if she had actually spent that much time and effort to pull all that information – especially considering how long it had taken a professional private investigator to do the same. And then he began to wonder if some "inadvertently shredded" documents had somehow been placed in her hands by McNaught or someone like him.

His neighbour had driven onto Jonathon's rented field, parked and gotten out of the cab, leaving the door open. So Jonathon shut down the tractor and jumped down from the driver's seat to go talk with him. His neighbour had something in his hand, and he held it about chest high.

"Hi," Jonathon said.

His neighbour squinted against the sun. Jonathon couldn't tell if he was smiling or not.

"Nice day," Jonathon said.

"Must be real nice," his neighbour began, "not having to pay your debts."

Jonathon paused. It was a video camera that his neighbour held. He hadn't been squinting against the sun. He'd been squinting at the view finder. Jonathon smiled and came a little closer. "We discussed all that in court already, my friend." He approached and stood with his hands on his hips. "And really, I don't want to argue with you, so maybe it's just best if you left."

"Don't you threaten me!" his neighbour said.

"I'm not threatening you!" Jonathon said. He was close enough to his neighbour that when the wind shifted, Jonathon could smell the stale tang of alcohol. "Look, maybe you should just leave. We can talk about it in the morning, when you've sobered up."

"Oh, I warned you! I warned you not to threaten me!"

His neighbour pulled out a bottle of bear spray and before Jonathon could throw up his arms or turn away, he sprayed it in Jonathon's face.

Jonathon shouted in pain and turned away. "Shit!" The neighbour raised his arm and doused Jonathon's head, trying to angle the can to get over Jonathon's upraised arms and continue spraying his face. Jonathon stumbled in the direction of his house.

Linda screamed his name. She'd been in the front lawn on high alert from the moment Jonathon had gotten off his tractor.

Jonathon coughed, and when he inhaled, he took in a cloud of the bear spray. It robbed him of his breath. He took another step, and then the pain really kicked in. He raised his hands to wipe the spray out of his eyes, but he knew he would only contaminate himself further. He stumbled blindly toward the house, wheezing, coughing and tearing up.

"Oh God, Jonathon!" Linda was suddenly at his elbow. He had no idea how far or how fast he'd gone, but she took him the rest of the way into the house, leading him up to the porch.

"Is he still there?" Jonathon wheezed. He could hear his two step-children asking what was going on, and if Jonathon was okay.

"He's gone," Linda said. "He just walked away. What was that all about?"

"Drunken bastard!" Jonathon heaved and coughed. "Help me get these clothes off..."

"It's all in your hair," Linda whined. "Your shirt is completely soaked." She coughed too. The fumes were suffocating. "Kids, get in the house. He'll be okay – you guys just get inside the house." Linda helped him out of his clothes, right down to his socks and underwear, then she pointed him in the direction of the downstairs bathroom so he could shower.

He had used handfuls of shampoo to try and get the stuff out of his hair, but the stench was everywhere, making his throat seize and his lungs burn. Every pore stung, and his eyes ran with tears.

"Jonathon," Linda said from the bathroom door. She pulled back the shower curtain. "I called the poison control line." She handed him an open bottle of olive oil. "They said you're supposed to rub this into your skin and then rinse it out. You're supposed to keep doing it until the stinging goes away, okay? I don't care if you use the whole bottle."

An hour later, he gave up. The spray no longer stung, but his skin, eyes, nose and mouth hurt. He came out wearing nothing but towels. Linda was in the kitchen with the kids.

"I called the police," she said.

"What, the Mounties?" Jonathon asked. His voice was hoarse.

"I had to report it, Jonathon. I know how you feel about them, but..."

Jonathon waved it off. "Thank you."

"Did you get it in your eyes?"

"No," Jonathon said. "No, I think it was just the fumes."

"Oh thank God..." She told him everything she'd learned from the Poison Control line. She'd even taken notes so she wouldn't forget anything in her panic. "He could have *blinded* you. What was he on about?"

"I don't know," Jonathon rasped. "Something about me not paying my debts – probably something about the lawsuit." He coughed. "The lawsuit from two years ago. I *told* the judge I'd filed personal bankruptcy in '92."

"I know, I know." She rubbed his back as carefully as she dared, and she poured him a glass of milk, hoping it would ease his sore throat. "And it's not like he's really out anything – he sold it to someone else in the end, didn't he?"

"God – as if I haven't already had enough trouble. Do even the neighbours have to turn on me too?" Jonathon sat down at the kitchen table. "They have no idea what I've been through – what *we've* been through. What gives them the right..."

"To judge?" she asked.

"To judge," he said, "to sentence, to execute..."

She shook her head. "They don't know," she said. "They don't have any idea. They can't see past their own narrow existence, and they can't see past their own injuries."

Jonathon sat with his frowning step-children and his wife for about an hour, talking it over. When they heard official-sounding footsteps on the front porch, Jonathon went upstairs to put on a pair of pants. Linda opened the door for the RCMP officer, and asked them to wait while Jonathon got dressed. He came down a few moments later, red from his scalp to his navel, especially on the side he'd turned to his neighbour. The officer shook his head and said, "I assume you'll want to lay charges," and he took out his notebook to start taking down Jonathon's witness statement.

Jonathon explained his past dealings with his neighbour, how the judge had awarded a quarter of a million dollars in favour of his neighbour, and how Jonathon hadn't been able to pay because of his personal bankruptcy. "I've had my fill of vindictive people," he said. "I'm sick to death of them. I'm just so…" He sighed. "Tired," he said, "of having to defend myself against false charges, and rumours, and accusations…" He hung his head. "No, I don't want to press charges."

The officer pointed at Linda and the kids. "You've got three witnesses. And if you tell me he had a video camera on you at all times, that's evidence that could be used in a court of law."

Jonathon tried to dismiss the idea with a wave of his hand. He was too tired even to talk.

"Assault is a criminal charge. An indictable offense," the Mountie said. "Mr. Parker, I'm obliged to lay charges, if you don't."

"Honestly," Jonathon said in a small voice, "I really don't care."

Softly, the officer said, "If I lay charges against him, I'll make it clear that it's me laying the charges, not you. But I'll need you to testify."

Linda ran her hands along Jonathon's shoulders, and he gave her fingers a squeeze. He looked up at her, and she nodded. She would stand by him, no matter what.

"I'll testify," he said.

A few days later, Jonathon was coming in for lunch, when there came a knock at the door. He opened the inside door; a woman in a business suit stood on the other side of the screen door. "Can I help you?"

"Jonathon Parker?"

"That's me."

"I have a package for you," she said. He opened the door, and she handed him a piece of paper. "You've been summoned."

He read the header of the court summons. It was a new suit filed by his ever-loving neighbour and the realty that had represented him, fil-

ing another civil suit against him, this time asking for $50,000. "God…"
Jonathon groaned, "this has got to stop…"

Jonathon booked an appointment and met his neighbour at the realtor's office to discuss an out-of-court settlement. He simply couldn't
afford his own legal defence. He was sick of seeing the inside of a court,
civil or otherwise.

"I'm sure we can come to some kind of an agreement," Jonathon
said to his neighbour. He felt like a rusted old robot reciting the same
bureaucratic phrases over and over again. "Because honestly, you're
going to lose. You know I'm bankrupt. You know I can't pay – it's on
record, and it's not going to change any time soon. This is nothing but
a frivolous law suit, and you know it."

His neighbour smiled. He was missing two teeth. "So?"

Jonathon clenched his jaw.

"I'll tell you what," his neighbour said. "Yeah. I'll drop the lawsuit.
We go into that court, you admit what you did to me was wrong, and
then you pay me half of that deposit you were supposed to give me."

"I told you already…"

He shook his head. "No, you were some kind of big shot businessman. You've got the money for it. I know you do. Your phoney bankruptcy shit is just a slick way to hide your money in your company
name."

"I told you already…"

"You can borrow it from somebody. Look, I don't really give a
damn, all right? That's the deal. You pay me twenty-five grand, I drop
the lawsuit. Don't, and you're gonna end up paying the full fifty grand,
plus court fees. It's your choice."

"Is that what it'll take to get you off my back?" Jonathon asked. His
neck hurt. "God, all this over five acres of land."

"Hey!" His neighbour pointed his finger at Jonathon. "This isn't
about the money, it's about the principle of the thing. What you did
was wrong, and you're gonna pay for it."

"Fine," Jonathon said.

"What did you say?"

"I said fine. If you want me to go to court and say I was wrong, then fine, but I won't lie in court. I'm not going to perjure myself, especially since I didn't do anything wrong. But if we're taking this to court, I won't contest. You can say whatever the hell you want, I really don't give a damn anymore."

His neighbour seemed a little stunned by the news. "Well…all right then." He glanced at the realtor, and said again, "All right."

The realtor made some noises about Jonathon making the right choice, and how he would personally see to it that the case went to court quickly, so they matter could be resolved soon.

When Jonathon left, he stopped outside his truck. Parked beside him was his neighbour's car. His ignition key was clenched in his fist. His neighbour's car was dusty, but otherwise pristine.

No one was around.

ARMSTRONG, B.C. FALL, 1998.

Jonathon sat at the table with his kids, trying to give them a reason to smile. He made a couple of jokes, and asked them about something they'd watched on TV. It was late afternoon, and it had been another bad day at school. It had been a rough day for Jonathon, too. He'd spent most of his day talking over the civil case with his lawyers and trying to make payment arrangements.

He had nothing left. Not money, not energy. And he was running low on hope, too.

Someone drove up the driveway, and a moment later, a car door slammed. Jonathon got up to meet the visitor on the porch.

He was glad to have shut the door behind him.

"Mr. Parker?" It was a young woman in a business suit.

Jonathon seriously considered changing his name.

"Are you Mr. Parker?"

"Yes, that's me."

The young woman came up the steps and handed him a court summons.

"Seriously?" he asked. He read the header. This time, he rolled his eyes shut and turned his face to the sky. In the preamble, the document said that, following an RCMP and B.C. Securities Commission investigation, he and Edward Keith were being summoned to court to account for the losses accrued by their investors, following the theft of monies by Bastienne, in Belgium.

Jonathon was sorely tempted to weep, right then and there. Instead, he breathed, thanked the woman for coming, then he went inside, said some meaningless words to his step-kids, went into the washroom and closed the door.

VERNON, B.C. FALL, 1998.

Jonathon was sick to death of 1998. He considered moving to Tibet and taking monastic vows. But he had a family to take care of. He'd already made vows to Linda, and she to him. He couldn't leave.

He couldn't leave her to face the fallout of her husband's name and image plastered over the front page news in Vernon. Things had been bad enough when there were only rumours flying about; now they had not one but three court cases with Jonathon's name somewhere on the docket. The kids took some of the public abuse, always at school, and the school did little to defend them against the "teasing." But Linda was taking the brunt. She'd had to leave her job at the bank already; they had to change their phone number. They considered moving. She wouldn't face it alone. She hadn't abandoned him when things were at their worst; he wouldn't abandon her when she needed him most.

This time, he was in criminal court, acting as a Crown witness against his admirable neighbour, who was trying to testify on his own behalf in the assault case. He pleaded leniency from the court, because he had a previous record of assault, he had a wife and three small children, and he would lose his job if he was convicted.

Jonathon turned to the Crown attorney and asked if they could request a recess. "I want to talk to this guy one-on-one," Jonathon said. *Why*, he wondered. *Why the hell am I doing this...?*

"I don't know about that," the prosecutor said. "You want to step outside the courtroom…and 'talk' with this guy." He'd made air-quotes when he said it.

"That's all I want to do," Jonathon said. "Please."

The attorney said, "Let me talk to the judge."

A few moments later, Jonathon was escorted to a conference room with his neighbour. An armed sheriff stood in the room with them, in case things turned ugly.

His neighbour's eyes were worn and red-lined.

"You're not helping yourself," Jonathon said. "You're floundering up there, and you look like an idiot, you know that?" The other man didn't respond. He looked like he was shrinking. "You know if I go up there and testify, you're going to jail. Have you ever been to jail before?"

"The drunk tank," he answered.

"A criminal charge like this one, it'll change your life."

"I know. Why do you think I'm pleading my own case?"

"Listen…" Jonathon heaved a sigh. *Tahiti*, he thought. *Change my name, move to Tahiti, and take up fishing for the rest of my life.* "Go back to the stand. Plead guilty."

"No, I can't!"

"Plead guilty, admit you acted out of drunken rage and tell the court that you're sorry. You apologize to me, on the record, and apologize to the court for wasting its time. You do that, and I won't testify against you."

"…You would do that?"

"I'm tired," Jonathon said. "I don't want to be here anymore than you do. Let's just get this over with." He closed his eyes. "Look, I know what it's like, all right? I don't want to see you lose your job – not for your own sake, dammit, because I think you're an asshole – but I'd do it for the sake of your wife and kids. You apologize, on the record, and I'll try to convince the Crown prosecutor to just…throw out the case or give you a slap on the wrist or whatever."

They came to an agreement, and they asked the sheriff to escort them back to the courtroom. Jonathon begged the indulgence of the court, and then proposed his solution: that if his neighbour would apologize on the record, that they accept his apology and not sentence him to jail. They agreed to hear the apology, and his neighbour delivered it sincerely. He even called himself an ass on the stand, which made the prosecutor smirk. They dismissed the charges.

His neighbour came up to him after the case was dismissed and the next was called up. "Why the hell'd you do that?" His eyes were wet. "Why would you do that?" He blinked and mashed a tear away with his fist. His bottom lip trembled, and he cleared his throat. "Nobody's shown me that kind of compassion ever before."

Jonathon nodded and said, "That's why."

And he left.

VERNON, B.C. DECEMBER, 2010.

By then, the daughter Jonathon had had with Linda was almost eleven years old. Jonathon's father and mother had moved back to Prince Albert shortly after the trials had all begun; Edward Parker had claimed illness, saying that he was now too old and too ill to keep working on the farm Jonathon had bought for them. Edward sold that farm back to Linda and Jonathon – in Linda's name – for more than what Jonathon had initially paid for it.

And, by then, things had been so bad for the kids that the family sold that same farm and moved to Coldstream, away from the ugly rumours and the harassment and the gossip. It was a clean start for them. Jonathon had changed his name, and though some had suspected who he was, it was a clean break for the kids, who, at least on paper, were no longer related to "that criminal" everyone had been talking about.

For twelve years, the case had been dragging on. In 1998, he and Edward Keith had been given an appearance notice to attend to civil court by the Law Society's Special Compensation Fund on behalf of the disgruntled investors. They were trying to get a judgment for the money they lost in the multi-million dollar theft committed by Bastienne. In 2005, after several hundred thousand dollars in legal fees, the civil law suit against Jonathon and Keith was dismissed. Edward Keith had developed throat cancer that same year.

A little over three years later, now more than twelve years after the event, and after a lot more legal fees, he and now-retiring lawyer Edward Keith were facing the end of the criminal-case side of the Bastienne affair. Both Jonathon and Keith were being charged with multiple counts of fraud and theft. In December of 2010, the judge was at last ready to hand down sentence. Keith ran out of money for his defence counsel, who had convinced him to plead guilty to six charges of theft and fraud. Keith's surrender left Jonathon with little hope of winning in his own defence, so his legal counsel negotiated a guilty plea with the Crown Prosecutor as well. He plead guilty to one count of theft, just so he could get the trial over and done with. Twelve years, despite having plead guilty, and only then was the judge ready to pass sentence.

"Edward Keith," the judge said, "having accepted your plea of guilty to these charges of theft and fraud, in light of the extreme and pro-longed stress of having waited for this matter to be resolved – a delay which was neither your fault nor within your control – this court is handing down a conditional sentence of two years less a day, during which time you will be under house arrest for the first eight months, and under a 9:00 p.m. to 6:00 a.m. curfew thereafter." He issued a simi-lar sentence but only for eighteen months for Jonathon. The judge went on to order restitution from both Jonathon and Edward Keith, who had already filed personal bankruptcy and had been disbarred for more than ten years, lost his law practice and any hope of a retirement fund.

Defeated and painfully weary, Jonathon was escorted home with his wife and children, to begin serving out his sentence.

EPILOGUE

12:01 AM, JUNE 3RD, 2012:

Today, this very minute is the first real opportunity for me to enjoy some semblance of freedom; it's the first day after expiry of what I can only hope is my last criminal sentence. And I'm tired. I'm tired of thinking about all of the reasons why I'm tired. I'm tired of trying to forget those same things. I'm tired of not being able to forget them. And I'm tired because I have to live with those memories that I'm tired of trying to forget.

It's been thirty-four years almost to the day since I first encountered two men called Ryder and Callaghan. It's been twenty-six years since I first encountered their friend, Elwood McNaught. I've referred to Ryder and Callaghan as the "Dynamic Duo" and to the three of them as the "Three Stooges" more often than I care to recall. What a disgrace those three have been to Canada's "finest", the Royal Canadian Mounted Police.

I'm tired of remembering how they affected my life. I'm tired of remembering what they were like as people. I'm tired of remembering them or anything about them, but I'm unable to forget them. I'm tired of not being able to forget them. Thank God I have forgiven them.

I'm tired of them manipulating control of my life. I'm tired of being blackmailed. I'm tired of having my liberty unjustly denied. I'm tired of having most of my life's income repeatedly stolen. I'm tired of always having to play financial catch up. I'm tired of paying legal fees to protect my innocence and to claim what was supposedly already mine.

I'm tired of remembering that I've paid more legal fees than two average households could earn in a lifetime. I'm tired of remembering that the Three Stooges stole more from me than three average households could earn in a lifetime. I'm tired of having already spent thirty-four years continually trying to recover from this. I'm tired, not because I was able to, but because they manipulated me into having to.

I'm tired of the Dynamic Duo chaining my hands behind my back and laughing while they beat the crap out of me. I'm tired of remembering how many times they did that to me. I'm tired of experiencing cuts, bruises, broken ribs, and stitches. I'm tired of creating explanations and dealing with interrogations about cuts, bruises, broken ribs and stitches. I'm tired of having lived for so many years in fear of more of this at any time without notice.

I'm tired of the Three Stooges threatening to steal from me. I'm tired of them stealing from me. I'm tired of them threatening to blackmail and blackmailing me. I'm tired of them defaming and assassinating my character. I'm tired of them framing me for criminal charges. I'm tired of the Three Stooges stealing from my friends and family members to put more pressure on me.

I'm tired of them stealing my money, my business partners' money, my family's money, and manipulating it so I was always blamed and often criminally charged with the theft of it. I'm tired of them committing crimes at my expense. I'm tired of serving criminal sentences for crimes they committed or caused. I'm tired of them having benefitted at my expense. I'm tired of trying to justify and explain these things to friends and family members. I'm tired of trying to defend myself to friends and family members. I'm tired of being judged.

I'm tired of not getting any support from friends and family members when I needed it. I'm tired of friends and family members not believing me when I have spoken truthfully. I'm tired of losing friends and family members. I'm even tired of trying to make new friends and I'm tired of trying to repair family relationships. I'm tired of not caring whether or not I have friends anymore. And I'm tired of not caring whether or not I have good relationships with many of my family members anymore.

I'm tired because many of my friends and family members have suffered these things without cause or even without ever knowing or being able to understand why. I'm tired because I've lost these friends and family members for no acceptable reason. I'm tired of remembering the hurt and disappointment they must have felt. I'm tired of being judged.

I'm tired because my remaining family still suffers unjustly for things they never had any control over. I'm tired because my family still suffers without the things they could and should have enjoyed. I'm tired because I still have to play financial catch up to enable my family to enjoy what they are entitled to. I'm tired because in spite of these things, I have always provided for and protected my family, beyond what they claim to have expected.

I'm tired of trying so hard to understand why I remain optimistic. I'm tired of trying to explain my continuing optimism to others. I'm tired of believing in what's right. I'm tired of maintaining faith in what's right. I'm tired because I know that I know what's right. I'm tired because what's right is not always expedient. I'm tired because what's right is not always easy. I'm tired because what's right is often very lonely. I'm tired because what's right often comes with huge costs and obligations. I'm tired of paying such a huge price, simply to do what's right.

But I'm relieved that the price of doing what's right is less than the price of doing what's wrong. I'm tired of knowing this too. And I'm tired of having this pointed out to me as if I were a complete idiot and needed the reminders. I'm tired of having doubts and I'm tired of experiencing uncertainties about this. I'm tired of everything that's happened to me and I'm tired of everything about me.

I'm so very tired of being tired and even more tired of trying to remember all of the reasons why I'm so tired. And I'm really tired of knowing I'll never be able to forget these things that make me so very tired. I'm just tired.

But I know that I will remain optimistic because I've been blessed with an inherent and unshakable optimism; exactly why I've been blessed with this I do not know. And I've been blessed with a few good friends and an amazingly wonderful family that demonstrates their unconditional love for me continually. This I cherish above all. And because they tell me so, I know this also; that they fully understand and accept why I'm so tired. For them, that have not judged, I remain inspired.

Jonathon Parker, tired, but not defeated.

31262588R00198

Made in the USA
Charleston, SC
09 July 2014